Lacan

The Seminars of Alain Badiou

The Seminars of Alain Badiou

Kenneth Reinhard, General Editor

Alain Badiou is widely considered to be one of the most important Continental philosophers of our time. Badiou has developed much of his thinking in his annual seminars, which he delivered in Paris from the late 1970s to 2017. These seminars include discussions that inform his major books, including *Being and Event*, *Logics of Worlds*, and *The Immanence of Truths*, as well as presentations of many ideas and topics that are not part of his published work. Some volumes of the seminar investigate individual thinkers and writers such as Parmenides, Plato, Nietzsche, Heidegger, Beckett, and Mallarmé. Others examine concepts such as infinity, truth, the subject, the present, evil, love, and the nature of change. These seminars constitute an essential part of Badiou's thinking, one that remains largely unknown to the non-Francophone world. Their translation is a major event for philosophers and other scholars and students in the humanities and social sciences and for the artists, writers, political theorists, and engaged intellectuals for whom Badiou's work has rapidly become a generative and inspiring resource.

For a complete list of seminars, see page 261.

Lacan

Anti-philosophy 3

Alain Badiou

Translated by
Kenneth Reinhard and Susan Spitzer

Introduction by Kenneth Reinhard

Columbia University Press
New York

Columbia University Press
Publishers Since 1893
New York Chichester, West Sussex
cup.columbia.edu

First published in French as *Le Séminaire—*
Lacan: L'antiphilosophie 3 (1994–1995)
© 2013 Librairie Arthème Fayard

Library of Congress Cataloging-in-Publication Data
Names: Badiou, Alain, author.
Title: Lacan : anti-philosophy 3 / Alain Badiou; edited by Kenneth Reinhard
and translated by Susan Spitzer.
Other titles: Seminaire-Lacan. English
Description: New York: Columbia University Press, 2018. |
Includes bibliographical references and index.
Identifiers: LCCN 2018018868 (print) | LCCN 2018029840 (ebook) |
ISBN 9780231548410 (ebook) | ISBN 9780231171489 (cloth) |
ISBN 9780231171496 (pbk.)
Subjects: LCSH: Lacan, Jacques, 1901–1981. | Psychoanalysis.
Classification: LCC BF173 (ebook) | LCC BF173 .B148 2018 (print) |
DDC 150.19/5092—dc23
LC record available at https://lccn.loc.gov/2018018868

Cover design: Julia Kushnirsky

Contents

Editors' Introduction to the English Edition of the Seminars of Alain Badiou

KENNETH REINHARD, SUSAN SPITZER, AND JASON E. SMITH

W
ith the publication in English of Alain Badiou's seminars, we believe that a new phase of his reception in the
Anglophone world will open up, one that bridges the
often formidable gap between the two main forms in which his published work has so far appeared. On the one hand, there is the tetralogy of his difficult and lengthy major works of systematic philosophy,
beginning with a sort of prelude, *Theory of the Subject*, and continuing with the three parts of *Being and Event*, *Logics of Worlds*, and the
recently published *L'Immanence des vérités* (*The Immanence of Truths*).
On the other hand, there are his numerous shorter and occasional
pieces on topics such as ethics, contemporary politics, film, literature,
and art. Badiou's "big books" are often built on rather daunting mathematical ideas and formulations: *Being and Event* relies primarily on
set theory and the innovations introduced by Paul Cohen; *Logics of
Worlds* adds category, topos, and sheaf theory; and *L'Immanence des
vérités* expands into the mathematics of large cardinals. Each of these
great works is written in its own distinctive, and often rather dense,
style: *Theory of the Subject* echoes the dramatic tone and form of a
Lacanian seminar; *Being and Event* presents a fundamental ontology
in the form of a series of Cartesian "meditations"; *Logics of Worlds*
is organized in formal theories and "Greater Logics," and expressed

in richly developed concrete examples, phenomenological descriptions, and scholia; and for reading *L'Immanence des vérités*, Badiou suggests two distinct paths: one short and "absolutely necessary," the other long and "more elaborate or illustrative, more free-ranging." Because of the difficulty of these longer books, and their highly compact formulations, Badiou's shorter writings—such as the books on ethics and Saint Paul—often serve as a reader's first point of entry into his ideas. But this less steep path of induction brings its own problems, insofar as these more topical and occasional works often take for granted their relationship to the fundamental architecture of Badiou's thinking and thus may appear to have a greater (or smaller) role in it than they actually do. Hence the publication of Badiou's seminars from 1983 through 2016 makes available a middle path, one in which the major lines of Badiou's thinking—as well as its many extraordinary detours—are displayed with the remarkable clarity and the generous explications and exemplifications that always characterize his oral presentations.[1] It is extraordinarily exciting to see the genesis of Badiou's ideas in the experimental and performative context of his seminars, and there is a great deal in the seminars that doesn't appear at all in his existing published writings.

The first volume of the seminars to be published in English, on Lacan, constitutes part of a four-year sequence on "anti-philosophy" that also includes volumes on Nietzsche, Wittgenstein, and Saint Paul. The second volume, on Malebranche, is part of a similar cluster on being, which also involves years dedicated to Parmenides and Heidegger. And the later volumes, beginning in 1996, gather material from multiple years of the seminars, as in the case of *Axiomatic Theory of the Subject* (which is based on the sessions from the years 1996–97 and 1997–98), and *Images of the Present Time* (which was delivered in sessions over three years, from 2001 to 2004).

Isabelle Vodoz and Véronique Pineau are establishing the French text of the seminar on the basis of audio recordings and

notes, with the intention of remaining as close as possible to
Badiou's delivery while eliminating unnecessary repetitions and
other minor artifacts. In reviewing and approving the texts of the
seminars (sometimes as long as thirty years after having delivered
them), Badiou decided not to revise or reformulate them, but to
let them speak for themselves, without the benefit of self-critical
hindsight. Given this decision, it is remarkable to see how consistent his thinking has been over the years. Moreover, each volume of
the seminars includes a preface by Badiou that offers an extremely
valuable account of the political and intellectual context of the
seminars, as well as a sort of retrospective reflection on the process
of his thought's emergence. In our translations of the seminars into
English, we have tried to preserve the oral quality of the French
edition in order to give the reader the impression of listening to
the original recordings. We hope that the publication of Badiou's
seminars will allow more readers to encounter the full scope of his
ideas, and will allow those readers who are already familiar with his
work to discover a new sense of its depths, its range, and its impli-
cations—perhaps almost as if reading Badiou for the first time.

The Seminars of Alain Badiou (1983–2016): General Preface

ALAIN BADIOU

The Seminars in English

It is a great pleasure for me to write this preface to the first volume of the English-language edition of the entire collection of thirty years of my seminars. It is hardly surprising that this project got its start in California, since it was there that my work and I were recognized early on in an English-speaking country, thanks in particular to Ken Reinhard, who has always had an original and profound insight into my work. I want to thank Columbia University Press for supporting what I know has been a long and difficult undertaking. And above all, I want to thank my friend Susan Spitzer, an incomparable translator who, for so many years, has been devoted to translating me, to transporting me from one language to another, with amazing creative zeal and accuracy, the fruit of her rich years in Paris. The information below is intended simply to shed some light on what these thirty years of public speaking have meant, to me and my various audiences, and why there may be some interest, or even pleasure, to be found in reading the seminars.

I. A Few Historical Reference Points

The word "seminar" should, in principle, refer to collective work around a particular problem. Instead, where these seminars are concerned, it refers to my own individual, albeit public, work on many different problems, all of which were nonetheless united by a philosophical apparatus explicitly claiming to be systematic.

Admittedly, the word "seminar" was already used in the latter sense with reference to Lacan's famous seminar, which, for me and many other people, has raised the bar very high when it comes to this sort of thing.

That a large part of my teaching took the form of such a seminar—whose ongoing publication in French (ten volumes have come out so far), in English now, and in Spanish at almost the same time, will show that it remained virtually free from any institutional authority—was originally due to pure chance.

At the beginning of the academic year 1966–67, while I was the senior class teacher at the boys' high school in Reims, I was appointed lecturer in an establishment that had just been created and that testified to the rapid expansion of higher education in the supremely Gaullist France of those years: the Collège universitaire de Reims, affiliated with the University of Nancy. Initially, only so-called propaedeutic [i.e., college preparatory] teaching was to be provided there (at the time, there was a first year of studies with that name, validated by a final exam that, if successfully passed, allowed students to begin their first year of university). So I was asked to teach the philosophy option in this preparatory year. But all of a sudden, thanks to one of those nasty betrayals so typical of academic life, the University of Nancy announced that, for the time being, it couldn't relinquish its philosophical powers to Reims and that there wouldn't be any philosophy option for the preparatory program to which my position was attached.

So there I was, a teacher of a nonexistent discipline. Given these circumstances, what else was there to do but hold an open seminar? And that's what I did for two years (1966–67 and 1967–68), before—I have to brag a bit here—an increasingly large audience and, what was even more flattering to me, one that was there out of pure interest since there was no final exam to reward their faithful attendance.

If I'd had the energy to look for my notes from that time long ago (when no one had either the idea or the means to bring in one of those big, clunky tape recorders to record my improvisations) and to revise those notes and turn them into a written text, I could have proudly begun this edition of the seminars with the one from 1966–67—fifty years of free speech!—, the year devoted to Schopenhauer, and then continued with the 1967–68 seminar, when my syllabus was focused on Mallarmé, Rimbaud, and Lautréamont, in that order. The *Chants de Maldoror*, however, which I had intended to begin dealing with in early May, was sacrificed on the altar of the mass movement.

And then, as a result of that May upheaval, which was to drastically change my life and my thinking about many issues other than academic appointments, I was appointed (since those appointments continued to be made nonetheless) Assistant Professor at the Experimental University of Vincennes, which soon became Paris 8.

The context in which I began teaching courses there was so feverish and politically so intense, the actions afoot there so radical, that the government decided that the philosophy degrees granted by Paris 8 would have no national accreditation! So there I was again, forced to give an open seminar since there was no state validation of our teaching efforts, despite the fact that they were highly innovative, to say the least.

This marginalization lasted for years. So—if, once again, the documentation really allowed for it—I could give an account of the free and open seminars of the 1970s, which, when all the exciting, frenetic collective action going on at the time allowed them to take place, were devoted in particular to the Hegelian dialectic, to Mallarmé again, to my beloved Plato, and to Lacan, always before audiences that were there out of pure interest alone, since there was no exam and therefore no academic credit to validate their attendance.

Actually, a synthetic account of that period does exist: my book *Theory of the Subject*, published by Seuil in 1982 under the editorship of François Wahl (English translation published by Continuum, 2009). It provides an admittedly very freely rewritten account of the seminars that were held between January 1975 and June 1979.

Beginning in those years, as a result of the so-called political normalization, things calmed down in the universities, even in the one in Vincennes, which had incidentally been moved to Saint-Denis. In the early 1980s, the government authorities decided that we of the glorious Department of Philosophy—where you could hear lectures by Michel Foucault, Michel Serres, François Châtelet, Gilles Deleuze, Jean-François Lyotard, and Jacques Rancière—deserved to have the national accreditation we'd lost gradually restored. It was from that time on, too, that the seminars began to be systematically recorded by several different attendees. Little wonder, then, that I decided to publish all of the seminars between 1983 and the present: for these thirty-odd years, abundant, continuous documentation exists.

Not that the locations, the institutions, and the frequency didn't change. Indeed, starting in 1987 the seminar moved to the Collège international de philosophie, which owed its creation in large part to the determined efforts of everyone in "living [i.e. non-traditional] philosophy" who felt put down and badmouthed by the University, Lyotard and Derrida being the two most emblematic names at the time. In that setting, I rediscovered the innocence of teaching without exams or validation: the seminar was now officially open and free of charge to everyone (for the reasons I mentioned above, it had actually always been so). It was held in the locales that the Collège secured or bargained hard to secure for its activities: the old École polytechnique on the rue Descartes, the École normale supérieure on the boulevard Jourdan, an industrial institution on the rue de Varenne, the Institut catholique on the rue d'Assas, and the main auditorium of the University of Paris 7 at Jussieu.

In 1998, when my seminar had been held under the auspices of the Collège international de philosophie for ten years, a crisis of sorts erupted: one faction of the Collège's administration viewed with suspicion both the form and the content of what I was doing. As far as the form was concerned, my status in the Collège was an exceptional one since, although I'd initially been properly inducted into it under Philippe Lacoue-Labarthe's presidency, I had never been officially re-elected as a member of the Collège. The content was viewed with suspicion because in those times dominated by the antitotalitarian ideology of human rights, rumors were going around that my teaching was "fascist." As I was unwilling to put up with such an atmosphere, I broke off my seminar midyear, thereby causing a lot of confusion.

I set it up the following fall at the École normale supérieure, where I'd been appointed professor. It remained there for fifteen years, which is pretty good, after all.

But this seminar was fated to always end up antagonizing institutions. I had to use the largest lecture halls at the ENS due to the sizeable audiences the seminar attracted, but at the start of the 2014 school year there was a dark plot afoot to deny me all access to those rooms and recommend that I accommodate around 250 people in a room that held only 80! After driving Lacan out, the prestigious ENS drove me out too! But, after all, I told myself, to suffer the same fate as Lacan was in its own way a glorious destiny. What happened to me next, however, can literally be called a "coup de théâtre," a dramatic turn of events. My friend Marie-José Malis, the outstanding theater artist and great renovator of the art of directing, was appointed artistic director of the Théâtre de la Commune in the Paris suburb of Aubervilliers. She offered to let me hold my seminar there, and I enthusiastically accepted. For two and a half years, in the heart of a working-class suburb, I stood on the stage before a full house and interspersed my final seminars, which were connected with the writing of my last "big" book, *L'Immanence des vérités*, with actual theatrical presentations. I was generously assisted in this by Didier Galas, who created the role of Ahmed in my four-play cycle, written in the 1980s and 1990s for the artistic and stage director Christian Schiaretti: *Ahmed the Subtle, Ahmed Gets Angry, Ahmed the Philosopher*, and *The Pumpkins*. On January 16, 2017, my Final Seminar took place in the Théâtre de la Commune in Aubervilliers, where pure philosophy, congratulatory messages, anecdotes, and theatrical productions all combined to celebrate the seminar's long history for one last time.

I'd always wanted the seminar to be for people who worked. That's why, for a very long time, it took place between 8 and 10 PM, on Tuesdays for a few years, on Wednesdays for probably twenty years, if not more, and on Mondays between 2014 and the time it ended in 2017, because theaters are dark on Mondays . . .

In these various places, there was a first period—five years, from 1987 to 1992—when the seminar had a feeling of spontaneity to it as it ran through philosophy's "conditions," as they're called in my doctrine: poetry, the history of philosophy (the first seminar on Plato's *Republic* dates back to 1989–90), politics, and love. It was over the course of those years, especially during the sessions on the rue de Varenne, that the size of the audience increased dramatically.

From 1992 on, I began putting together large conceptual or historical ensembles, which I treated over several consecutive years: anti-philosophy, between 1992 and 1996; the Subject, between 1996 and 1998; the twentieth century, between 1998 and 2001; images of the present time, between 2001 and 2004; the question of subjective orientation, in thought and in life, from 2004 to 2007. I dealt with

Plato, from 2007 to 2010; then with the phrase "changing the world," from 2010 to 2012. The final seminar, which was held, as I mentioned above, in a theater, was entitled "The Immanence of Truths."

I should point out that, although it was a more or less weekly seminar at the beginning, it was a monthly one for all of the final years of its existence.

II. The Seminar's Form

As I mentioned at the outset, my seminar ultimately took the form of an ex cathedra lesson, the venerable old form known as the "formal lecture" [cours magistral]. But this was the outcome of a long evolution. Between 1969 and, let's say, the late 1980s, there were questions from the audience. It was obviously a lot easier to entertain questions in a room with 40 people at Vincennes than in a theater with 300. But it was also a matter of the time period. Initially at Vincennes, every "class" was a sort of steeplechase in which the hedges, which had to be jumped over elegantly and efficiently, were the constant hail of questions. It was there, as well as in the tumultuous political meetings I attended, that I learned how to stay unfailingly focused on my own thinking while agreeing with perfect equanimity to answer any question calmly, even if it was clearly a side issue. Like Claudel's God, I took crooked paths to reach my goal.

I must admit that, little by little, with the "normalization," I was able to rely on the audience's increasing unwillingness to listen to overly subjective rambling, rants with no connection to the subject under discussion, biased ideological assaults, complaints about not understanding or boasts about already knowing it all. Ultimately, it was the dictatorship of the masses that silenced the frenzied dialectic of interruptions without my having to change, on my own, my relationship with the audience. In the Jules Ferry auditorium at the ENS or in the Théâtre de la Commune, nobody interrupted anymore, or even, I believe, considered doing so, not out of fear of a stern refusal on my part but because the ambient opinion was no longer in favor of it.

I never ruled out having someone else come and speak, and thus, over time, I extended invitations to a number of people: François Regnault, to speak on theater; Jean-Claude Milner, to speak on Lacan; Monique Canto, to speak on Plato; Slavoj Žižek, to speak on orientation in life, etc. These examples give you a sense of my eclecticism.

But in the final analysis, the seminar's form, solidly in place for about twenty-five years, remained by and large that of a one-man show. Session by session, I began with careful preparation, resulting in a set of lecture notes—I never really wrote out a seminar—that provided the basic outline, a few summary sentences, and the quotations or references used. Often, I gave out a handout containing the texts that I would read and comment on. I did this because my material was nothing like philosophical references in the traditional sense of the term. In particular, I had frequent recourse to the intellectual concentration that poetry allows for. Naturally, I also engaged in logico-mathematical formalism. However, it's very difficult to make extensive use of that resource before large audiences. I usually reserved it for another seminar, one that could be called arcane, which I held for a long time on Saturday afternoons and which contributed directly to my densest—and philosophically most important—books: *Being and Event* and *Logics of Worlds*. But for the time being there are no plans to publish these "other" seminars.

III. What Purpose Did the Seminar Serve?

It's hard for me to say in what respect my seminar was useful for people other than myself. What I noticed, however, was that its transmission of sometimes very complex subjects was of a different sort from that of my writings on these same subjects. Should it be said that the seminar was easier? That's not exactly the point. Clearly, philosophy has always combined oral activity and writing and has often privileged the oral over the written, as did its legendary founder, namely, Socrates. Even those—like Derrida—who promoted the primacy of writing were very careful never to overlook physical presence and the opportunities oral presentation provides for transference love, which Plato already theorized in his *Symposium*.

But I think that the oral presentation, as far as I myself and no doubt many attendees were concerned, conveyed the movement of thought, the trajectory of the investigation, the surprise of discovery, without having to subject them to the pre-established discipline of exposition, which is largely necessary whenever you write. It had the musical power of improvisation, since my seminar was not in fact written out. I met many seminar attendees who hadn't read my books. I could hardly commend them for it, obviously. But I understood that the thinking-on-the-spot effect of the oral presentation had become the most important thing to them. Because if the seminar "worked" as it should—which was naturally not guaranteed—the audience felt almost as if they themselves had thought up what I was talking to them about. It was as though all I'd done, in Platonic parlance, was trigger a recollection in them, whereas philosophical writing per se demanded sustained and sometimes unrewarding effort. In this respect, the seminar was certainly easy, but such easiness also left traces, often unconscious ones, of which attendees who thought they'd understood everything would have been wise to be wary.

For me, there's no question that the seminar served as a laboratory. I tested out ideas in it, either already established ones or even ones that emerged during my public improvisations, by presenting them from a variety of perspectives and seeing what happened when they came in contact with texts, other ideas, or even examples from contemporary situations in politics, art, and public opinion. One of the great advantages of oral presentation is to be able to repeat without really boring your audience—which would be very difficult to do in writing—because intonation, movements, gestures, slight accentuations, and changes in tone give repetition enough charm to make it not just acceptable but even retroactively necessary. So the seminar went hand in hand with the inner construction of my thought, something Deleuze would have called the moment of invention of the concept, and it was like a partly anarchic process whose energy could later be captured by prose in order to discipline it and incorporate it into the philosophical system I've created, whose final, and I daresay eternal, form, is nonetheless the written form.

Thus, some of the seminars directly became books, sometimes almost immediately, sometimes later. For example, *Saint Paul: The Foundation of Universalism* (the 1995–96 seminar, published by Presses Universitaires de France in 1997; English translation published by Stanford University Press in 2006); *Wittgenstein's Antiphilosophy* (the 1993–94 seminar, published by Nous in 2009; English translation published by Verso in 2011); and *The Century* (the 1998–2001 seminar, published by Seuil in 2005; English translation published by Polity in 2007). In all three of these cases, the content of the books is too similar to that of the seminars for there to be any need for the latter to be published for the foreseeable future.

But all the seminars are in a dialectic with books, sometimes because they exploit their effects, sometimes because they anticipate their writing. I often told my seminar attendees that I was without a doubt throwing myself on the mercy of their attention span (a two-hour seminar before such an audience is truly a performance), but that their presence, their degree of concentration, the need to really address my remarks to them, their immediate reaction to my improvisations—all of that was profoundly useful to my system-building efforts.

The complete set of volumes of the seminar may, in the long term, be the true heart of my work, in a dialectical relationship between the oral and the written. Only the readers of that complete set will be able to say. It's up to you now, dear reader, to whom every philosopher addresses himself or herself, to decide and pronounce your verdict.

Introduction to the Seminar on Lacan

KENNETH REINHARD

Why does Alain Badiou begin the project of publishing his seminars with the year on Lacan? Badiou often names Lacan as one of his three primary "masters," along with Sartre and Louis Althusser; but Lacan is certainly more than just one of several influences in Badiou's intellectual development. In his 1991 essay "Truth: Forcing and the Unnameable," Badiou writes, "A contemporary philosopher, for me, is indeed someone who has the unfaltering courage to work through Lacan's anti-philosophy."[1] For Badiou, it is not Sartre or Althusser or any other twentieth-century thinker, but *Lacan* whose challenges every contemporary philosopher worth his or her salt must confront.[2] The present volume of Badiou's 1994–95 seminar, the culmination of his three-year study of modern anti-philosophy with the special case of Lacan, makes good on this assertion, and demonstrates that in these terms Badiou is truly a—perhaps *the*—contemporary philosopher of our time.[3]

As Badiou indicates in this statement, it is not exactly Lacan's work as a whole that he considers urgent for philosophers today (and in this seminar he is concerned exclusively with the later Lacan), but Lacan as an "anti-philosopher." The term "anti-philosophy" was first used by several French Counter-Enlightenment figures to describe their reactionary opposition to the *philosophes*, and Lacan takes it up, perhaps with a touch of irony, in the 1970s.[4] Badiou, in turn, repurposes the expression, while preserving some aspects of its Lacanian inflection; for Badiou, anti-philosophy is not the antithesis of philosophy, but a transhistorical mode of thinking and doing that is both *critical* of one or more key philosophical concepts (such as truth or the good) and proposes a kind of *act* that it regards as in excess of philosophy's conceptual horizon. Badiou's list of anti-philosophers thus involves figures conventionally included in the history of philosophy, such as Blaise Pascal, Jean-Jacques Rousseau, Friedrich Nietzsche, and Ludwig Wittgenstein, as well as thinkers whose work falls outside philosophy proper, such as Saint Paul and Lacan. But however inside or outside, antagonistic or sympathetic, the anti-philosopher may be vis-à-vis philosophy, the philosopher has much to learn from their encounter, which at the very least may assist philosophy in clarifying its own agenda through the challenges of this particularly vexing other. Anti-philosophy overlaps at points with philosophy's other two historical antagonists, sophistry and religion, but its methods and ends are distinct from theirs. Like ancient and modern sophistry, anti-philosophy is skeptical about truth; and like religion, anti-philosophy seeks meanings outside the organons of knowledge. But anti-philosophy is neither a technique of persuasion or deconstruction nor a hermeneutics of revelation or redemption. Most essentially, anti-philosophy aims at an act that it believes is an unconditioned break, a transformation without determination, a groundless leap into the new. There is of course an element of the performative in both sophistry and religion that at moments might seem to align them with anti-philosophy. The anti-philosophical act properly speaking, however, is not in the service of some other aim (such as persuasion or belief), but is purely for its own sake. And whereas sophistry and religion are philosophy's competitors and often explicit enemies, the encounter of philosophy and anti-philosophy is more complicated, at times like that of therapist and patient, at others, like hysteric and master, and at best perhaps like that of neighbors—occasionally mutually beneficial, but uneasy and requiring careful minding of borders.[5] The philosopher is well-advised not only to tolerate anti-philosophy, but to study it, to take its critiques seriously (if not necessarily to heart), to look to anti-philosophy in order to clarify the topology of philosophy: what is proper to it, what is improper to it, and even perhaps what, to echo Lacan, is "extimate" to it—in philosophy *more than* philosophy.

Let us return to Badiou's statement that "a contemporary philosopher, for me, is indeed someone who has the unfaltering courage to work through (*traverser sans faiblir*; literally 'to traverse without weakening') Lacan's anti-philosophy." The term that Badiou uses in this statement, *traverser*, has a special Lacanian resonance, appearing in the well-known expression "to traverse the fantasy" which denotes a moment of subjective transformation or conclusion in an analysis—a moment of the *act*.[6] For Lacan, the aim of psychoanalysis is not self-understanding, but for the subject to "traverse" into a new position in the topology of the Other, the position of the object in its fundamental fantasy, in an act which involves the "destitution" of the subject itself.[7] Badiou's imperative that a contemporary philosopher must traverse Lacan's anti-philosophy would then urge us not merely to think it through and appropriate it, the way, for example, Continental philosophy has explored and absorbed the lessons of structural linguistics and anthropology. Rather, the traversal of Lacan implies something transformative for philosophy, a shift in its fundamental position or orientation in thought through the encounter with the work of this self-proclaimed anti-philosopher.

For Badiou, the essential philosophical ideas are the *subject*, *truth*, and *being*, and to "traverse" Lacan requires unflagging strength and the courage to rise to the real challenge that Lacan poses to these fundamental philosophical topics. Both Badiou and Lacan regard the subject not as the foundation of consciousness, but as something occasional and evanescent. But whereas for Lacan the subject is a vanishing point, merely a disturbance of the symbolic order represented by the petrification of one signifier in relation to the movement of the other signifiers, for Badiou the subject is a "rare" but real achievement, the local instantiation of a truth process, with which an individual may affiliate and thereby attain a kind of nonindividual immortality as a subject.[8] Badiou frames *Being and Event* with discussions of Lacan, clarifying the similarities and differences between his and Lacan's positions on being and the subject. In the opening Meditation, Badiou aligns his fundamental decision on being—there is no "one"; "oneness" is a secondary operation performed on a primary multiplicity—with Lacan's assertion in his later seminars that there is only a process of "some oneness" (*ya d'l'Un*), and that psychoanalysts must resist the temptations of the metaphysical One, which, like the possibility of a sexual relationship, is the yearning for something "worse" (in Lacan's elaborate coinage, *s' . . . oupire*, which we translate here as "yearsening"[9]). But in the closing Meditation of *Being and Event*, Badiou points out that whereas Lacan defines the *subject* as merely a gap or void, a "thing of nothing," in Hamlet's phrase, for himself it is *being* that is constituted by the void and its concatenations (or, in the mathematical language of ontology, the empty set). If *Being and Event* opens with a profound gesture of affiliation with the Lacanian project in terms of ontology, it concludes with a crucial distinction on the nature and significance of the subject. Yet on this point too Badiou is perhaps closer to Lacan than to most of his philosophical contemporaries, for whom the subject remains a metaphysical concept, irredeemably tied to essentialism and humanism.

Finally, whereas most anti-philosophers disparage the idea of truth and elevate the local effects of meaning in its place, Lacan never entirely abandons some notion of truth (even if in his later work he insists that it can only be "half-said") and dramatically devalues the category of meaning, which, as a function of the imaginary, he regards as an illusion of consistency closely linked to that of the ego.[10] Although Badiou agrees with Lacan in distinguishing truth from both knowledge and meaning, truth for him is the originary and essential philosophical idea. Badiou's understanding of truth derives from Plato, but breaks with most traditional philosophical definitions of truth in terms of correspondence, coherence, or pragmatic value, which Badiou refers to as "veridicality." For Badiou, truth is the emergence of something new in a world on the basis of what is most generic, hence most invisible and least localizable, within it. Truth is not a representation of the generic, but its *extension*. Truth is always produced under certain specific conditions depending on the realm of its production (art, politics, science, or love), but it is intrinsically trans-worldly, universal, infinite, and eternal. Badiou's philosophical accounts of truth, the subject, and being are all markedly different from Lacan's anti-philosophical accounts; but unlike other anti-philosophers, Lacan *repurposes* these concepts for psychoanalysis rather than merely rejecting them as unreal. And this makes Lacan a most unconventional and especially persistent anti-philosopher.

Lacan seems compelled to revisit the history of philosophy to an unusual degree for an anti-philosopher, and frequently berates the analysts in his audience for not doing likewise. For Lacan the obligation to read philosophy is not simply a question of "knowing your enemy," although there is certainly an element of that; rather, as Badiou points out, Lacan "puts philosophy to a test," seeks to ascertain whether philosophy has any purchase on the real or account of the act.[11] Thus some of the singularity of Lacan as an anti-philosopher is due to the fact that he feels obligated not merely to reject philosophy, but as Badiou writes, to "traverse" it, endlessly probing its history for traces of the real—perhaps the way Doubting Thomas probes Christ's wounds in Caravaggio's painting—not only as the contrast to but also as the detritus of the decisive psychoanalytic act.[12] Like Badiou, Lacan has a special affinity for Plato, the philosopher reviled above all others by most anti-philosophers. And Lacan's relationship to other anti-philosophers is not entirely positive; as Badiou writes, Lacan has "an anti-philosophical relationship to anti-philosophy itself." Hence we might say that for Badiou Lacan's work not only constitutes a key instance of modern anti-philosophy, but is itself the *traversal of anti-philosophy*, its subjective destitution, both fulfillment and dissolution. As such it also marks what Badiou calls the "closure" of modern anti-philosophy, the end of a certain formal and historical sequence. So it is clear why Lacan's anti-philosophy poses a singular challenge for Badiou and everyone who would be a contemporary philosopher, everyone, that is, who would contest the sophistic and hermeneutic claim of philosophy's death—that is, anyone who would ask, as Badiou does, what Lacan's anti-philosophy—the traversal and closure of a certain anti-philosophical sequence—*opens up*, for the philosopher willing to encounter it.

But what is distinctive about Lacan as an anti-philosopher? In what way is his critique of philosophy different from that of other modern anti-philosophers? Why does Badiou insist that Lacan is the single anti-philosopher with whom a contemporary philosopher *must* grapple; and why does this require "courage"?

Badiou begins the seminar by recapitulating the argument he had developed over the last few years that there are various distinct types of anti-philosophers, depending, on the one hand, on the different "subject matter" or materials on which they operate (that is, the particular realm of thinking that they endeavor to intervene in and transform) and on the other, on the different ways in which they locate and practice the all-important anti-philosophical act. For example, Nietzsche's subject matter and the material in which he makes propositions, according to Badiou, is "art," while his act is "archi-political," as expressed in his famous announcement,

"We have just entered into great politics, even into very great politics . . . I am preparing an event which, in all likelihood, will break history into two halves."[13] That is, Nietzsche's medium is writing as creative invention, as rhetorical and poetic production; but the act that his entire life calls for is "archi-political," an intervention in the conditions or source of political action, in which he himself embodies a radical break in world history. In the case of Wittgenstein, the subject matter of his anti-philosophy, according to Badiou, is "language," understood as the material form of logical and conceptual construction, whereas his act is "archi-aesthetic," insofar as its central gesture is an act of showing or "letting-be" at the originary limit between the sayable and unsayable.[14]

Perhaps surprisingly, Badiou asserts that the material on which Lacan's anti-philosophy operates is "love"—rather than, as one might assume, *jouissance* or desire, which are arguably both more "material" than love for Lacan and more central to his theory and practice of psychoanalysis. In his earlier work, Lacan generally regards love as misrecognition, the result of transference, and connected with the imaginary aspect of the ego, but in his later thinking he assigns it a place of proximity to the real: insofar as love "makes up for the sexual relationship," whose impossibility comes to define the real for Lacan, love marks and holds open the place of that missing relationship.[15] For Badiou, of course, love will come to be understood as one of the four "truth procedures" (along with politics, art, and science) that are the conditions of philosophy.[16] Moreover, psychoanalysis is not just a theory, but a practice, something that *takes place*, and as such it seems to constitute an *event* in the truth procedures of love; as Badiou writes in his *Manifesto for Philosophy*, "In the order of love, of the thinking of what it conveys with respect to truths, the work of Jacques Lacan constitutes an event" (81). As we will see, one of the key elements of Lacan's critique of philosophy is that it puts a mere semblance of love (philo-sophia as the love of truth) at the center of its discourse. In doing so, according to Lacan, philosophy obscures the fact that, although love may be "imaginary," always transferential, merely a repetition, it nevertheless substitutes for something much worse: the illusion of the possibility of a sexual relationship.[17]

Lacan's anti-philosophical act, according to Badiou, is finally *archi-scientific*, an attempt to transform the relationship between knowledge, truth, and the real. Badiou cites Lacan's 1970 statement, "truth may not convince, knowledge passes in the act," as a key account of the act and its affiliation with knowledge rather than truth. Whereas most anti-philosophers regard the all-important act as a break with knowledge, whose value they minimize or relativize, for Lacan the act "passes" knowledge—which is not to say it "surpasses" knowledge, but on the contrary, that it *transmits* a kind of knowledge in the form of Lacanian "mathemes," by means of the particular psychoanalytic act known as "the pass."[18] But the questions of what counts as this "passed" knowledge, its distinction from truth, and its embodiment in Lacan's mathemes are complicated, and will require a good deal of Badiou's attention in this seminar.

If, according to Lacan, philosophy seeks "knowledge about the truth of the real," it is because philosophy assumes that the real is the way things are, however that may be defined, and that there is an essential truth of this real, however complex that truth may be. Furthermore, philosophy sees knowledge as the attempt to establish the coherence of truth and its correspondence to the real, and to articulate it in meaningful and adequate representations. Badiou shows that for psychoanalysis-as-antiphilosophy there can be neither truth nor knowledge of the real. For Lacan the real is not an object with an essential truth that a subject can know, but a constitutive contradiction at the heart of subjectivity, a failed or missed encounter (the impossibility of a sexual relationship). Philosophy's fusion (or confusion) of knowledge, truth, and the real on the basis of these reflective correspondences resembles what Lacan calls the "imaginary tripod" of psychosis—the pseudo-symbolic structure that lends a fragile stability to the psychotic's delusions, temporarily forestalling complete breakdown.[19] For Lacan the coherence of each of these dyads is illusory, and the three terms can only be understood as the irreducible strands of a Borromean knot in which no single term or link is self-sufficient. There is no representation adequate to the real, according to Lacan; it presents only the absence of meaning, or as he will put it in his 1972 essay "L'Étourdit," the real is "*ab-sens*," in excess of the philosophical opposition between sense and nonsense.[20] The term "ab-sense" in Lacan (and what appears to be its equivalent, "ab-sex sense") signifies the absence or lack of a sexual relationship, the rock of the real on which subjectivity is both founded and founders.

So whereas most anti-philosophers champion the always local and contingent practices of meaning-making against the philosophical certainty that there can be global knowledge of the truth of the real, for Lacan there is indeed a kind of knowledge in the form of a matheme that can be integrally transmitted through an act—the pass—a knowledge that cannot be reduced to a meaning, is distinct from nonsense, and has nothing to do with truth. Furthermore, this knowledge can only emerge with the dissolution of the analysand's supposition of the analyst's knowledge, which structures the transference in the initial stages of an analysis. Truth is a problematic concept for Lacan, especially in his later work, where he argues that it has the linguistic structure of fiction or a lie, it is always incomplete and can only be "half-said"[21]; yet the very impossibility of its full symbolic articulation gives truth some purchase on the real.[22] As Badiou points out, for other anti-philosophers there is usually something transcendent in the act, which reaches for a mystical or prophetic meaning beyond knowledge; for Lacan, however, the psychoanalytic act produces a knowledge that is both purely immanent and entirely transmissible.

Badiou isolates three statements Lacan makes about philosophy in order to identify the critical elements of Lacan's idiosyncratic anti-philosophy: the claims that philosophy (1) is blocked by mathematics; (2) plugs the hole in politics; and (3) has love at the center of its discourse.

It is a common anti-philosophical complaint against philosophy that it is too enthralled by and dependent on mathematics, which anti-philosophers tend to consider as not really a mode of thinking at all, but merely the manipulation of signs. Modern anti-philosophers such as Nietzsche and Wittgenstein locate philosophy's primal error in the moment when, under the influence of Plato, it defined its project as continuous with the discoveries of mathematics and geometry. But Lacan's anti-philosophy is quite atypical in its assessment of mathematics: when Lacan says that philosophy is "blocked" by mathematics, according to Badiou, he does not mean that it is too much under its sway, but, on the contrary, that it has failed to fully comprehend mathematics. According to Lacan, philosophy is blinded to mathematics by its belief that the signs and formulas it uses are intended to discover or produce meanings linked to the world. Such a semantic or hermeneutical function is completely foreign to mathematics' real work, according to Lacan, which is based on purely axiomatic decisions. In Lacanian terms, mathematics is an act of "saying" (*un dire*) rather than a statement, a meaning that is "said" (*un dit*). Badiou agrees with Lacan's account of mathematics, at least on this point, but he will object that Lacan's critique of philosophy here is too sweeping: it is true that such a reduction of mathematics to semiotics is an ongoing temptation for philosophy but, Badiou insists, it is a temptation that philosophy also actively resists. Philosophy is always in the process of separating itself from religion, understood as the discourse of "meaning" par excellence; hence there is always some lingering trace of the hermeneutical that philosophy tries to eliminate from its thinking, and this may appear at times in the form of such misapprehensions about the nature of mathematics. But the originary philosophical gesture, according to Badiou, is to distinguish the truths that are its conditions from opinions and the encyclopedias of knowledge as such. And contrary to the suspicions of most anti-philosophers, philosophy's closest ally in this project is mathematics. In this sense, Badiou argues, philosophy can "unblock" mathematics, allow mathematics to realize its unique status as ontology.

Badiou's account of Lacan's critique of philosophy as "plugging the hole" in politics is more complicated and requires explication, in classic Lacanian fashion, in terms of the imaginary, the symbolic, and the real. There is a certain ambiguity in Lacan's formulations, moreover, as to whether there is a hole *in* politics that philosophy conceals or whether politics *is* itself a hole that philosophy obstructs with its metaphysical theorizations. First of all, Badiou points out that for Lacan philosophy fails to see that politics functions as an "imaginary hole in the real," a hole that functions, paradoxically, as a "glue" that produces solidarity in the face of capitalism's intrinsically fragmentary forces. This is indeed politics as denial of the real of capitalism, but it is also politics as shelter from or compensation for the trauma of that real; politics, in this sense, we could say, makes up for the impossibility of authentic human relations under capitalism. Secondly, Badiou shows that, in a sort of dialectical reversal of his first argument, Lacan also sees politics as a "symbolic hole in the imaginary," insofar as politics cannot be reduced to communitarianism, the imaginary coherence of the group, but involves "symbolic authorization" in a discourse, such as "collective will," beyond any organization based on individualism, a discourse that produces knowledge as a hole in the imaginary unity of the nation or state. Finally, Badiou demonstrates how politics for Lacan acts as a "real hole in the symbolic," as the de-completion of the impersonal order of political ideals and law. And here Badiou cites Carl Schmitt's theory of the sovereign decision on life and death as an example of such a "hole," the real exception that constitutes the symbolic law in the very process of exceeding it.

For Lacan, philosophy, beginning with Plato, has done nothing but obscure the nature of these political inconsistencies with theories that would grant politics one form or another of consistency.[23] Badiou argues that for Lacan, on the other hand, the definitive political gesture is neither the foundational chartering of a collective nor the sovereign suspension of its laws, but the act of *dissolving* a group as such—a frequent occurrence in the history of Lacan's psychoanalytic associations themselves. For Lacan, a political organization is always contingent and temporary; it has a task to accomplish rather than a status quo to prolong, and the authentic political decision is the determination of the proper moment to liquidate the political structure that has served its purpose.

The third element Badiou points out in Lacan's critique of philosophy is the claim that philosophy puts love at the center of its discourse, in the form of the "love of truth." Badiou shows that for Lacan, when philosophy voices the superego-like command to "love truth," this is finally the imperative to love one's own impotence or symbolic castration as a speaking being, since truth is structurally incomplete, can only be "half-said"—the truth of the subject *is* its impotence. Philosophy promotes a lie about truth (that it is powerful) in order to conceal that truth is a lie, that it is limited by the conditions of linguistic structure, only available in the form of paradoxical spoken statements such as "I am lying." Badiou shows that for Lacan, philosophy could achieve a modicum of power by acknowledging that the truth it loves is merely a defense against its own impotence, and finally the lack of a sexual relationship as such, which it would prefer to know nothing about; only in this way could philosophy intervene in the all too human passion for ignorance. Philosophy has also erred, according to Lacan, in its promotion of happiness (which Lacan associates with "the American way of life") as the affect connected with truth. And Badiou agrees that happiness is both the aim of philosophy—although perhaps not in the "American" sense—and the affect of the truth procedure of love.[24] For Lacan, however, what philosophy and American ego psychology call "happiness" is only a defense against *jouissance* and the anxiety that is its affect. As Lacan indicates, in a passage cited by Badiou, "the psychoanalyst holds his act in *horror*."[25] Instead of this impotent love of truth and pursuit of happiness, psychoanalysis, according to Lacan, involves the *love of knowledge*, a love that, in Lacan's aphoristic formulation, "raises impotence to the level of impossibility."

For Badiou, this is perhaps the single most precious of Lacan's many "verbal treasures," and one that he suggests, most remarkably, may also provide a precise definition of philosophy. Lacan articulates versions of this formulation at various points in his later work, including the summary of his 1971–72 seminar, . . . *ou pire*: "In psychoanalysis, it's a question of raising impotence (which accounts for the fantasy) to logical impossibility (which embodies the real)."[26] Badiou argues that for Lacan philosophy loves and lingers in its own impotence, cherishing the fantasmatic cloaking whereby everyday castration, the limitations that we take on in acceding to the symbolic order, is accepted as an unavoidable "truth" of the human condition—an imaginary "realism" that philosophy prefers to the traumatic encounter with the real. Lacan takes a stand against impotence not by denying it (and proclaiming instead the reality of power, in the mode of Nietzsche) but by an act of "raising" or "elevating" impotence to the level of "impossibility"—which might seem even less potent. But whereas the "impotence" of castration involves a structure of fantasmatic compensation (finally, the unconscious belief in a fully potent Primal Father), "impossibility," as Lacan indicates, "embodies the real"—the real, precisely, as the impossibility of a sexual relationship. We may hear an echo in this formulation of "raising" of Lacan's account of the dynamics of sublimation in the1960s, in which "the object is elevated to the dignity of the Thing."[27] But the effective work of psychoanalysis as an act of "lifting up" something imaginary or symbolic (potency or impotence) to the level of the real (impossibility), does not have the "dignity" associated with the cultural work of sublimation. As Badiou points out, the psychoanalyst can only feel anxiety and "horror" at the prospect of this act. It cannot be faced with equanimity, insofar as it requires the analyst to enter into the place of the *objet a*, the wretched waste product of the analysand's act. Yet in neither case can this "lifting up" be reduced to the endless displacements and condensations of the unconscious, but involves an interruptive and transformative act, and the production of something new. Badiou uses Lacan's account of this elevation of symbolic "impotence" to real "impossibility" to schematize the movement of the analytic treatment: if the first phase of psychoanalysis involves a process of interpretation, in which the primal fantasy that accounts for the analysand's impotence is formalized as a movement of signifiers, the second phase occurs when an *impasse* in that work of formalization is encountered. Such a formal impasse, the impossibility of passage, is the condition of a real act; the work of the analyst is not to bring the analysand to the realization that an act or real change is "possible"—an act that is possible is, in fact, no act at all. An act that appears as possible in a given situation can only remain within that situation. Rather, it is only by demonstrating its *impossibility*, by reaching an impasse in interpretation, as if with one's back to the wall, that the "pass" of a real act can emerge.

Some readers may find elements of Badiou's reading of Lacan unorthodox, quixotic, or even outrageous, especially coming from someone who does not hesitate to confess that he is "unanalyzed," has never been either an analyst or an analysand.[28] Badiou is not concerned about whether his ideas correspond with the doctrinal interpretations of one or another Lacanian school; he does not take a position about the various polemics that animate and divide them. Nor is Badiou interested in criticizing Lacan's anti-philosophy, although he points out what he takes to be limitations in some of Lacan's descriptive accounts of philosophy. Lacan's anti-philosophy is the only one that the philosopher really must work through, the only one that does not merely reject truth and knowledge, but rethinks their relationship with each other and to the real. The locus and matter of this thinking, according to Badiou, is love, and the philosopher cannot afford to ignore Lacan's evental irruption within the field of one of philosophy's four fundamental conditions. Finally, Lacan's project of elevating everyday impotence to real impossibility for the sake of a radically transformative act provides a working model for the intrepid philosopher of change. The philosopher who rejects the finitism and relativism of today's dominant ideology of what Badiou calls "democratic materialism" (ruled by the assertion that there are no truths, only bodies and languages) will find guidance and inspiration in Badiou's presentation of Lacan's singular anti-philosophy, and pointers towards a "materialist dialectic" which must encounter and traverse that impossibility.

About the 1994–95 Seminar on Lacan

ALAIN BADIOU

Since the late 1950s, Lacan has been as indispensable a companion along my intellectual journey as he has been a difficult one. He's been indispensable because it was through him that I found the means to effect a synthesis between the idea of the free Subject, which I'd enthusiastically embraced in my Sartrean youth, and that of the importance of formal structures, inspired by my long-standing admiration for Plato, my love of mathematics, and the Structuralist current that had begun to dominate the intellectual scene. And he's been difficult, because, even though Lacan constantly worked "with" philosophers, from Plato and Aristotle to Heidegger by way of Descartes, Kant, Hegel, and Kierkegaard, he not only refused to be identified as a philosopher—increasingly so as his system of thought took shape—but he also made a point of playing up a marked difference between the discourse of psychoanalysis and the discourse of philosophy. He ultimately summed up his position as being that of an "anti-philosopher," an eighteenth-century term that he revived. Since a rigorous practice, the analytic clinic, was the real on which his thinking was based, Lacan could only see in the philosophical discourse a pretension of thought to dispense with the real.

Before I began the seminar you're about to read, I had written a great many texts on Lacan, right from the time I was involved in the *Cahiers pour l'analyse*, during the years 1966–1968.[1] The most important of these can be found under the general heading "Philosophy and Psychoanalysis" in my book *Conditions* (Seuil, 1992; English edition, Continuum, 2008). It is clear to me, on rereading them, how they counterbalance an unqualified admiration for almost everything to do with the pure doctrine of the Subject against a stubborn resistance to almost everything to do with the Subject's linkage to both the real of being and the arrangements of the symbolic order, with the crux of the issue ultimately concerning what might be called "the being of truths."

I should add, and this is of no little importance, that the last chapter of *Being and Event*—Meditation 37—is entitled "Descartes/Lacan" and that I therefore conclude my ontological treatise with my paradoxical relationship to two of the foremost contributors to the ongoing renewal, in which I presume to participate, of the category of Subject.

There is no better evidence that this vexed, or vexatious, fidelity has lasted up until today than Lacan's strategic position in my second "big" systematic treatise, *Logics of Worlds* (Seuil, 2006; English edition, Continuum, 2009). Book VII, the last book in it, tackles the very difficult problem of the "body" of truths, hence of their material existence in determinate worlds. The author of reference, to whom the whole second section of Book VII is devoted, is none other than Lacan. I agree almost entirely with his theory of the subjective functions of the body, except that I have to reject his position that the Absolute is, in his words, "an initial error in philosophy" (*Television*, 108), which, as he sees it, seeks to "suture the hole [*béance*] in the subject." He's clearly a difficult companion, Lacan.

The 1994–95 seminar is part of a tetralogy devoted, as it happens, to the most well-known anti-philosophers. Although the tetralogy concludes with a key apostle of anti-philosophy, namely, Saint Paul, it deals first with modern anti-philosophers—Nietzsche (1992–93), Wittgenstein (1993–94), and Lacan—as opposed to the trio of classical anti-philosophers—Pascal, Rousseau, and Kierkegaard—to whom I may one day devote seminars. They amply deserve as much and are moreover already very frequently mentioned in my books.

As regards Lacan, the aim of the seminar was to focus more closely on the foundations of his anti-philosophy rather than to provide a general overview of his work. So the texts most often used were from Lacan's last "style," which, in privileging the real over the symbolic and topology over algebra, attempts to structure the analytic experience less on the basis of a logic—such as the logic of the signifier—than on the basis of the dialectic between knots and cuts, mazes and gaps, tangled paths and random clearings. Along with this, as a major shift, there is a strategic function of the mysterious *jouissance*, whereas in the first part of his project Lacan had instead attempted to isolate desire—to distinguish it from demand—by using a strictly symbolic determination of its object.

As you'll see, disagreement is constantly mixed with amazement at the Master's creative ideas. You make your way as best you can, in the underbrush at times. But you come across so many crucial formulations! Of all these verbal treasures, the one that stands out for me is that the goal of analytic treatment is to "raise impotence to impossibility."[2] The ultimate paradox is that this may well be the definition I've been seeking for ages (and which Lacan had already come up with long ago for a completely different purpose): the definition of . . . philosophy.

Alain Badiou, February 2013

Abbreviations of Lacan's Works Cited in the Text

AE   *Autres écrits*. Edited by Jacques-Alain Miller. Paris: Seuil, 2001.

É   *Écrits: The First Complete Edition in English*. Translated by Bruce Fink. New York: Norton, 2006.

EN   *The Seminar of Jacques Lacan, Book XX: Encore: On Feminine Sexuality: The Limits of Love and Knowledge*. Edited by Jacques-Alain Miller. Translated by Bruce Fink. New York: Norton, 1975.

F   *The Seminar of Jacques Lacan, Book XI: The Four Fundamental Concepts of Psychoanalysis*. Edited by Jacques-Alain Miller. Translated by Alan Sheridan. New York: Norton, 1998.

M   "Monsieur A." *Ornicar?* 21–22 (Summer 1980) / *Le Séminaire, Livre XXVII: Dissolution (1979–1980)*. Unpublished.

OP   *Le Séminaire, Livre XIX: . . . ou pire*. Edited by Jacques-Alain Miller. Paris: Seuil, 2011.

T   *Television: A Challenge to the Psychoanalytic Establishment*. Edited by Joan Copjec. Translated by Denis Hollier, Rosalind Krauss, Annette Michelson, and Jeffery Mehlman. New York: Norton, 1990.

Lacan

Session 1

November 9, 1994

This year, we are going to complete the series of seminars on contemporary anti-philosophy that began two years ago. We started with the foundational position, Nietzsche's, then, last year, we examined Wittgenstein's position, and we'll conclude now with Lacan.

This will impose two related tasks on us.

The first, of course, will be to determine in what sense Lacan is an anti-philosopher, a task made easier by the fact that, unlike the other two, he explicitly says he's one. Ultimately, as you know, identifying an anti-philosophy in the contemporary sense of the term always presupposes determining what I've proposed to call its subject matter and its act. We'll have a chance to come back to this as we go along, but let me just remind you, in this regard, that I identified Nietzsche's subject matter as artistic, while his act was archi-political.[1] And, as for Wittgenstein, I identified *his* subject matter as ultimately linguistic, or, more precisely, logico-mathematical, while his act had to be considered archi-aesthetic. A first proof will therefore concern the identification of Lacan's anti-philosophical subject matter and act. The difficult issue, since, as usual, it's the crucial one, will be the question of the act. You know what my hypothesis is—I've made no secret of it,[2] the theorem, if not its proof, is known in advance—namely that the Lacanian act is of an archi-scientific nature. So much for the first batch of questions. The second task will be to determine why Lacan can be regarded not just as an anti-philosopher but as someone who brings contemporary anti-philosophy to a close. Because if Lacan can be identified as someone who brings contemporary anti-philosophy to a close, that closure must presuppose not only an anti-philosophical relationship to philosophy but also, of course, an anti-philosophical relationship to anti-philosophy itself. There is no closure clause that is not based on a particular, determined relationship to what it closes. To say that Lacan is in a position of closure with respect to contemporary anti-philosophy as opened by Nietzsche is an odd thesis that needs to be grounded, not empirically in the fact that he's the last anti-philosopher we know of (because in that case there'd be no reason to say he's in a position of closure) but in the fact that the Lacanian position on the questions raised by anti-philosophy is such that one can, in effect, speak of closure. The issue of closure becomes complicated if we ask what it opens up to, since every closure is also and at the same time an opening. So if we say that Lacan closes contemporary anti-philosophy, the question immediately arises as to what this closure opens up to in the general dispositions of thought (along with, of course, my own particular penchant for posing the problem of what it opens up to in philosophy). In other words, what does Lacan's closure of contemporary anti-philosophy testify to with respect to what is opened up in philosophy?

So that's the core group of the very precisely formulated problems that we'll attempt to solve this year, which are as follows:

- the distinctive nature of Lacanian anti-philosophy in terms of its subject matter and act;
- the question as to in what sense it's a closure where anti-philosophy is concerned; and

– the question as to what this closure opens up to in terms of philosophy. Or, to use a metaphor I already used in connection with
Nietzsche: What is passed down to philosophy by Lacanian antiphilosophy as a closure?

⎯⎯∞⎯⎯

I'd like to begin today with a very specific issue, which has to
do with the subjective dimension. There's a recurring subjective
feature in anti-philosophy that I would call the anticipated certainty of victory as a subjective disposition with respect to one's
discourse.[3] Take Nietzsche in *Ecce Homo*, for example: "My philosophy will triumph one day."[4] This is the anticipated certainty of
victory in the strictest sense. Then there's Lacan in "L'Étourdit":
"It is not I who will triumph but the discourse that I serve" (*AE*,
475). And, finally, there's Wittgenstein, in the Preface to the
Tractatus, where the emphasis is different but is subjectively the
same: "On the other hand the *truth* of the thoughts communicated
here seems to me unassailable and definitive."[5] In all three statements you can hear the subjective disposition of the anticipated
certainty of victory.

Two comments can be made about this. The first is that the
anti-philosophical subjectivity is, as a rule, a subjectivity of victory
in the present. What I'm saying is true, what I'm presenting, what
I'm demonstrating, what I'm proposing, what I'm setting forth, is
in the element of truth, and its address, in this sense, is at once in
the present and timeless. In anti-philosophy there is, as usual—I've
really stressed this point—the subjective dimension of a delayed
temporality, which, in this case, is expressed in the anticipation of
the inexorable, ineluctable nature of victory. The anti-philosophical
discourse will triumph.

And here's the second comment: We might wonder what this certainty is based on. It is not, as might be imagined, the result of a facile critique, of a subjective presumptuousness. Consider Lacan's statement: "It is not I who will triumph but the discourse that I serve." What we actually have here is the very anti-philosophical dimension of service, meaning that the discourse is less proposed than served. Along with it there is an elision of the self or the subject precisely so that the anticipated certainty might emerge.

Even in Nietzsche's case, as I pointed out two years ago, the same holds true. We know—and this is the difference that will have an impact on everything I'll be saying this year—that Nietzsche himself absolutely had to appear on the stage of his act. So he couldn't avoid saying, in a certain way: "I will triumph," because he had to come to the gaping place of his act as a sort of *thing*. It is moreover this coming to the gaping place of his act that has come to be called his madness. Nietzsche comes between two worlds, but, as he is careful to say, it is not a self that comes there, in the sense of a presumption of the self. Indeed, Nietzsche will say very precisely that what comes there, between two worlds, is a *destiny*. Consider the chapter of *Ecce Homo* entitled "Why I Am A Destiny." It is only after answering this question that this "I" qua destiny can be said to come to the place of the act. Better yet, what comes to the place of the act is a thing, a something. Remember that amazing letter of February 12, 1888 that Nietzsche sent from his boarding house in Nice to Reinhart von Seydlitz:

> Between ourselves . . . it is not inconceivable that I am the first philosopher of the age, perhaps even a little more, something decisive and fateful that springs up between two millennia.[6]

So, "philosophy will triumph" or "It is not I who will triumph but my discourse" can be identified here in the notion of an emergence, an unprecedented upsurge, of which the "I," the self, is merely a dimension, a parameter, or a service, as Lacan puts it. And it is at the point of this inevitable upsurge, separate from the self, which, here, is but the emergence of a something between two worlds, between two discursive tenses, between two millennia, as Nietzsche puts it— it is only with regard to this emergence or unprecedented upsurge that the anticipated certainty of victory can be established. Incidentally, this is also why, in the Preface to the *Tractatus*, Wittgenstein can state, without either arrogance or humility:

> How far my efforts agree with those of other philosophers I will not decide. Indeed what I have here written makes no claim to novelty in points of detail; and therefore I give no sources, because it is indifferent to me whether what I have thought has already been thought before me by another. (3)

This statement, "it is indifferent to me whether what I have thought has already been thought before me by another" shows that the anticipated certainty of victory has nothing to do, either, with any presumption of originality. Originality, as far as an anti-philosopher is concerned, is ultimately just an academic notion. The point is not originality; it is the upsurge, which, as such, is unprecedented or unrepeatable. And therefore, even assuming that others might have said one thing or another resembling, or even identical to, what I have thought, it is truly a matter of indifference.

This is why the anticipated certainty of victory as a subjective feature of anti-philosophy is clearly of the order of the act: it is on the basis of the act that this certainty is guaranteed. And if the certainty is anticipated, if I say in the future tense "I will triumph" or "My discourse will triumph," it is because we can only be sure of the act by its effects. The act itself can only be grasped as the certainty of rupture on the basis of its visible effects. That's why, inasmuch as certainty is at the heart of the act, it can only be *anticipated* certainty, because victory becomes legible in the general system of the act's effects.

Let me remind you that, for Nietzsche, the archi-political act is an act that "breaks the history of the world into two halves"—that's his catchphrase—and as such, it will render the demise, the breakup of the world, or, as he puts it, the transvaluation of all values, visible. For Wittgenstein, the archi-aesthetic act (or the archi-ethical act, which is absolutely the same thing, or indistinguishable from it), will open up access to the mystical element, the silent principle of salvation, which, as the principle of the silence of salvation, will also only be legible in the system of its effects on the personal life of someone who submits to it.

So how is this issue presented in Lacan? What is at the heart of the anticipated certainty of victory, as expressed by Lacan in his statement to the effect that it is not he who will triumph but the discourse he serves? It's the analytic act, of course. That is why our whole approach will be to attempt to identify it as the real of the anti-philosophical act. One very tricky question will then be to determine whether the two can be equated or not, whether it's the emergence of psychoanalysis that puts an end, in a way, to philosophy, exposing it as a sham, and whether this emergence, whose proper (and, as Nietzsche would have said, "fateful") name is Freud, is reducible to the pure and simple existence of the analytic act. The analytic act that has, as we know, its own scene, a subjective scene where it is not directly a question of philosophy, or of anti-philosophy. Incidentally, I would remind you that anti-philosophy was characterized by Lacan as merely being *connected* with the analytic discourse.

But what exactly does "being connected" mean here? This will be one of our guiding threads. If there is an act, as there must be an act at the heart of the anti-philosophical disposition, how is that act connected with the analytic act? And how can this connection—for the time being still completely enigmatic—be the guarantee of a victorious certainty? The path we're going to follow, which, I must admit, is a grueling one that I'll only be giving a sketchy description of today, is the path of the act—in the Lacanian sense of the term, the act truly grasped in its activity as such, or, in other words, in what it guarantees in terms of victorious certainty—the path on which the act is not exactly of the order of truth. Or, more precisely, what is convincing in the act has far more to do with the inner resource of knowledge.

I'm mentioning this thesis, whose legitimation alone is complicated, right away, so that we can already see in it a dispute with philosophy that will become strained at the point of the linking, which is also an unlinking, of truth and knowledge. In a nutshell, for those of you who attended my seminar last year, we will see that, in Lacan's anti-philosophical strategy, the question of the truth/knowledge dis-relationship occupies a position that is ultimately comparable to the question of the truth/meaning relationship in Wittgenstein.

In this regard—and it was like a starting signal, the opening bell of a fight for me—I'm amazed by the last sentence in Lacan's "Closing Address to the Congress of the École freudienne de Paris" in 1970. In that speech, Lacan said, and this is really the last line of it, "Truth may not convince, knowledge passes in the act [*La vérité peut ne pas convaincre, le savoir passe en acte.*]" (*AE*, 305).[7] If I can explain, to myself as well as to you, what that sentence means this year, we will have pretty much achieved the goals we set for ourselves. So, now, I'm only saying, or repeating, the sentence: "Truth may not convince, knowledge passes in the act." It is because we can identify the act as the passing, or the "pass," of knowledge (the pass—we'll be seeing what *that's* all about![8]) that slowly, step by step, we'll be able to say that the act, for Lacan, is archi-scientific, or rather, as we'll see, that it gradually became so. This is why I'm using the sentence in question as the epigraph for what I'm going to attempt to say this year.

Truth may not convince, knowledge passes in the act.

I'd like to clarify this sentence with two comments that are quite unrelated, as you'll see, but that will open up a whole terrain of investigation for us.

Remember, first of all, that, to stick with what we know for certain, the basic gesture of every anti-philosophy involves a destitution of the philosophical category of truth. It could even be said that the essence of modern anti-philosophy—which is descended from Nietzsche—is the attempt to destitute, by various means, the philosophical category of truth.

This is perfectly clear in Nietzsche's work, where there's a plethora of passages in which we can observe the fact that the category of truth is ultimately a category of *ressentiment* and that the typical figure found in it is the priest. The most famous passage—I'll quote it for you—may be in *Twilight of the Idols*, which Heidegger discussed at length. But what gives the passage its force is that it ties the abolition of truth to the Dionysian affirmation in which the act dissolves. Between the twilight of truth, which, when all is said and done, is the philosophical idol par excellence, and the Dionysian affirmation, there is really a sort of unity of gesture, a unity of action. Let me remind you of this famous passage, in which, moreover—keep this in mind—truth is correlated to world: it is the "true world." It is thus the intelligible world, the Platonic "world-behind," but, in the end, it's the status at once philosophical and "worldly" of the category of truth.

Nietzsche writes:

We have abolished the true world: what world is left? the apparent world perhaps? . . . But no! *with the true world we have also abolished the apparent world!*[9]

Then, we find:

Noon; moment of the shortest shadow; end of the longest error;
zenith of humanity.... (51; trans. modified)

So there you have it! This comes as close as possible to the feeling
of the act, i.e., something that's an abolition—not a contradiction or
a sublation but an abolition—to which there is juxtaposed, and is at
the same time indistinguishable from it, the most dazzling, radiant
affirmation. It is both "the shortest shadow" and "the end of the
longest error," and the name for all this is *Noon.* Noon!

There is a whole thinking of noon. And over a long history, modern
history included, it has been counterposed to a thinking of midnight. It's important to understand, including in terms of the issues
we're dealing with here, what the metaphorical resource of noon and
midnight is in thought.

In Nietzsche, noon is virtually the name of the act itself. It's the
sun's zenith at the moment when shadow dwindles away to nothing. But I think one can simply say that any decision of thought
(philosophical, anti-philosophical, or other) opts metaphorically for
either noon or midnight. All thought is meridian, Paul Celan would
have said, but it is either diurnally or nocturnally meridian;[10] it is in
the wavering balance between the hours, the middle of the hours.
But being in the noontide middle of the hours isn't the same thing
as being in the midnight middle of the hours.

I think there's actually a poetic injunction that's always prior to
this choice. This question of noon and midnight may be one of the
points where the decision of thought is irremediably in the space
of a prior poetic injunction. In a sense, it's always from the poem
that we have already gleaned what noon and midnight dictate for

thought, since it's poetry that reveals the metaphor. And poetry will express it, in its division, in its scission. It will express the two sides of noon and the two sides of midnight poetically. There is already—and Lacan should be mentioned in this connection—a "topology of surfaces" here, which can be found in the metaphorical choice between noon and midnight, and in their respective divisions.

Let's explore, shall we, this division, which will be of use to us later, even though it may seem remote from our problems right now. Let's think, for example, about what both links and opposes Friedrich Hölderlin's and Stéphane Mallarmé's midnight, since we're dealing with the prior poetic injunction.

Hölderlin's night (there's also a whole problematics of day in his work) and his midnight proper are the time of the sacred treasure and the time of the holiness of oblivion. It is really in the holiness of oblivion that thought meditates as midnight. For Mallarmé, on the other hand, midnight is precisely the time of the undecidable, that is, also the time of gambling, of chance. These are really two very different midnights: one, like a midnight of repose but in the sense of receptiveness, of a wakefulness in sleep itself, and the other, a midnight that is on the contrary the midnight of the act, the midnight of "A Throw of the Dice."

Here are two excerpts I'll read you so that we can experience the resonance of this, not just the injunction. Let's take, for example, the second long stanza of Hölderlin's elegy "Bread and Wine" (translated by Michael Hamburger), perhaps his greatest nocturnal poem, in which the thinking of night is put into play. You'll see that this night is a remembrance, a place of memory, where sleep and wakefulness are side by side.

> Marvellous is her favour, Night's, the exalted, and no one
> Knows what it is or whence comes all she does and bestows.
> So she works on the world and works on our souls ever hoping,

Not even wise men can tell what is her purpose, for so
God, the Highest, has willed, who very much loves you, and therefore,
Dearer even than Night reasoning Day is to you.
Nonetheless there are times when clear eyes too love the shadows,
Tasting sleep uncompelled, trying the pleasure it gives,
Or a loyal man too will gaze into night and enjoy it,
Yes, and rightly to her garlands we dedicate, hymns,
Since to all those astray, the mad and the dead, she is sacred,
Yet herself remains firm, always, her spirit most free.
But to us in her turn, so that in the wavering moment,
Deep in the dark, so that there shall be something at least that endures,
Holy drunkenness she must grant and frenzied oblivion,
Grant the onrushing word, sleepless as lovers are too,
And a wine-cup more full, a life more intense and more daring,
Holy remembrance too, keeping us wakeful at night.[11]

That's what Hölderlin's night is: the traversal, at the height of wakefulness,[12] of a midnight of infinite guarding of the sacred treasure of both memory and oblivion.

If we take Mallarmé's night now, in the plot sequence of "Igitur," which is sort of a summary of the meaning of midnight, the overall sequence is presented as follows, in *4 Pieces*:

1. Midnight
2. The Stairs
3. The Dice Throw
4. Sleep on the Ashes, after the Candle is Snuffed Out

> More or less what follows: Midnight sounds—the Midnight when the dice must be cast. Igitur descends the stairs of the human mind, goes to the depths of things: as the "absolute" that he is. Tombs—ashes (not feeling, nor mind) dead center.

He recites the prediction and makes the gesture. Indifference.
Hissings on the stairs. "You are wrong": no emotion. The
infinite emerges from chance, which you have denied. You
mathematicians have expired—I am projected absolute. I was
to finish an Infinite. Simply word and gesture. As for what
I am telling you, in order to explain my life. Nothing will
remain of you—The Infinite at last escapes the family, which
has suffered from it—old space—no chance. The family was
right to deny it—its life—so that it stayed the Absolute. This
was to take place in the combinations of the Infinite face
to face with the Absolute. Necessary—the extracted idea.
Profitable madness. There one of the acts of the universe was
just committed. Nothing else, the breath remained, the end
of word and gesture united—blow out the candle of being, by
which all has been. Proof.[13]

And then, in parentheses, there is: ("Think on that") . . .

—⸎—

So there you have it—the double midnight, if you will! It's quite
clear: between the midnight of "there one of the acts of the universe
has just been committed," which is the time when the dice must
be thrown, and the luminous midnight of receptiveness where memory and wakefulness are side by side, there are what could be called
the two original poetic inscriptions of a possible midnight.

And to help you understand how a philosophy can be under this
possible double injunction of the metaphor of midnight, it could be
argued that this double midnight is inscribed, for example, in Hegel,
on both its sides, on both its surfaces, in what must simply be called
the nocturnal dimension of philosophy. As you know, for Hegel, the
owl of Minerva only takes flight at dusk, which means that philosophy
takes place when everything has already taken place. So philosophy

is in a certain way the midnight of the day of thought. That's why it's accomplished when, also, and at the same time as history itself has come to its end. But it's absolutely clear that, for Hegel, the philosophical midnight, which is the basic retroactive effect of the coming-to-self of the truth of being, will signify simultaneously a peaceful end—the culmination of the becoming of spirit—and something like an absolute decision, something in which the absolute decision of sense achieves self-consciousness. The Hegelian nighttime of philosophy is of course the ultimate abatement of the contrary deployment of spirit in its historial figures, but it's also the moment when philosophy, in this case Hegel's, decides about it with a decision that is absolute, final, and irreversible. A decision that is *last* philosophy.

Now what about noon, the noon that, in a way, will be of more interest to us? It, too, is inscribed in the poem's division. It, too, has two sides. There is what could be called a heavy, leaden noon, a noon at once defeated and triumphant: the "Noon, king of summers" . . .[14] But, more to the point, in terms of what concerns us here, it is noon as the name of thought dissolved in the splendor of day, or, closer to my own thinking, noon is basically the annihilation of the void of being by the radiance of what is [*l'éclat de l'étant*]. Due to the extreme brilliance [*suréclat*] at noon of what is, its own bedazzlement, the void, the withdrawal of being themselves disappear and there is nothing but this radiance, which is the radiance of what is as a figure of the moment when thought is in reality discordant with what has withdrawn behind this blaze of presence.

The poet who focused most obsessively on this figure is without a doubt Paul Valéry. This is why Jean Beaufret[15] could almost always draw a sort of specifically French line connecting Heidegger and Valéry.[16] Valéry focused on noon because, for him, the question of the coexistence of appearing and light was crucial to his own conceptual framework.

I'm going to read you one of his most well-known, but also most striking, passages on this issue: stanzas three and four from "Sketch of a Serpent," an excerpt from the collection entitled *Charms*:

The sun, the sun! . . . You dazzling fault!
You, sun, who mask mortality
Under the gold and azure vault
Where flowers keep their secrecy;
You, by unfathomable delight,
Proudest accomplice and the height
Of all my insidious traps,
You keep all hearts from ever seeing
The universe is just a lapse
In the purity of Non-being!

Great Sun, you whose alarm so rings
For Being, who follow up with heat,
Then close it in a sleep that brings
The landscapes painted with deceit,
Feigner of joyful phantoms there
That render visible in air
The dubious presence of the soul
I'm always pleased the way you shoot
The lie about the Absolute.
O flame-made King of shadows!. . .[17]

"O flame-made King of shadows!" That's what this noon is! In other words, the noon in which the radiance of appearing, in its very appearance, is actually the annihilation of shadow, of an essential withdrawal with which thought can no longer be in harmony. You could say that noon so conceived is thought dominated by the One. This is why, in "Le Cimetière marin" ("The Graveyard by the Sea"),

Valéry would connect this figure of noon with the figures of Parmenides and Zeno, right from the beginning of the poem. The maritime noon into which thought disappears will be the name for Eleatic thought, in which being and the One are in a relationship of absolute co-belonging.[18]

But there's another noon in poetry, and this has always been the case, because the poetic pre-inscription is originary. There's another noon of thought that is, on the contrary, the noon of the most important decision—not the noon of the stupor of being but the noon of division, or of a break. Let me mention right off the bat Paul Claudel and his play *Partage de midi* (*Break of Noon*). The noon that can be divided is clearly a different noon from the undivided one of the radiant appearing of what is. At that moment, noon will be the name of the real event, the meridian name, hence the name without number, the name that is not a number, the noon that counts nothing but the sun's zenith again, and will be the name of the real event. That is, the name of the turning point of life: at noon, something irreversible will happen and will consequently bear the name not of changelessness or the specific way in which thought is dissociated from being by the successive flashes of appearing, but, on the contrary, the name of the impossibility of stopping. After noon, stopping will become impossible because Noon has become the name of the irreversible.

⸺❧⸺

With regard to this extremely important issue, I'm going to read you the end of Act I of *Break of Noon*, in the second version of the play, since *this* noon is only found in the second version. In the first version it's not yet noon.[19]

But first a word about the context, for those of you who might not be familiar with the play. The first act of *Break of Noon* takes place aboard a ship bound for the Far East as it is going through the Suez

Canal. There are a woman and three men. The woman is Ysé. Then, there are her husband, De Ciz; her lover, Amalric; and the man who's madly in love with her, Claudel, portrayed under the name of Mesa. So this woman is surrounded by a set of men the whole question of which is its completeness. And aboard this ship, at noon, Mesa and Ysé's love will be determined to be a real—that is, impossible—love. Noon is the name of the irruption of this real, of the sudden, silent irruption of this real. The whole play will be about how this noon, which is the name of love as the impossible real, can nevertheless be the locus of a division. It will be the story of the division or break of noon as a division of the real of love at the point of the impossible.

―⸺―

In Act I, nothing is declared. Obviously, the event arrives, as Nietzsche put it, "on doves' feet," but nothing is declared, except that the noon whistle, the ship's siren that will announce noon, will be the stand-in for this unspoken declaration:

> YSÉ (*stretches out on the rocking chair*): Now we have really passed
>   Suez.
> MESA: We shall never pass it again.
> *Pause.*
> AMALRIC: In a few minutes it will be noon.
> MESA: We are going to hear the siren. What a queer name that is!
>   Siren!
> YSÉ: There is no more sky, and no more sea. There is nothing left but
>   the void, and in the middle, striking terror, is that species of fossil
>   animal which is going to begin to bray.

Just as an aside, you can see that the depiction of noon as nothingness, which was already evident in Valéry, is taken up again here, but for a completely different purpose, because, in the midst of this nothingness, noon will be the name of the break, not of the lack of distinction, between the radiance of what is and the essence of appearing.

MESA: What a cry in this desert of fire!

YSÉ: The brontosaur is going to begin to bray.

DE CIZ: Shh! Look!

> *He opens the awning with his finger.*

YSÉ: Don't open the awning, for Heaven's sake!

AMALRIC: I'm blinded as though by a gunshot. That's not what I'd call sun anymore.

DE CIZ: It's like lightning! You feel reduced and consumed in the reverberating furnace.

AMALRIC: You feel horribly visible, like a louse between two panes of glass.

MESA (*near the crack of the tarpaulin*): How beautiful! How fierce!

The sea with its shimmering back

Looks like a cow thrown to the ground to be branded with a red-hot iron.

And her lover, as they call him, you know, the sculpture you see in museums, Baal,

This time he's no longer her lover, he's the executioner who sacrifices her!

It's no longer kisses he gives her, it's the knife in her womb!

And face to face she trades him blow for blow. Formless, colorless, pure, absolute, enormous, fulminating.

Struck by the light she answers in kind.

YSÉ (*yawning*): Oh, this heat! How many more days to the lighthouse at Minnicoy?

MESA: I remember that little nightlight on the water.

DE CIZ: Do you know how many more days, Amalric?

AMALRIC: God only knows! And how many days exactly since we left? I've no idea.

MESA: The days are so much alike they seem to form one single, endless, black and white day.

AMALRIC: I like this great, motionless day. I feel perfectly at ease. I admire this great shadowless hour.
I exist, I see,
I don't perspire, I smoke my cigar, I'm satisfied.

YSÉ: He's satisfied! And how about you, Monsieur Mesa? Are you satisfied? Well, I am not satisfied.

She laughs, but the solemn silence which is settling down is stronger.[20]

Note that this laughter occurs just as Mesa is about to name the event, the irreversible that will be declared by him, the impossibility of stopping in any place. Let me continue:

MESA: There is no place where we could stop if we wanted to.

DE CIZ (*pulling out his watch*): Be quiet! The hour is going to sound...
Long pause. Eight bells.

AMALRIC: Eight bells.

MESA (*raising his finger*): Noon.[21]

This excerpt was about the division of noon, in symmetry—albeit in staggered symmetry—with the division of midnight, where we nevertheless come back to the issue of whether we're dealing with the amiable discordance of being or with the point of undecidability and irreversibility of the act. Note that, with Claudel, as so often in the theater, the division is personified. Amalric's noon is all about feeling satisfied, while Mesa's noon is doomed to impossibility.

Note that here, too, as I mentioned about Hegel in connection with midnight, it's perfectly possible to say that Nietzsche's noon, which exists implicitly in Claudel's noon, consists of both noons at once: Mesa's and Amalric's, with Ysé suspended between the two. It can't be completely reduced to only one of them, even if Amalric could be said to be more Nietzschean, in the usual sense of the term, than Mesa. Nietzsche's noon is, on the one hand, the absolute, undifferentiated unity of affirmation, namely, one of Nietzsche's ideas according to which the Dionysian noon must affirm things without distinguishing between their values. In other words, it is the lack of distinction between the positivity and negativity of any evaluation, since all of it must in some way be completely affirmed. Thus, noon will be the name of complete affirmation. But, in addition, noon will of course also be the name of the sheer flux of life, that is to say, the ever-recurring event: the fact that there is nothing about this affirmation itself that supports it in its sameness; it's just as much the variety, the invariably ceaseless proliferation, of life. Nietzsche's noon is both the will to power and the eternal recurrence at one and the same time. Noon must be the name of both of them—the will to power as the complete resource of the constantly creative affirmation and the eternal recurrence as the particular way in which this affirmation must bring back what there is in its entirety.

<hr />

After this overview of the poetico-philosophical injunctions of the operation of noon and midnight, we might wonder: How does Lacan come into all this? Or another way of asking the question might be: Is Lacan a man of noon or a man of midnight?

To be sure, it's not really metaphor that guides him. Metaphoricity is essential to Lacan's thinking; there is an important theory of metaphor in it, but it's not metaphor that guides him. Rather, it's connection, the portmanteau word, or the matheme, let's say. But still, it's obviously no coincidence that he states that truth can only be half-said. There is a half-saying of truth, and if you take the particular way in which this is formulated in "L'Étourdit," you'll say—this is the exact sentence—"Truth can only be half-said" [*De vérité il n'y a que mi-dit.*] (*AE*, 449). Yes! Isn't that so? The fact that truth can only be half-said [*mi-dit*, a homonym of *midi*, "noon"] can't be purely coincidental. The fact of the matter is that truth can only be half-said. As you can imagine, if Lacan were reading this sentence, he couldn't fail to say that this "half-said"—*mi-dit*—is also a noon—*midi*—and that it could be expressed in the following way: Truth can only be *mi-di(t)*. The problem is whether we're doing credit to truth by connecting it to noon. Is it essentially a statement about truth? Or is it essentially a statement about saying [*le dire*]? This might seem like a rhetorical question, but it's not—especially if you recall everything I said about the Wittgensteinian connection between truth and the sayable, and if you recall that the entire anti-philosophical tradition is based on a unique and special proposition concerning this relationship between truth, saying, and act (the great triangulation of the anti-philosophical machinery). I've already had occasion to show this in Pascal. The triangulation of saying, truth, and the act is constitutive of the Pascalian apparatus of thought and ultimately of the apparatus of thought of every anti-philosophy. So it's vital to know whether, when truth is connected to the *mi-dit*, taken in its double sense of "noon" and "half-said," it is a statement in which the emphasis should be placed on truth or one in which the emphasis should be placed on saying. So, of course, we're also prompted to ask whether it would be true to say that truth is harmful [*nuit*, from *nuire*, "to harm," and a homonym of *nuit*, "night"] or that it is half-harmful [*nuit à demi*]. Is truth that which is half-harmful [*mi-nuit*, a homonym of *minuit*, "midnight"]?

This is the problem we'll start with, since the destitution of the philosophical category of truth is the basic gesture of every anti-philosophy. I would remind you that in an anti-philosophy, the aim, when it comes to truth in its philosophical sense, is not to refute that truth but to discredit it. This is even the reason why anti-philosophical polemics is not, strictly speaking, a philosophical polemics. Anti-philosophy's aim is to show that the category of truth is harmful—in short, that the half-said is harmful [le mi-dit nuit].

This is perfectly obvious in Nietzsche, the founder. But it's no less evident in Wittgenstein, especially in the further development of Wittgenstein's thinking. Remember: the defining feature of an anti-philosophy is that it's always a curative treatment. It's not a critique but a treatment. The point is not to critique philosophy but to cure people of philosophy, which has made them terribly sick: to cure humanity of the Plato-disease, as Nietzsche put it. And in Wittgenstein's case, to cure it of the philosophy-disease altogether, the latter being the propensity, which must be explained, to make absurd, senseless propositions. Thus, the issue of truth being harmful is not a mere language game here; it is absolutely intrinsic to anti-philosophy. Did Lacan say—did he end up saying, or can we assume that he might say, or that he did say, or would have said— that, just as truth can only be half-said, so, too, truth—in a certain sense—is that which is half-harmful? This is an enigmatic point, and it's a provisional line of inquiry.

With Wittgenstein, the destitution of truth is clear right from the *Tractatus*. Once again, I'll use the Preface, in which can be noted a somewhat crazy subjective arrogance—but which needs, on the contrary, to be understood literally as a sort of integrity. This is always the problem with the anti-philosophers: you have to understand as integrity what is clearly a sign of insanity. Wittgenstein writes:

I am, therefore, of the opinion that the problems have in essentials been finally solved. And if I am not mistaken in this, then the value of this work secondly consists in the fact that it shows how little has been done when these problems have been solved. (4)

This passage comes right after the sentence I quoted a little while ago about truth. Here's the whole passage again, in the Pears-McGuinness translation:[22]

> On the other hand the *truth* of the thoughts that are here communicated seems to me unassailable and definitive. I therefore believe myself to have found, on all essential points, the final solution of the problems. And if I am not mistaken in this belief, then the second thing in which the value of this work consists is that it shows how little is achieved when these problems are solved.[23]

The destitution of the category of truth begins in the following way: I have purified the notion of truth, I have eliminated its philosophical sense, I have fundamentally and definitively solved all the problems. And after doing all this, I realize that almost nothing has been accomplished. Hence: "how little is achieved when these problems are solved."

So Wittgenstein's thesis is twofold. First of all, the category of truth in its philosophical sense is harmful because it's linked to nonsense. But second of all, even if we were to unlink it from nonsense by proposing an anti-philosophical category of truth, this would in any case not be very important. So there's a double critique of the category of truth: first, its usurpation by philosophy is absurd, and second, even rectifying it only provides us with the solution to problems that, when all is said and done, are devoid of interest. The essential remains to be done, and this, for its part, is of the order of the act and no longer the true proposition. I don't have the time here, but it could be shown that the destitution of the philosophical category of truth always has this double meaning in an anti-philosophy: showing that the philosophical category of truth is harmful and, on top of that, showing that, assuming that what's harmful about it were removed from it (that's the rectification, or the treatment), well, it still wouldn't be very interesting or of great import as compared with the definitive resource of the act.

—∞—

What will it be possible to say about Lacan in this regard? The problem—as you can see right away—is a lot more complicated, because it's perfectly possible to argue that Lacan restored and, in a certain sense, re-established, the category of truth. In this re-establishment we find, of course, the gesture of destitution of the *philosophical* category of truth, while, at the same time, Lacan had to traverse that category. In his traversal of it, he set it aside in favor of another concept that he put in the very place of the analytic act. So Lacan cannot be said to be an anti-philosopher for whom the category of truth is, as such, in a central position of opposition. On the contrary, he kept up a long, tortuous flirtation with that category. And it can easily be argued, once again, that he is someone who re-established it.

What I'm nevertheless going to try to show here—and I want to point out that, as part of his research at the Collège international de philosophie, François Balmès had already paved the way where Lacan is concerned—is that from the 1970s on (let's use those years as a reference point) a long, uneven process of destitution of truth in favor of knowledge, or, let's say, of sidelining truth in favor of knowledge, was very much underway. Everything will have to be reconsidered: what does "in favor of" mean? How does one concept's prevalence over another come to be constituted in Lacan's work? What is this sidelining all about? These questions will gradually become the core content of our inquiry.

I think the problem was articulated in two statements that I'm taking from Seminar XX, *Encore*, from 1973—two statements that Lacan himself felt were hard to reconcile. The first statement was made in the May 15, 1973 session, the tenth session in Jacques-Alain Miller's transcription in the Seuil edition [translated as "Rings of

String" in the English edition(118)]. This is how it's formulated: "There is some relationship of being that cannot be known" (*EN*,119). The other statement, from March 20, is taken from the eighth session, to which Jacques-Alain Miller gave the title "Knowledge and Truth" (90). In it, Lacan says that the essence of analysis, i.e., what defines it, is that "knowledge about truth can be constituted [on the basis of its experience]" (91).

Two statements, then: "There is some relationship of being that cannot be known" and "Knowledge about truth can be constituted." Why is reconciling them so complicated, and why is there a tension between them? Of course, one is tempted to say that this relationship of being that cannot be known only concerns truth, and to that extent it would make a hole in knowledge and would be subtracted from something that cannot be known, something that belongs irreducibly to the order of the unknown and supposedly communicates with anything you like, including the unconscious. But, on the other hand, the essence of analysis is precisely the fact that knowledge about truth can be constituted. So it could be said that the tension, which I think is one of the most powerful moments in the final Lacan's work, could be expressed in the following way: On the one hand, truth is supreme insofar as it is unknown; there is some relationship of being that cannot be known, and, since this is the case, it is the language of truth to which the mastery of the unknown is linked. But, on the other hand, the essence of analysis is precisely to constitute knowledge about truth, or, in other words—let's face it—knowledge about the unknown. This is unavoidable, and it's a Freudian insight, after all: analysis does in fact consist in bringing unconscious knowledge to light. But if the essence of analysis is to constitute knowledge of the unknown as knowledge about truth, it is *knowledge* that's crucial, since it ultimately becomes that to which the analytic act will be related.

What I'll try to show, in fact, is that the key to this tension, to this enigma, has a name in Lacan's work and that name is the *matheme*.

I'll try to show that this is the name Lacan coined for what renders thinkable, simultaneously, and through writing—that's the whole point—the fact that there is some relationship of being that cannot be known, on the one hand, and, on the other, that there is nevertheless knowledge about truth, i.e., that there can be knowledge about the unknown. It's in this respect that, in Lacan, with a good deal of retroaction and anticipation, the matheme alone will provide the meaning of a statement that I think is wonderful, which can also be found in the 1970 "Allocution de Clôture du Congrès de l'École freudienne de Paris" ["Allocution sur l'enseignement"]. The statement is: "Knowledge constitutes the truth of our discourse" (*AE*, 302). It's a statement whose meaning is not self-evident, considering everything I've just said, but it happens to be crucially important in terms of the tension I mentioned and dates from only a few years later.

The aim of my overall approach is to account for this extraordinary conflict between knowledge and truth on the basis of the Lacan of the 1970s. As I said earlier (this was my first enigmatic formulation): the analytic act, as the "passing" of knowledge, as "the knowledge that constitutes the truth of our discourse"—what will it be? As far as understanding it goes, I don't know whether we'll have made much progress by July . . . but in any case, it's fair to say that, in its Lacanian conception, the analytic act is first and foremost the fall of a knowledge that is supposed in the subject, the knowledge that the analysand presumes the analyst possesses. There has to be a fall of this figure of the subject-supposed-to-know in order for there to be an act in the act itself. [24] So long as the analyst-subject's supposed knowledge is maintained or reinforced, the act cannot occur. The act—whose stake is the Subject that the analysand, the "patient," is to become—therefore involves the taking on of a knowledge that the analysand must stop supposing is possessed by the analyst. But what does an unsupposable knowledge mean? An unsupposable knowledge means a transmissible and, if possible, integrally transmissible, knowledge—a knowledge that is no longer dependent on the singularity of a subject, no longer dependent on the analyst's position, because it can be integrally transmitted to anyone at all.

If there is to be an analytic act, it will simultaneously be the destitution of a knowledge supposed in the subject and the taking on of an integrally transmissible knowledge. This obviously recalls the upsurge, in Nietzsche, of "something fateful between two millennia," of something between two eras, of something that drops off, of something that is unsupposed in the subject and is therefore positively transmissible. Yes, this reminds me of something about the matrix of the anti-philosophical act in general, in which we always see that truth is merely in eclipse, since the act is, so to speak, the in-between of supposed knowledge and unsupposable knowledge. Truth is merely in eclipse behind two different types of knowledge. It has to be there, of course. What does "has to be there" mean? We shall see. But the particular way in which it is there is ultimately, in terms of the act, in eclipse behind two types of knowledge—the knowledge supposed in the subject and the unsupposed and transmissible knowledge—meaning, in the final analysis, behind two types of knowledge one of which is subjective, even imaginary, and the other of which is impersonal. But an impersonal knowledge, as far as Lacan is concerned, is either a matheme or it's nothing.

And that now reminds us in exemplary fashion of Mallarmé's midnight: something has happened that causes the impersonal, transmissible idea, regardless of how much chance is involved in it, to suddenly appear as the idea of chance itself, as knowledge that cannot be supposed in any particular subject. So, in order for truth to be half-said [mi-dite], knowledge must be half-harmful [mi-nuit] in that sense. And this will provide a framework for much of our endeavor this year to explain the Lacanian statements I cited, along with a few others, and perhaps to understand—since we're in the interval between noon and midnight—what crucial connections there are between truth as *mi-di(t)* in Lacan's sense of the term and the ultimately Mallarméan act that takes place at the time when the dice must be cast, enabling the move from supposed to unsupposable knowledge and conveying—as philosophers, now, would say—an impersonal truth.

⸺∞⸺

So much for the first of the two points I said I would make; and here is the second. I told you right from the outset, with no guarantees, that the Lacanian act was both anti-philosophical and archiscientific. Am I getting ahead of myself again, or can we build on these questions, the way I did with respect to the destitution of the category of truth? I think we can understand the act especially from the Lacan of the 1970s on—and we'll only be concerned with that Lacan—by situating the triangulation of philosophy, psychoanalysis, and mathematics in his thinking. It's not through a mere face-off between philosophy and psychoanalysis that this question can be dealt with in the post-1970 Lacan's space of thought. This was already somewhat the case before, but after 1970 it becomes blatantly obvious. To understand Lacan's anti-philosophical dimension, it needs to be approached through a triangulation that includes mathematics.And it's regarding this triangulation that I want to give you a few reference points.

The first of these is from "L'Étourdit," where Lacan says:

> As it is the most appropriate language for scientific discourse, mathematics is the science without conscience that our dear Rabelais promised, the science by which a philosopher can only be blocked. (*AE*, 453)[25]

After the philosopher is identified as someone who can only be blocked by mathematics, there comes the following note by Lacan about the philosopher, a note that's very important:

The philosopher is inscribed (in the sense a circumference is said to be inscribed) [*he's an all-around truthful guy, isn't he?*] in the discourse of the master.[26]

You can see what he means: the philosopher is what's truthful in the discourse of the master, the philosopher is what runs true in the discourse of the master, or what makes it go round.[27] "He plays the role of the Fool in it," adds Lacan. *That* I like. You probably know that when Lacan was young, he wrote on the wall of the teaching hospital staff room: "Not just anyone who wants to can go crazy."[28] If we're playing the role of the Fool, this can at least be rewritten as: "Not just anyone who wants to can become a philosopher"—which is still pretty good!

This doesn't mean that what he says is foolish [*Lacan goes on, and this, in my opinion, is a laudable concession!*]; it's even more than usable . . . Nor does it mean, mind you, that he knows what he's saying. The court fool has a role to play: being truth's stand-in. He can play it by speaking like a language, just like the unconscious.[29] That he is himself unconscious is of secondary importance; the important thing is that the role should be played.

So the philosopher is someone who runs true in the discourse of the master. He plays the role of the fool in it, i.e., the stand-in for truth, who's absolutely unconscious of what he's saying and, as a result, is required only to play this role.

Thus, Hegel [*Lacan concludes, and this is of interest to us regarding the triangulation I mentioned*], although he spoke as accurately about mathematical language as Bertrand Russell did, nevertheless missed the boat: the fact is, Bertrand Russell is within the discourse of science.

This last comment suggests that Hegel said something essentially identical to what Russell would say about mathematics and yet it had no effect: it missed the boat because it was expressed from the standpoint of the circumference inscribed in the discourse of the master. Thus, Hegel may have spoken truthfully, but he was still blocked by mathematics.

⸺⸎⸺

Let's keep a few of this passage's points in mind. The philosopher as the master's fool. Fine. And what he aspires to is science with consciousness, so he's blocked, as a result, by mathematics, because mathematics is in exemplary fashion science *without* consciousness. You'll note the very subtle difference here between Lacan and Wittgenstein concerning the philosopher's relationship to mathematics. Wittgenstein's thesis is that the philosopher is deluded about mathematics in that he thinks—and this is not at all Lacan's thesis—that there's an absolutely unique resource in it, a resource that Wittgenstein will make every effort to show is *not* in it. The philosopher, according to Wittgenstein, has—ever since Plato—hypostatized mathematics: he has made it the paradigm of a thinking completely cut off from experience, not subject to the anthropology of language and thereby constituting a consistent body of universal truths. The philosopher thinks that that's what there is in mathematics. And the treatment, anti-philosophy's way of treating the philosopher's relationship to mathematics—the triangulation does indeed exist— will consist in showing that what the philosopher thinks there is in mathematics is not really in it, that mathematics is just a language like any other. Thus, for Wittgenstein, the philosopher is deluded about mathematics, and the treatment consists in dispelling this delusion. As far as Lacan is concerned, the philosopher is blocked by mathematics, which is not at all the same relationship. The treatment, then, doesn't involve putting an end to the delusion but possibly unblocking the philosopher. Wittgenstein is the philosopher's psychiatrist, while Lacan is his plumber.

Anti-philosophy (and this has absolutely been the case since Pascal) always deals with philosophy's relationship to mathematics— philosophy's relationship to science, but especially philosophy's relationship to mathematics. And, every time, anti-philosophy shows that there's something wrong with that relationship. Only, in Wittgenstein's view, something's wrong with mathematics because the philosopher has a false image of it. It's a delusion, a sort of paranoia that must be treated as such: it's a thought disorder, so it needs to be cured. Whereas, in Lacan's view, if there's something really wrong with philosophy, it's because it's blocked by mathematics. Even if it knows mathematics, it doesn't understand it.

Finally, the last comment that can be made about this passage is that philosophy is usable. It's even "more than usable." What does that "more" mean? I have no idea. It's not just usable but . . . but what? Is it ultimately a form of knowledge? In any case, it's more than usable. This notion of being usable is absolutely important, absolutely crucial. It's what I myself translate as the Lacanian obligation to traverse philosophy. Anti-philosophy cannot do without philosophy; in other words, not only is philosophy usable, but it's a good thing that it is, because, in fact, it absolutely *has* to be used! And Lacan, as is well known, used it more than anyone. It's what I call the traverse operator. The anti-philosophical act itself needs to traverse philosophy and to perform a certain number of operations on it: destitution of the category of truth; unblocking with regard to mathematics, in Lacan's case, and putting an end to the mathematical delusion, in Wittgenstein's case. In short, anti-philosophy needs to establish the particular way in which it traverses philosophy. This is imperative for it. And this is what is recapitulated here by the fact that philosophy is quite, or more than, usable, and so it must indeed be used. So much for the first overview of the triangulation. If you really want to understand the operations by which anti-philosophy traverses philosophy and why Lacan talks all the time about those poor philosophers such as Hegel, Plato, Aristotle, Descartes, and many others, who are blocked by so many things, you need to identify what this essential imperative is.

The second sentence that I'd like to use for support, once again in "L'Étourdit," is an extremely important statement. But here, too, we'll only see why later on. I'll just give it to you as such so you can think about it:

> This is why the mathemes on the basis of which the mathematizable—itself definable as what can be taught of the real—is formulated in impasses, are likely to be coordinated with this absence from the real.
> (*AE*, 479)

Here, "absence from the real" is the absence of the sexual relationship. "Real," in the Lacanian period in question, often means that "there's no such thing as a sexual relationship." In any case, here, as the absence from the real, it means the absence of a sexual relationship and especially its absence in any mathematization, or, in other words, its absence in writing. But let's leave that aside for now. Let's simply examine the intelligibility of the sentence and just say that there is a real determined by an absence and with respect to which the mathemes on the basis of which the mathematizable is formulated are in impasse. There's the real, which, in this case, is the absence of sexual relationship; there's "what can be taught of the real," which is the mathematizable; and there are the mathemes, as the impasse of the mathematizable. It is here, to my mind, that the archi-scientific emerges in the place where the act will appear as what can only be called—a phrase Lacan would find abominable—"a real of the real." Before we overdo it, let's say more precisely: the writable real of the real that is taught. The matheme will be at a point of impasse, but this point of impasse is the point of the real. So the matheme will be at the real point of the mathematizable, which is "what can be taught of the real." So we are justified in saying that the matheme is what inscribes the real as an impasse—but the real of what? Well, of what can be taught of the real. For the time being, let's just make do with this formula that uses the phrase I'm suggesting, "the real of the real," in which, quite obviously, the two occurrences of the real are not of the same kind.

Once again, I'd like to make a brief comparison with Wittgenstein. For him, a truth that can be taught *about* the world—let's take "world" as the equivalent of "real"—is what can be expressed of the real in the form of propositions whose meaning is true. The sense of the world—not a truth *about* the world or *in* the world but the truth of the world as such, hence of life as such—the sense of the world is what cannot be expressed of the real in the form of true propositions. These things are very similar, very closely related to each other, if you think about it. In Wittgenstein's case, at bottom, you also have the mathematizable, i.e., the proposition as what can be written of the real, so to speak, in truth, that is, as a proposition that says something true about the world. And you have the sense of the world, namely, what really matters, in Wittgenstein's eyes—ethics, aesthetics—which, since it can't take the form of true propositions, will be termed "unsayable." The sense (the unsayable truth) of the world will thus be that aspect of the real, which, since it can't be spoken about, one must keep silent about.[30] Lacan will add: what cannot be expressed in speech can be expressed in writing, in the formula. What must be kept silent about, in Lacan's view, is indeed that real of the real that cannot be spoken about but only written. Such is precisely the matheme.

For Lacan, in what is absent as real there is what can be taught of this real; there is science. Then, of what can be taught of this real, there is what is at the real point of its impasse—what I call "the real of the real." And at that point there is not, strictly speaking, what can be taught; rather, there is what can be transmitted, which is not the same thing. Consequently, in terms of structure, the Lacanian matheme is the exact same thing as Wittgenstein's mystical element, since he calls "mystical element" anything that cannot take the form of propositions and is nevertheless what matters in the highest degree to us. Thus, the matheme is structurally equivalent to Wittgenstein's mystical element, except that there is a writing of it. If we move between Lacan and Wittgenstein, the matheme is like written silence.

This is the thesis I mentioned to you before, which I'll now argue: the matheme, which is the key to the act insofar as it is the "passing" of a knowledge, is the name of the archi-scientific. You can clearly see why it's the archi-scientific: because it's at the point of impasse of science, and not *in* science. The matheme will be the name of the archi-scientific, that is, what is capable of writing the real of what can be said of the real. This is not a saying of the real but rather what inscribes the real of what can be scientifically said of the real—if "what can be said" is taken as a synonym of "what can be taught." True things can be said about the real: that's what science is. This sayable or teachable aspect of the real can also be written in the real: that's what the matheme is.

We have already seen that the anti-philosophical act, whatever its requirement or special nature, always necessitates this torsion: not a cleavage of the real, which would be too obviously dialectical, but a *double occurrence* of the real, which is ultimately situated at the point of the act, that is, which cannot be distributed, which cannot be supposed in a subject, which cannot be classified, which is not predicative. It's a double occurrence of the real, which is at the point of the act as torsion.[31] Here, the torsion occurs between the real as the real of science and the real of "what can be taught of the real," as a matheme. The double occurrence is science and the matheme, or, as is stated very precisely in the Lacan passage I cited, the mathematizable and the matheme, hence, in the final analysis, mathematics and the matheme. And the matheme is archi-scientific because it is not mathematics, being at the point of the real of mathematics itself. If it were mathematics, the matheme would be scientific. But we've just seen that, on account of the torsion, it can't be mathematics, precisely because it touches the real of mathematics itself, which is why it is archi-scientific.

Of course, there still remains to be proven (and it's a lengthy process to undertake) that there's a sort of reciprocity between act and matheme. This, as we shall see, hinges on the thesis that's so difficult to defend (but which I'll nevertheless defend) that, for Lacan, the analyst's desire is the matheme. This means that, in a sense, the matheme must also be in the position of an object, since that's a general law: only something that is in the form of the object can be the cause of desire. So if we claim that the matheme is at the point of the act, that the matheme is ultimately the new name Lacan came up with for what causes the analyst's desire, we'll have to accept that the matheme can function as an object and that what the analyst, like Rimbaud, desires is to find the formula.[32]

Let me conclude this long, complicated lecture by giving you our starting point for next time. I purposely got way ahead of myself today so as to give you a glimpse of the general space we'll be moving around in, with, I hope, greater precision. We're going to start over, simply and calmly, with the anti-philosophical operation properly speaking. And, by incremental steps, we'll reach the unbreathable heights of the matheme.

We'll begin with two statements. The first of these, which I already gave you, can be summed up simply as: "The philosopher is blocked by mathematics." The second is an extremely interesting and fascinating passage that you can find in the introduction to the German edition of Lacan's *Écrits* in *Scilicet* 5 [*AE*, 554]. It's a text from October 7, 1973 (we shouldn't completely lose sight of the chronological dynamics of all this), which reads as follows:

> For my "friend" Heidegger [*The word "friend" is in scare quotes. Can you imagine, one day, when the matter has been thoroughly dealt with—maybe Roudinesco[33] has already done so, I have no idea—can you just imagine the snide question that might be asked: When do these scare quotes date from? Were they in the manuscript or were they added on the proofs? When did "Heidegger" become untouchable?*] . . .

Anyway, it reads as follows:

> For my "friend" Heidegger [*just above this, he had said "a German I feel honored to know." And he added, in parentheses, " . . . (the way we express ourselves to indicate that we have made someone's acquaintance)"*] . . .

Anyway, it reads:

> For my "friend" Heidegger, invoked with the great respect I have for him: in the hopes that he might take a moment—a wish I'm expressing purely gratuitously since I know he won't do so—to take a moment, as I say, to consider the idea that metaphysics has never been anything and can only continue by plugging the hole of politics. That is its province. (*AE*, 554–55)[34]

So here, and under the auspices of his "friend" Heidegger, a second thesis about philosophy, related to the one about the philosopher being blocked by mathematics, is introduced: the thesis that the essence of metaphysics is to plug the hole of politics. Thus, Lacan suggests this wonderful idea to Heidegger, although he takes the precaution of saying he knows that Heidegger won't use it in any way, perhaps precisely because Heidegger, when it came to plugging the hole of politics, had already done his bit! But this text is truly very interesting. When counterposed to the other one, it raises two questions.

The first one is: does the word "metaphysics" have a meaning distinct from the word "philosophy" here? Lacan doesn't say it's philosophy that's engaged in plugging the hole of politics but metaphysics. Does Lacan then accept, here, the Heideggerian operator of metaphysics? The first question is: Should we make a distinction between philosophical thinking in general and metaphysics, giving "metaphysics" the quasi-technical meaning defined and introduced by Heidegger?

Once that problem's been dealt with, we'll ask: What's the connection between "being blocked by mathematics" and "plugging the hole of politics"? Is it because one plugs the hole of politics that one is blocked by mathematics? Or is it the other way around? Or are these two things completely unrelated? If that's the case, why the close proximity, so to speak, with the metaphor of the hole, the plugging and unplugging, the mental plumbing? As you can imagine, this issue is of the utmost importance to me, because I myself think two things about it.

First of all, as opposed to Lacan, I claim that philosophy ever since Plato has been precisely what *unblocks* mathematics as far as its status in thought is concerned. And I'm absolutely opposed to Lacan's thesis when he says (let me remind you):

> Thus Hegel, although he spoke as accurately about mathematical language as Bertrand Russell did, nevertheless missed the boat: the fact is, Bertrand Russell is within the discourse of science. (*AE*, 453)

I think the exact opposite. If there's a locus of thought that is blocked by itself, it is surely mathematics, because it's essential for it to be unaware of its own ontological significance. As a result, since mathematics is an active, creative truth procedure (contrary to Wittgenstein, I fully recognize mathematics as a form of thought) that nevertheless has a blocking point when it comes to its own ontological nature, I maintain, contra Lacan, that philosophy has constantly, and ever since Plato, been attempting to *unblock* it. The philosopher isn't someone who is blocked by mathematics but someone who attempts to unblock it with regard to itself.

Similarly, I think the other ongoing task of philosophy is to help reopen the hole of politics, which is constantly blocked, not at all by itself, as is the case with mathematics, but by the continuous efforts of very powerful people to ensure that a true politics—of emancipation, of equality, communist, or whatever you want to call it—to ensure that a true politics, therefore, doesn't exist.

In neither case can philosophy be confused with what it unblocks. It is not the same as either mathematics or politics. It clarifies the true nature of the one and provides assistance, at a still formal level, to the other against its enemies. But if you've got to choose between plumber metaphors, you can see that I situate the blocking and unblocking operations very differently from Lacan.

I would really like to see clearly into these various blocked sewers. So let's say that, two weeks from now, we'll begin by asking: What connection is there, in this Lacanian anti-philosophical business, between *blocking* and *unblocking*?

Session 2

November 30, 1994

Last time, as you'll recall, we'd gotten up to connecting two of Lacan's statements about philosophy. These two statements were: "Mathematics is the science a philosopher can only be blocked by" and "Metaphysics has never been anything and can only continue by plugging the hole of politics." That's a lot of blockages where philosophy is concerned, and the anti-philosophical tone is, after all, already very much in evidence here.

The interesting thing is that something other than philosophy is being referred to in these statements. Philosophy is grasped in terms of a unique relationship to mathematics, on the one hand, and to politics, on the other. In my terminology, this means that Lacan is explicitly referring to two *conditions* of philosophy: its political condition and its mathematical condition. And it is indeed as conditions that he uses them. It's very important for him that the philosopher be blocked by mathematics, in the very identification of philosophy. As for metaphysics being the hole-plugger of politics, the statement I quoted shows that, for Lacan, following Heidegger's lead, that is practically its essence. Metaphysics has never been anything and can only continue by plugging the hole of politics. Which, by the way, means that metaphysics only exists to the extent that there's this hole, otherwise the philosopher-plugger would have nothing to plug.

Is politics a hole? Does it have holes in it by definition? That's yet another kettle of fish. But we'll come back to it.

—— ◦◦◦ ——

The preliminary question I'd like to address today is this: Does Lacan's use of the term "metaphysics," rather than "philosophy," with regard to the hole-plugger of politics, have a particular significance?

Just as an aside, in the talk he gave at the "Lacan avec les philosophes" conference,[1] a talk devoted to Sophocles's *Antigone* entitled "On Ethics: Apropos of Antigone," Philippe Lacoue-Labarthe remarked, in passing, about Lacan: "Didn't he once say that politics was the hole of metaphysics?" That's not exactly what Lacan said, that politics was the hole of metaphysics. Of course, it served Lacoue-Labarthe's purposes to say so, but it's not exactly what Lacan said. He said that metaphysics plugged the hole of politics, but he didn't say that that hole of politics was a hole of metaphysics. Where is the hole, ultimately? What is this hole the hole of? What has a hole in it? If anything, you get the impression that metaphysics is the plug for a "hole of politics," about which Lacan didn't immediately say what sort of hole it was or from what breach it resulted. At any rate, he didn't say it was the hole of metaphysics.

This slip of the tongue made by Lacoue-Labarthe, who assumed that metaphysics was the historial destiny of philosophy, alerts us to an issue: What can Lacan possibly mean here by "metaphysics"? Especially since, as I told you last time, the passage in which this sentence appears contains a dedication to his "friend" Heidegger. So it does indeed seem as though metaphysics is being invoked here as a Heideggerian category. It is moreover a piece of advice he gives Heidegger—"You'd be well advised, dear 'friend,' to consider that metaphysics plugs the hole of politics"—even though he knows, he says, that Heidegger won't do anything with this suggestion.

In any case, "metaphysics" is most likely taking the place of "philosophy" here, in line with Heidegger. But a question then arises, a basically very simple question but one that, to my mind, hasn't been addressed head-on. It's this: Is Lacan, implicitly or explicitly, in agreement with Heidegger's historial framework? Which amounts to asking: Does Lacan, in one way or another, endorse the Heideggerian category of metaphysics, which is a category of the history of being? Of course, if Lacan was in agreement with Heidegger's metaphysical problematic—I'm not saying with Heidegger overall but with this particular issue that I call Heidegger's historial framework, i.e., with the Heideggerian category of metaphysics—or if Lacan saw himself as being contemporaneous with the idea of the end of metaphysics, of its closure, then the question of his anti-philosophy takes on a different meaning. That's what's important; it's this question that's crucial as regards Lacan's relationship to Heidegger.

The question of that relationship has two common forms, even though they may give rise to some rather sophisticated analyses.

The first, which is the low form, the "celebrity" form, is whether it was wise of Lacan to have lunch with Heidegger, whether, in hobnobbing with an unrepentant ordinary Nazi and an unreformed ordinary anti-Semite, he wasn't being a little foolhardy. Was it wise of him to invite his "friend" Heidegger, with or without scare quotes, to his home, knowing what we know, what he knew, what everyone had known for ages about Heidegger and national socialism?

The second form of the question can be expressed this way: In what terms can Lacan be linked with what I'd call Heidegger's antihumanism? Antihumanism in the deepest sense, that is to say, in the sense of a seizing by speech taken to the poetic point at which "man" is an obsolete category. Of course, we know that Lacan translated Heidegger's essay "Logos" from the German. But the interesting thing is that this essay, "Logos," is focused on Heraclitus's Fragment 50:

Not after listening to me, but after listening to the account [*logos*],
one does wisely in agreeing that all things are one.[2]

And, in effect, what I'd call the figure of Heideggerian-type antihumanism can be detected in Lacan's interpretation of this statement of Heraclitus's and of Heidegger's commentary on it. In this
context, "antihumanism" amounts to saying: it's never I who must
be listened to but something that transfixes and seizes me, whose
historial figure holds total sway over me, and that, here, takes the
name of *logos*.

But, ultimately, the most important question concerning Lacan
and Heidegger goes far beyond the explicit citations and references
that do in fact touch mainly on the question of the *logos*, or, in other
words, on the question of the specific way in which thought is based
on the originarity of a saying [*un dire*]. This issue is very evident,
but above and beyond it there is really the question: Did Lacan see
himself as being contemporaneous with the declaration of the end
of metaphysics—and therefore contemporaneous, in one way or another, with the category of metaphysics itself? Or again: Did Lacan,
either directly or indirectly, make use of the category of metaphysics as a singular figure confronted with its own closure? And, in
that sense, is there a contemporaneity between Lacan's project and
Heidegger's thematics of the end of metaphysics—that is, of the end
of philosophy in favor of a thinking whose origin lies with the poets?

I would venture another remark, namely that what's essentially at stake in this question, in terms of what we're concerned
with here, becomes clear if we connect it with another question,
which I don't intend to deal with right away. That question is: Isn't
Heidegger himself an anti-philosopher? If so, isn't Lacan's consonance with Heidegger ultimately the anti-philosophical consonance
itself? I already spoke a bit about this last year. To my mind, there
are two major figures in philosophy about whom the question of

anti-philosophy arises: there's Kant, and there's Heidegger. This is because, in both cases, there would seem to be a declaration of the end of the entire earlier philosophical apparatus, superseded by a new type of thinking: Critique, for Kant, and the "new God" for Heidegger.

Of course, the impasse of philosophy (conceived of by both of them as metaphysics) isn't the same for them. For Kant, it is the critical impossibility of any theoretical metaphysics, an impossibility demonstrated in the Transcendental Dialectic: it is impossible to anchor philosophy's traditional assertions in a consistent body of knowledge. So we must give up maintaining them. For Heidegger, it is metaphysics as a figure of the history of being that has reached the exhaustion of its essence and calls for its own end and its replacement in thought. Is this anti-philosophy, then, where both of them are concerned?

Well, no, actually. It could be shown—albeit, once again, this would have to be done in great detail, and it would amount to a long digression—but it could be shown that neither Kant nor Heidegger is an anti-philosopher, in the sense I attribute to that word. And this is so for two reasons I'm only going to briefly outline here.

The first reason is that the space of apprehension of philosophy, in both Kant and Heidegger, is still that of an acknowledgment, either historial or precritical, but in any case an acknowledgment. The distinctive operation and tone of radical discrediting that is characteristic of the anti-philosophical gesture is not evident in these writers. The question of philosophy remains the starting point for them, even if only to invalidate its apparent authority. But there's no proposition of a radical surpassing that denounces philosophy, from one end to the other, actually, as a pathology. This was already not the case with Kant, who, as a man of the Enlightenment, shared the rationalist and scientific ambition of all the classical philosophers. And it's even less the case with Heidegger since, for him, metaphysics is an epoch of the history of being. And insofar as it is the history of being, it remains an essential, and in a certain sense necessary, vection of the specific way in which the destiny of being is fulfilled. There is a destinal element that obviously cannot be dealt with in the figure of absurdity or of the purely pathological, in which, by contrast, Nietzsche's priest or Wittgenstein's senseless propositions are grounded.

The second reason—and I'll leave it at that for today—has to do with the fact that there's no alternative act, strictly speaking, in either Kant or Heidegger. They don't identify a distinctive anti-philosophical act that would both undermine philosophy and signal the advent of a different, unprecedented, completely unexpected disposition of thought. There may be a promise—that's the case with Heidegger—but the figure of the promise needs to be absolutely distinguished from the figure of the act. OK, let's leave this aside now. In the final analysis—and this is what I wanted to say— I will not contend that the connection between Lacan and Heidegger is based on the anti-philosophical gesture itself.

So we've got to go back to our point of departure: Is there, in Lacan's thinking, a clear identification of metaphysics or philosophy as a historial figure that has entered the period of its completion or closure?

I'd like to start with a passage from *Radiophonie*, which dates from 1970 (*Scilicet* 2/3) [reprinted in *Autres écrits*]. It's right at the beginning. In it, Lacan attempts to determine the impact of linguistics on the general theory of the symbolic, in response to the first question he was asked, which was as follows:

> In the *Écrits* you say that, without realizing it, Freud anticipated Saussure's and the Prague Circle's research. Can you explain what you mean by this? (*AE*, 403)

For our purposes, his answer contains three important statements. First, Lacan mentions the success that linguistics has achieved in its own field and says—this is the first statement, which is expressed clearly:

> It is thought that this success [of linguistics] could be extended to the whole network of the symbolic order by admitting meaning only on condition that the network guarantees it and the impact of an effect, yes, a content, no. (*AE*, 404)

This first part of the passage tells us that meaning is thinkable as an effect of the symbolic, an effect that is itself attributable to the symbolic's being defined as a network. All well and good. This statement already foregrounds the question of meaning, and that, of course, puts us on alert, since we know, and will confirm, perhaps even more precisely this year, that the question of anti-philosophy hinges to a very large extent on that of the meaning/truth opposition. Here, we are told that meaning is thinkable as an effect of the symbolic. Lacan continues as follows:

> The signified will be scientifically thinkable or not depending on whether a field of signifiers, which, by its very material, is distinct from any physical field obtained by science, can hold together or not. (*AE*, 404)

This second part of the passage indicates that we know that meaning is thinkable as an effect of the symbolic order conceived of as a network. From the symbolic order as a network we shift to the field of signifiers, a field that, if it holds together, i.e., if it is consistent, renders the signified scientifically thinkable. But on the other hand—and it is here that we move toward the *meta*-physical—the field of signifiers is, by virtue of its material, distinct from any physical field. It's a nonphysical field, hence unrelated to what can be obtained as a physical field by science. So the field of signifiers is not physical, and its consistency—the fact that it holds together even though it is not physical—guarantees that the signified is scientifically thinkable. This is where science comes into play. The signified will be scientifically thinkable to the extent that this nonphysical field of signifiers—and Lacan is very explicit about it being nonphysical, that is, not able to be obtained by scientific means—has consistency. This should be understood in the following way: some science—let's not say *a* science—exists, or at any rate something scientifically thinkable exists, whose condition is not physical in the scientific sense. So something scientifically thinkable exists whose condition—the consistency of the field of signifiers—is not physical in the scientific sense. Insofar as it is not physical it is *meta*-physical. Which is what Lacan will say—in fact, he goes on:

> This entails a metaphysical destitution, which should be understood as an act of dis-being [*désêtre*].[3] No meaning will henceforth be held to be self-evident. (*AE*, 403)

You see how the word "metaphysical" occurs here. Metaphysics, as conceived of here, appears as a dis-being of meaning. What is prohibited by this metaphysical operation is the fact that meaning can consist by itself, can consist in its being of meaning [*son être de signification*]. "No meaning will henceforth be held to be self-evident": this is really an operation of dis-being, because meaning cannot be thought—scientifically perhaps?—or, in other words, cannot enter the realm of the thinkable under the assumption that it derives this thinkability from its being. So being must be subtracted from meaning in order for meaning to be thinkable. All in all, everything is clearly articulated: a metaphysical condition of the thinkable exists as soon as thinkability has to do with meaning. This thinkability of meaning, requiring metaphysical consideration, which is itself linked to the consistency of the field of signifiers, can be said to produce a truth of meaning. But it will then be necessary to say that this truth can only be obtained as scientific truth (as "scientifically thinkable") under condition of a subtractive *meta*-physical operation, an act of dis-being, a destitution.

What, then, would Lacan's question be in relation to Aristotle's definition of metaphysics? Let's not go back to its beginnings but just take "metaphysics" in the clear definition Aristotle gave it. Lacan emphatically states here that physics does not exhaust the thinkable, not even the scientifically thinkable. Since "physics" is understood as that aspect of nature that comes to be scientifically thinkable, Lacan concurs with Aristotle about the fact that that aspect of nature that comes to be thinkable, which can be called a physics in its generic sense, does not, in fact, exhaust the thinkable. And so there must be a metaphysics.

But Lacan obviously objects right away that, in this meta-physics required by the thinkability of meaning, it's certainly not a question of a science of being qua being, as is the case with Aristotle. And this is even what must be expressly prohibited since the idea that meaning has a metaphysical truth in the realm of being must, precisely, be prohibited. It's not in being that we'll find what is thinkable of meaning, but, on the contrary, in an act of dis-being, that is, a destitution of being. It's only by prohibiting being from the consideration of meaning as thinkable that meaning can be guaranteed to be effectively scientifically thinkable.

That said, it's striking that this subtractive operation, this destitution, is precisely, in the strictest sense of the term, what Lacan calls metaphysics: what is not determined by any physics. So this is of course closely related to what was stated at the outset, namely that meaning is not thinkable as *content*; it is never of the order of content. To the extent that it's thinkable—let's leave aside the question of its being, since we need to remain within the logic of dis-being—to the extent that it's thinkable, or, in other words, under the condition of the destitution of its being, meaning is not of the order of content. It is of the order of the effect. Fine.

This is a very strong and coherent statement, and it defines metaphysics as (1) Aristotelian, since what comes after or along with physics forces us to see that it's not true that physics exhausts the thinkable; and as (2) anti-Aristotelian, so to speak, inasmuch as it's not a matter of the science of being qua being, let alone of substance, as is the fate of Aristotle's metaphysics (substance: what is there in what consists) but, on the contrary, of a radical dis-being that eliminates all thinkability of a content in favor of the thinkability of an effect.

We could say that Lacan both acknowledges and has reservations about metaphysics: he acknowledges it because the thinkable can't be contained within the strict realm of the physical, however broadly the word is defined; and he has reservations about it in the sense that, even if it's not a question of the physical, it's nonetheless not a question of the content of meaning in terms of its being, nor is it a question of ontology—which Lacan liked to write, as you know, with an *h: hontology*.[4] On another occasion he would say: "Onto-shamelessly now, I will say something . . .".[5] Well, from this point, we can shamelessly pick up the thread of our original question: Is metaphysics the same thing in Lacan's sense of the word and Heidegger's?

We could cut right to the chase and say no, because "metaphysics," for Lacan, is not in the space of metaphysics in the Heideggerian sense for a reason that seems obvious: for Heidegger, modern science, the scientifically thinkable, is prescribed by metaphysics as the history of being. So science, for Heidegger, is a figure that is itself dependent on the metaphysics of the subject, whereas, for Lacan, the point is to establish a science of meaning—or, at any rate, to make meaning scientifically thinkable, by taking on, by performing, a metaphysical operation, a metaphysical destitution that, far from having to do with the historiality of being, is constitutive of a dis-being.

You can see that it's absolutely clear that, for Lacan, neither science nor Descartes, who represents the thinkable condition of the subject of science, are, strictly speaking, figures of metaphysics as he understands it. The problem is, this angle overlooks a lot of questions and doesn't allow us to accurately gauge—to take the full measure of—the difference between Lacan's operation with regard to philosophy and the scheme of Heidegger's historial framework. We need to be more demanding and rigorous. We will therefore work our way through Heidegger so that everyone has as clear a view as possible of the parameters of the question.

⁂

Ultimately, what, for Heidegger, is the "distinguishing feature of metaphysics," as he himself calls it? We need to go back to this question with precision, because the whole little world of philosophy is in such agreement about the idea of the closure of metaphysics that, in the end, no one knows what's closed or open any more.

In this connection, let me refer you to a text by Heidegger that I'm very fond of, which has the peculiar advantage of not being a text. It's actually the notes you'll find in Chapter 9 of *Nietzsche*, published by Gallimard, located at the very end of Volume 2 under the title "*Projets pour l'histoire de l'être en tant que métaphysique*" ("Sketches for a History of Being as Metaphysics").[6] These notes date from 1941. In this text, written almost in shorthand, Heidegger tries to tell the history of being to himself. It's the history of being as told to children. I don't know if it's a story that would be enchanting enough to make them fall asleep, but it's the history of being reduced to its bare bones, although at the same time it is—albeit very elliptical, at times almost just lists of words—very important. The operations of metaphysics, as Heidegger attempts to narrate them, will reveal the ultimately distinguishing feature of this metaphysics.

As you know, there is first—this is the beginning of "philosophizing" as such—the Platonic, or what can be called Platonic, operation, which Heidegger describes as the subjugation of *aletheia* by the *idea*, or as the subjugation of truth as unveiling or unconcealment by the delimitation as presence of the Idea.[7] This shift will establish the "appearing as presence," or the delimitation of the entity, as imposing its dominance over the movement of the primordial disclosure of being. What was given in proximal immanence as the disclosure or the figure of the unveiling of being will be placed under the yoke of the delimitation of the idea as the figure of presence of the thinkable. As a result, the entity ensures its predominance in the order of thought over the very movement of being, because it forces being to be thinkable only in the guise of the "what-it-is." This shift from the question of being to the idea's delimitation of the "what-it-is," of the *ti esti*, will turn being into a normative position. This point is all-important. Instead of being the original movement of disclosure, or of the coming to self of its own essence, or of the return to self of unconcealment, being will become the very norm of what is, i.e., of the entity, in the guise of the "what-it-is."

But what I think is the fundamental point is that this comes about because the idea is counted as one. That is the fundamental operation of delimitation: something comes to be counted. This exposure to the count, which is the most basic prescription of the delimitation of the idea, is being as quiddity. What's that? What on earth is that? Insofar as the idea counts as One, the "whatness" of what there is—which is called "quiddity" in the scholastic tradition—causes being to be thought as quiddity, that is, as the normative principle of the *quid* of the entity.

Which leads Heidegger to say that this whole movement amounts to assuming the One. Let me quote this concluding passage, which will take us back to Lacan:

> The predominance of quiddity brings forth the predominance of the entity itself each time in what it is [*The delimitation of the idea will bring about a subjugation of the movement of displacement or disclosure of being in the form of the entity*]. The predominance of the entity fixes Being [*so a fixation occurs*] as *koinón* [*as common reason*] on the basis of the One. The distinguishing feature of metaphysics is decided [*so it's decided by that, at that very moment*]. The One as unifying unity becomes normative for the subsequent determination of Being. (55; trans. modified to conform to the French)

It is to this that the whole initial movement of the history of being leads us: the distinguishing feature of metaphysics is the enframing of being by the One. That is the distinguishing feature of metaphysics, which could be expressed as: the predominance of the entity, the advent of onto-theology, the forgetting of being. But in terms of the distinguishing feature of metaphysics, it is the enframing of being by the One. This means that the One as unifying unity in thought is really the norm for any subsequent determination of being. Consequently, the distinguishing feature of metaphysics can't be understood if it is not related to the question of the One. So we'll have to reformulate our question: What is the status of Lacan's thinking of the One? Is the Lacanian One, in all its various meanings, the decision of a normative position with regard to being? Is the One thinkable, the way psychoanalysis counts [*compte*] and recounts [*conte*] it, as the key figure of the metaphysical disposition? By itself, this problem provides a measure of the real degree of thinkable proximity between Lacan's conceptual framework and Heidegger's historial notion of metaphysics.

Unfortunately . . . Unfortunately, the question of the One is extremely complicated in Lacan. You'll say: everything's complicated in Lacan. More or less. But the question of the One is *really* very complicated. In my opinion, there are two extremely complicated questions in Lacan's work: the question of the One and the question of love, which are closely interrelated. We're going to get to that eventually; it's our trajectory.

I'm not going to give you a ready-made Lacanian theory of the One here. But since we're interrogating it now from the particular angle of the question of metaphysics, I'll give you a few things to think about, taken from the summary—hence a written text—of his Seminar XIX, . . . *ou pire* [. . . *or worse*], a summary you can find in *Scilicet* 5.[8] Bear in mind that we're interrogating this text in light of the fact that the key to metaphysics is that sort of diversion of the thinking of being toward simple commonality, the indiscriminate *koinón* under the normative authority of the One, itself derived from the delimitation of the idea.

Lacan begins by saying that the One is what one "yearsens for" [*s' . . . oupire*].[9] It's written as one word; it comes from the verb *s'oupirer*, *s*-apostrophe-*oupirer*. Then Lacan adds a crucial sentence:

> Those I characterize as yearsening are led to the One by doing so [*c'est à l'Un que ça les porte*]. (547)

In this sentence it's clear that there is an aspect of normative imaginary in the One, since one is led to the One in the dimension of yearsening, which, let's face it, is a dimension of getting worse or worsening, as Lacan will specifically point out a moment later. What I mean by this is that it's not good to yearsen. And Lacan says that not yearsening is, as he puts it, "a point of pride with me." So not yearsening is the pride of thinking. And those who do yearsen, well, they are led to the One by doing so. So not being focused on the

One is the pride of thinking—something Heidegger would whole-heartedly agree with.

Lacan then explains the pride the psychoanalyst can take in not letting himself be corrupted by the position of the One:

> Analysts can't accept being set up as abject pieces of trash in the place defined as being rightfully occupied by the One, with the added insult that this place is that of semblance. (*AE*, 548)

This is why analysts yearsen and for that very reason are led to the One. If you're an analyst and you don't want to yearsen, well, you'll have to accept being set up as an abject piece of trash in the place that's the One's place, which is that of semblance. Lacan seems to think that most analysts have no desire to end up as an abject piece of trash in the completely imaginary place occupied by the One. Which explains why they continue to yearsen for the One to stay in its place, and for them to stay in theirs, which is to be a wonderful Subject supposed to know all about the poor analysand who consults them.

Let's glean what we can from all this. Clearly, the One is associated by Lacan with a sort of discovery of the real that's blocked by a semblance. The One is in a place that belongs to semblance and that will have to be occupied, if you're an analyst, in real degradation and abjection. For our purposes, let's keep in mind that the One, which it's already not a good thing to yearsen for, marks the place of a subjugation of the (abject) real by (glorious?) semblance. That's without a doubt what Lacan is saying. If the One connotes a sort of localized subversion of the real by semblance and if that's why one yearsens for it, it could be said that this is not so different from the idea that the metaphysical diversion of being is the subjection of the disclosure of being to the normative One. Especially because the normative aspect can be found in Lacan, since the poor analysts' yearsening leads them to the One.

The third thing that should be noted in this text—and here, thank goodness, we're not really dealing with Heidegger anymore!—is that, as Lacan says:

> [A] woman ... doesn't yearsen for the One, since she's Other ... (*AE*, 548)

Note that, inasmuch as a woman, since she's Other, doesn't yearsen for the One, the One now seems to be associated with the universal mastery of the masculine—which could be called the mascul-One—position. A woman is its breaching, such that she's always Other, whereas men do yearsen for the One, thereby participating in the subjugation of the real by the demarcation of a place of semblance.

Incidentally, if a woman doesn't yearsen for the One since she's Other, then it must be admitted that this whole text of Lacan's, this whole summary of the . . . *ou pire* seminar, is feminine in essence, since Lacan expressly says that he prides himself on not yearsening: "Others yearsen, but I pride myself on not doing so."

Even if its tone is absolutely unique, all of this is still more or less in line with the distinguishing feature of metaphysics as defined by Heidegger, and therefore also in line with a critique of metaphysics as the normative subjugation of the real by the One placed in a position of semblance. What Lacan calls a metaphysics in the subtractive sense—that is, the metaphysical operation of dis-being that alone allows for a truth of meaning—is indeed a critique of metaphysics in Heidegger's sense of the term, namely, the subjugation of the real by the normative authority of the One. So the Lacan/Heidegger consonance would seem to be proven. But, as usual when it comes to Lacan, we're going to have to give things one more twist again or we'll end up being played for fools. Lacan takes a first precaution, which he thoughtfully alerts us to in the same text:

Moreover, I didn't propose a thinking of the One, but based on say-ing that there's some One [*qu' "y a d' l'Un"*], I tracked how it's used, so as to turn it into psychoanalysis. (547)

So we have to be careful: everything I just said about the One Lacan does not claim is a thinking of the One. But what is it, then? Well, it's the definition of its operation. There is an operation of the One. The One is only of interest to Lacan to the extent that there is some One, whose use can be tracked so as to turn it into psychoanalysis.

Here we've reached an absolutely, intrinsically fundamental point. Lacan's thesis is as follows: if you interrogate the One in terms of its being, you come back to that history of metaphysics as dis-being, you propose a thinking of the One in the Heideggerian sense, you interrogate the One in terms of its being with regard to the fate of the ontological question. That much I think can be said. But this is "bad" metaphysics, which ultimately leads you to the One, makes you yearsen. Any approach to the question of the One in terms of its being is never anything but yearsening. However, the One can also be thought in terms of a "good" metaphysics, namely, in terms of its dis-being, not its being. This will mean thinking the One in terms of how it's used, i.e.,—and this is completely consistent with our point of departure regarding the question of dis-being—thinking the One in terms of its *operations* in no way involves you in yearsening.

The basic distinction Lacan makes here about the question of the One is between (1) a thinking of the type "the One is," and it must be questioned in terms of its being—this type of thinking is metaphys-ical yearsening, because, in this case, you don't escape the normative authority of the One that subjugates the real in the very place of semblance; and (2) a thinking of the type "there's some One." But "there's some One" is a different thesis, a completely different one, from "the One is." It doesn't require thinking the One in terms of its being but simply noting that there may be some One in a realm of operations that's important, as Lacan says, "to turn into psychoanalysis." And the thesis that there's some One is itself subtractive, that is, consistent with the principle of dis-being. It will think the One as an empty place, as a demarcation or as an operation, but not as normative subjugation.

I'd simply like to point out that this Lacanian distinction between the One thought in terms of its being—the thesis that the One is—and the thesis "there's some One" as the power of the count, as the operative power of the count-as-one, is the very first thesis of my book *Being and Event*, its absolute point of departure. That goes to show the importance I attach to the whole of this difficult, fraught discussion. It is in fact the thesis on which will be based the proposition that, in terms of being, there is nothing but the multiple, the multiple without One. Meeting the challenge of thinking all the way through what a multiple without One is, a multiple that's not a multiple of units, is precisely the very starting point of my ontological project. Now, it must be acknowledged that this distinction is a Lacanian one. It's Lacanian because it links the existence of a being of the One to the distinguishing feature of metaphysics in Heidegger's sense and reserves the thesis "there is some One" for a metaphysical use in Lacan's sense—that is, in the sense of destitution and dis-being.

At this point, there are ultimately two possible meanings—regardless of the words Lacan himself uses—of the term "metaphysics." There's the Heideggerian meaning, definable as the subjugation of the real by the One and related to the thesis "The One is." And then there's the Lacanian meaning, which connotes a subtractive operation whereby all being is withdrawn from meaning so that meaning can be thought exclusively in the realm of the effect. It's from this second meaning of the One that Badiou could be said to have developed his ontology! Now that this has been more or less clarified, let's ask ourselves if we can discern an aspect of anti-philosophy in it.

⎯⎯⎯⎯⎯

We now have at our disposal a totally new and precise form of the anti-philosophical (in Lacan's sense) interrogation of philosophy. It can be expressed like this: Does the philosopher yearsen? I'd like to point out that, in the text we began with, the people Lacan has it in for are not *us* for once, not the philosophers but the analysts! They're the ones who take a beating. The analysts who have abandoned their own essence as analysts—the poor guys, they yearsen for the One because they don't like being relegated to abjection, to the point of real of the Thing.

But *we* can ask ourselves the following question: If, as Heidegger claims, metaphysics in its entirety, that is, philosophy in its destinal history, really consists in the subjugation of being by the normative authority of the One, then this statement, as interpreted by Lacan, could be written in a very elegant way: philosophers, for the past two thousand years, have been yearsening. Is that really what Lacan means?

Well, no, not at all! Because everything Lacan just said about the operational function of the One, as distinct from the bad One that's yearsened for, he will attribute . . . to *Plato*, Heidegger's designated culprit! Indeed, after his discussion of the One, Lacan writes: "Which is already in the *Parmenides* (Plato's dialogue)," and then adds this phrase that I just love: "owing to a strange avant-garde" (*AE*, 547). Far from being the initiator of an eternal yearsening, the great Plato introduced the true operational thinking of the One, the thinking Lacan wants to promote. Philosophy as the avant-garde of anti-philosophy! It's mind-boggling.

From this point on, we can refocus this Lacan/Heidegger comparison. In fact, for Heidegger, the metaphysics of substance in its Aristotelian sense is called metaphysics because it is the forgetting and the erasure, via the subjugation by the One, of what is expressed by the word "physics," namely, *phusis*. However, *phusis* is the primordial disclosure of being in its most originary effects. Heidegger says: *phusis* means to return to itself. He even renders it that way: "to return to itself." So it could be said that, for him, metaphysics is, in a sense, the forgetting of physics. Not of physics in Galileo's sense, but of physics in a much more fundamental sense, the one that allows us to still hear *phusis* in the word "physics," or, in other words, the disclosure of being in truth. Thus, "metaphysics," in its historial sense, is, for Heidegger, a sort of forgetting or erasure of what, originally, was heard in the word "physics," understood in its "most primordial Greek" sense, or anything of that sort—a German history of *Urnatur*, for example.

For Lacan, on the other hand, metaphysics is a subtractive definition of physics (indeed, what is scientifically thinkable of meaning is metaphysical, not physical), but still within the scientifically thinkable. This also means that it can be a science of the operations of the One. It's only by relating to the One though yearsening that there is metaphysical decline in Heidegger's sense of the term. But actually, for Lacan, metaphysics, in its strongest and most authentic sense, is the possibility of the scientifically thinkable that is *not* physical and is therefore not subject to physics. But since it remains scientifically thinkable—and that's the key point—the metaphysical is an extension of the scientifically thinkable and not an erasure or a forgetting of physics in its most fundamental sense of *phusis*. This, it must be said, is why Lacan is a lot closer to the Stoics than to Heidegger. Indeed, there's a key Stoic thesis about incorporeals, not in the sense of a suprasensible imaginary but in the sense of that which language, signs, provide perfectly empirical examples of. In the final analysis, Lacanian metaphysics should be understood as: there can be a science of incorporeals. The signifier is in fact not a body, in the sense of anything physics can define as a body. So it is of the order of the incorporeal. The Stoics had already acknowledged and made room in their own doctrine for incorporeals as substantial rationalities. We could say that, in terms of its inspiration, Lacan's metaphysics is Aristotelian-Stoic rather than Heideggerian.

So we're back at the heart of the question of Lacan's relationship to philosophy. Of course, for Lacan, there is a diversion of thinking by philosophy (which, for Heidegger, is metaphysics itself); there is a metaphysical yearsening. But—and this is a crucial point for Lacan's anti-philosophy—this diversion turns out to be divided right from the start: there is no single history of philosophy's diversion of thinking. That's precisely why there are two meanings of the word "metaphysics." At the very moment Lacan suggests that yearsening might well be philosophy itself, he says: "Right, but with Plato there is an avant-garde position." In other words, for Lacan, there's no one history of being, certainly not. Let's say that there's no one history of being that can bear the name "metaphysics." There's a very complicated, divided history that runs through what is known as metaphysics. It's fair to say that for Lacan—to use a metaphor of Heidegger's—the history of philosophy is conjointly (in the sense of a disjunctive conjunction, as Deleuze would say) the divided history of being and dis-being. In the historical field of philosophy's operations something like a yearsening history of being can certainly be observed, and there, in effect, Lacan is on many occasions close to Heidegger, including as regards the One. But the gradual construction of the operation, itself metaphysical, of dis-being can also be seen. As a result, Lacan's relationship to philosophy, and consequently the terrain of his anti-philosophy, is far more complex than Heidegger's. It's a really convoluted relationship. Heidegger's relationship to philosophy, when all is said and done, is that of a Hegelian-type historicity, with its own investigatory categories, its originary site, its successive stages, its present distress, and so on. It can be shown how Plato, then Descartes, then Kant, then Hegel, and finally Nietzsche all constitute systems of thought through which the history of being as metaphysics takes shape. But there's nothing like that in Lacan, even when there are flirtations with Heidegger—the reason for which, as I pointed out, basically revolves around the yearsening for the One. There, yes, something of metaphysics persists. But Lacan's fundamental relationship to philosophy is completely different. It's not a historial relationship, because what he wants to do is to put philosophy to a test. That's what he undertakes on the terrain of anti-philosophical operations. It's a matter of putting philosophy to the test of the analytic act. It's when put to the test of that act that the philosophical position will be discerned, divided, and made to appear as an inextricably tangled web of operations on being and operations on dis-being.

We'll have occasion to come back to the act. But let's take one of Lacan's countless provisional definitions in Seminar XX, *Encore*. When does the act occur? It occurs when [*says Lacan*] "there emerges [*as soon as you're involved in the act, you're involved in the emergence*] a speaking (*dire*) that does not always go so far as to be able to 'ex-sist' with respect to the words spoken (*ex-sister au dit*)(*EN*, 22).

So it's the emergence of a speaking that is not always able to exsist with respect to what has been spoken. A speaking has to emerge in which something of what has been spoken irremediably in-sists. A sort of fusion of the speaking and the spoken? Yes, but in that case a speaking that emerges and carries off with it a part of the unspoken that is attached, as it were, to the spoken, riveted to the spoken. At that moment, the act has occurred. This is why the act isn't the speaking but the emergence of a speaking-spoken [*un dire-dit*].

Do I understand what this means? I sort of understand it. Because, when you come right down to it, you could say that it's still very similar to Wittgenstein. It's the sudden emergence of a speaking whose relationship to silence (to what cannot be said) is essential. That is the moment of the act.

Lacan then says:

> That is the acid-test (*épreuve*) by which . . . a certain real may be reached. (*EN*, 22, parenthetical gloss in original)

So the act is a test that's an emergence, the emergence of a speaking, and through this test a certain real may be reached. This temporary description will suffice for the time being. But it's what Lacan adds that's of interest to us, and it's terrific:

> [A]n even bigger pain in the ass for us this year will be to put to this test (*épreuve*) a certain number of sayings (*dires*) from the philosophical tradition. [*Can you imagine?!*] (*EN*, 22, parenthetical gloss in original)

That was the syllabus of Lacan's 1972–73 seminar, and having to put the sayings of philosophy to the test of the act was a big pain in the ass! *That* is Lacan's real relationship to philosophy. This relationship, as you can see, is not a theoretical one. Sure, it's as theoretical a relationship as you like, but in its heart of hearts it's not a relationship of theoretical sampling or conceptual reference, not at all. Lacan's relationship to philosophy is a relationship of testing: philosophy will be put to the test of the analytic act, meaning that philosophy's sayings will be put to the test of the singular emergence of a speaking-spoken. Philosophy will have to traverse this emergence of a speaking that is heteronomous to every philosophy. And then we'll be able to see what is destroyed in the test and what survives.

When Lacan deals with philosophy, it's always in the context of that test. You'll notice that here and frequently elsewhere he uses the phrase "the philosophical tradition." I think that, ultimately, for him, metaphysics is not in fact a closing figure of the history of being. Instead, although the philosophical tradition of course conveys the two meanings of the word "metaphysics"—its meaning of being and its meaning of dis-being—it nevertheless does not constitute a history, only a corpus passed down by tradition, any given saying of which can be put to the test of the analytic discourse and its act.

But why are the sayings of philosophy, put to the test of the analytic act, such a pain in the ass? Why are they the biggest pain in the ass? To my mind, if they're a pain in the ass, it's because the origin of this tradition lies in its double-sidedness. It's not easy to grasp. There's something fundamentally and primordially double-sided about the sayings of philosophy. And the test of the philosophical tradition by means of the act is largely the test of this double-sidedness. This can easily be seen in the figure of Socrates. Lacan's Socrates will have to be written about someday . . . There are Nietzsche's Socrates, Hegel's Socrates, Aristophanes's Socrates, Kierkegaard's Socrates, Plato's Socrates, Xenophon's Socrates, and there's Lacan's Socrates. He's an incredible character, Lacan's Socrates! But if there's one thing we know, it's that Lacan's Socrates is a double-sided character. There's a Socrates, or rather Plato, who's simply dependent on the figure of the master, and then there's a Socrates, Socrates himself, who is more of an analyst. There's an identification of Lacan with Socrates. There's no doubt about that. There's a dimension of dis-identification, too. But this double-sidedness of the figure of Socrates is a double-sidedness it would be very interesting to compare with that of Nietzsche's relationship to Socrates. These two different double-sided figures really ought to be compared. Such a comparison would shed light on the very status of philosophy put to the test of the analytic act.

There's a passage in *Encore* that has always fascinated me, an exemplary passage about this issue and virtually about the origin of the difference between Lacan and Heidegger, too. Lacan points out that there is such a thing as the Other, that the Other is a hole, that it founds truth, and so on, and he then speaks about science. Here's what he says:

The fact that thought moves in the direction of a science only by being attributed to thinking—in other words, the fact that being is presumed to think—is what founds the philosophical tradition starting from Parmenides. (*EN*, 114)

Here, once again, he's on the side of metaphysics, except that this time—something Heidegger wouldn't like—he includes Parmenides in it. Metaphysics doesn't begin with Plato but earlier, with Parmenides, because Parmenides is the one who'd supposedly already instituted the subjugation by the One, by presuming that being thinks. And Lacan goes on:

Parmenides was wrong and Heraclitus was right [*the unity of the original make-up of philosophy is shattered*]. This is clinched by the fact that, in Fragment 93, Heraclitus enunciates: . . . 'the prince . . . who prophesies in Delphi neither avows nor hides, he signifies' . . . (*EN*, 114; trans. modified to conform to Badiou's paraphrase)

Thus, Heraclitus's theory of signification opens an alternative to Parmenides's theory of the identity of being and thinking. Note that, for Lacan, there isn't even any originary matrix; there's no Heideggerian inception. This is very striking because, as you know, Heidegger provided a great many analyses, sophisticated ones moreover, to show that, fundamentally, the movement of thought in Heraclitus and Parmenides was the same. It could even be said that, for Heidegger, thinking that what Parmenides said is contrary to what Heraclitus said is a typical symptom of metaphysical forgetting. Read all of Heidegger's texts on this subject. A typical symptom of metaphysics is to have said that Parmenides is the metaphysics of the One and being, and Heraclitus is the metaphysics of becoming. A whole very subtle operation of Heidegger's consists in showing that this distinction, this opposition between a thinking of becoming or of incessant flux on Heraclitus's part and a thinking of changeless being on Parmenides's part, is merely a metaphysical reinterpretation of the inception of being. And if you take a closer look at this inception, you'll then see that, in reality, Parmenides's and Heraclitus's systems of thinking are identical.

Now what does Lacan say here? He explicitly says the opposite: "Parmenides was wrong and Heraclitus was right." Therefore, there's no doubt for him that there is an originary split and not a single origin. For Heidegger, there is an originary site, an original disclosure of which Parmenides and Heraclitus were the inextricably entangled and intertwined instances of thought. For Lacan, there is an original alternative: either you're on the path of the co-belonging of being and thinking—Parmenides's path, in other words—or you're on the path of the dis-being of signification. For that's what's meant by the god's "he neither avows nor hides": there's no question of concealment or unconcealment of being in Heraclitus's interpretation. There's simply: "he signifies." Such is the Heraclitean path, the path of the dis-being of meaning.

As you can see, though, this originary split between the two paths is there right from the start of the philosophical tradition. It's not the evental cut of psychoanalysis that constitutes it, at least not in this passage. It's not something Freud introduced; it's philosophy's dual nature. Philosophy will be marked by the dual coexistence of the two paths: Parmenides's path and Heraclitus's path. Naturally, as a result—and this will be a conclusion of sorts regarding the question I asked at the outset—it's not on a history of being that the expression "philosophical tradition," which we'll henceforth use as denoting Lacan's overall relationship to philosophy, can be based. But what's a real pain in the ass is the fact that this philosophical tradition didn't begin with one simple origin; it began with an original duality. So where does the unity of this so-called tradition lie, a unity that's necessary if one is to declare oneself an anti-philosopher? Lacan, in his typical fashion, then makes a pirouette by saying that the key can be found in *love*—which will make things even harder for us.

Indeed, Lacan says:

[L]ove . . . People have been talking about nothing else for a long time [*this time, it's to be our one and only theme, our non-dual simplicity*]. Need I emphasize the fact that it is at the very heart of philosophical discourse? (*EN*, 39)

After all this, what do we know? We know that the philosopher (1) is blocked by mathematics, (2) plugs the hole of politics, and (3) places love at the very heart of everything he speaks about. It's this that we'll have to deal with in our difficult quest, namely, what is Lacan's anti-philosophical identification of philosophy?

It is on the basis of a complicated knot, not a simple history, that Lacan's anti-philosophical position is grounded. For there's apparently no way out of this conundrum without bringing in not just the two terms we have already had to deal with, mathematics and politics, but ultimately three, since we've got to work our way through love. It is in this triangulation of love, politics, and mathematics that "philosophy" can finally take on meaning, as we'll see next time when we undo the Gordian knot of the matheme, the hole, and the compensation love provides.

Session 3

December 21, 1994

Last time, I singled out three statements that could be considered a first attempt by Lacan—and by the post-1970 Lacan, the one we're primarily concerned with here—to identify philosophy. Let me give you those three statements again:

– The first one points up a relationship of philosophy to mathematics: the philosopher is blocked by mathematics.
– The second defines a relationship of philosophy to politics: metaphysics, Lacan explicitly says, plugs the hole of politics.
– And the third defines the relationship of philosophy to love: at the heart of the philosophical discourse there is love.

Now, we're going to deal with a very unique and interesting protocol, namely, the way in which an anti-philosophy, of whatever sort, identifies philosophy. We know that this identification strategy is always a discrediting strategy: the identification is linked to the effort to stigmatize philosophy in its very essence. Nevertheless, it's still possible to isolate identification protocols that differ depending on the various anti-philosophies concerned. It's fascinating to isolate one of these protocols from the philosophical standpoint and to see how, in what terms, and on the basis of what paradigms a given anti-philosophy proposes a thinking of what it calls philosophy.

I'll run through a few classic examples of anti-philosophers so that you have a good understanding of this identification protocol, because one of the challenges of this year's seminar is that Lacan's protocol for identifying philosophy is extremely complicated. I'd even say that there's an element of indirection in his anti-philosophy. And it is essential to think through this indirection because it is what justifies the thesis I'll attempt to argue: that, in a way, Lacan brings contemporary anti-philosophy to a close. Not anti-philosophy in general but one period of contemporary anti-philosophy. He brings it to a close by establishing with philosophy not just a simple relationship of direct discrediting but a very special kind of indirection.

Let's begin by noting that every anti-philosopher has his own favorite philosopher, his own personal whipping boy. If we ask how Pascal identifies philosophy, it's clear that for him it's Descartes. But in what Pascal is targeting above and beyond Descartes there is a general identification of what can be called "philosophy." Now, there's no doubt that, for Pascal, philosophy is a sophisticated form of diversion [divertissement]. Philosophy diverts us in that it takes us as far afield as possible from acknowledging what our real situation is. And philosophy's singularity lies in the fact that it is specifically the diversion of thought. There can be diversions of mood, of existence, of the body. The theory of diversion is complicated, but at the heart of the diversion of thought itself there is philosophy. And this is so for one main reason: philosophy claims to deal with God. The classic opposition, of course, is that between the God of Abraham, Isaac, and Jacob, on the one hand, and the God of the philosophers and scholars on the other. In reality, the identification of philosophy depends on the identification of God. And the philosophers' conceptual God—the concept-God we could call it—is, at bottom, the ultimate form of diversion with respect to what, in real life, can be tied to the true

God, to the God felt by the heart, and to the God of Revelation. Philosophy is grasped in its real heart as that which, owing to its concept of God, diverts us from the true God, namely, from the God who can only reveal himself as an intimate aspect of existence.

There is clearly another feature that is typical of Pascal's anti-philosophy but can be found in pretty much all of them: it's the fact that the identification of philosophy, the identification of the concept-God, of the demonstrable God, goes hand in hand with the appearance of what we might call, following Deleuze, a counter-figure, that is to say, a counter-figure to the philosopher. Indeed, one aspect of anti-philosophy—sometimes overlooked but in my opinion absolutely crucial to the anti-philosophical strategy—is that the anti-philosopher always speaks as if there were no point in addressing philosophers. This is a very important twist. You can find it even in Lacan. He is always careful to say, in his writings about the philosopher, that everything in them is intended for the analysts. It is by no means a question of engaging in a discussion in which you debate with the philosopher. The philosopher's case has already been settled or lost. What I call the counter-figure is the figure addressed in this very process of identification of philosophy, and that figure is never the philosopher. A true anti-philosophy is always an apparatus of thought that is intended to tear someone away from the philosophers, to remove him from their influence. That someone, whom I call the counter-figure, is the person who will have to be brought around to the act. The anti-philosophers think there's no hope of bringing philosophers around to the act since they are precisely the ones in relation to whom the act is constituted as anti-philosophy. This is why, in Pascal, the negative identification of philosophy is intended for the libertine. He's the one who's being spoken to. He's the man who's addressed in this whole business. And the libertine is not Descartes, he's another figure, another configuration. He's the person who might possibly be influenced by Descartes or fall under his sway. The libertine is the one who needs to be wrenched away from philosophy and returned to true thought, which is Christianity as Pascal conceives it.

Who is Lacan's counter-figure? Well, it's the psychoanalyst. Not the analyst as someone identical to Lacan's anti-philosophical position but the analyst as a wavering, vacillating position. Lacan always maintains that, ultimately, the analysts shouldn't be trusted. They always have to be forcibly led back to the analytic act. It would be really great to put together an anthology of the insults Lacan heaps on the analysts! An anthology like that would be fascinating, wouldn't it? No opponent of psychoanalysis would dare say even a small fraction of the things Lacan says to the analysts, especially to the ones who come to listen comfortably to his seminar. But when he insults them, it's on the basis of something crucial that's being addressed to them, which the insults themselves constitute. Just as, for Pascal, the libertine is truly the lost soul and yet he's the one being addressed, so, too, it could be argued that, for Lacan, the analyst is the lost soul. He's always treated as if he were in a lost condition. There are countless texts in which Lacan explains that the analysts—especially and even exclusively them—have of course not understood a thing of what he's been saying for the past twenty years. But even so, it's still to them that he speaks, with the patience of a saint. The same kind of patience can be noted in Pascal vis-à-vis the libertine. But these two instances of patience are obviously correlated with *impatience* vis-à-vis the philosopher, who will doubtless be lucky enough to end up being a little less insulted, simply because the anti-philosophers have always refused to speak to him. The very rare remarks addressed to philosophers that can be found in Lacan's work—I mentioned one with regard to Heidegger—are clearly throwaway remarks, remarks that admit they have no chance of being heard. This is perfectly clear. However, Lacan never says he has no chance of being heard by the analysts, albeit he notes, even as he whips and kicks them, that they haven't understood, that they don't understand, that they'll have to understand, that maybe someday they'll understand, that they'll understand a hundred years from now, and so on. It's hand-to-hand combat, an antagonistic way of addressing them. Such is the counter-figure, namely, the anti-philosopher's true addressee, even in the identification of philosophy. The point to keep in mind is that the anti-philosophical identification of philosophy is not intended for the philosophers but for the counter-figure. The counter-figure may be the libertine, the free thinker, the sensitive soul, the existent individual, the analyst, and so on. They comprise the gallery of counter-figures to whom anti-philosophy is addressed. Therefore, when we philosophers try to get wind of this identification we ought to be aware that it is not meant for us and that we're only hearing it through the keyhole. It's a matter between Pascal and the libertine, between Lacan and the analysts, or his analysts. It's a matter between Nietzsche and the handful of free men he tries to identify. This exercise in identifying the counter-figure to whom the anti-philosopher speaks could also be applied to Rousseau, Kierkegaard, and Wittgenstein. And, in every case, the inquiry would be over when we had both shown the protocol for identifying philosophy and isolated the counter-figure, i.e., the addressee of the identification.

In Rousseau's case, it's interesting that the philosopher is someone very specific: the bad man. And "bad" is a category. He even makes a doctrine out of it. Of course, Rousseau is targeting the philosophy of Voltaire, or Hume. And in a philosopher of that sort—the Enlightenment philosopher, in its traditional sense—Rousseau discerns a distinctive subjectivity, which is a "bad" subjectivity in the very conceptually elaborate sense that it does not open up to the voice of the heart, that it is the closing of the heart, that it turns heartlessness into a doctrine. The philosopher is someone in whom there is a deliberate obstruction of sensitivity—sensitivity in the deep sense of that which animates subjectivity. It is around this figure that the protocol for identifying philosophy, even when very complex, will coalesce. This in turn gives rise to the sensitive man-of-the-people as a counter-figure, the milk-drinking peasant with his simple belief in a God of goodness, a figure Rousseau tries to exempt from philosophical badness constituted as a paradigm.

There you go! Now you can try your hand at showing how Kierkegaard's protocol for identifying philosophy has to do with the Hegelian dialectic, whose basic aim is purely and simply to eradicate subjective existence, to dissolve the irreducibility of existence in the vast, abstract, and spurious dialectic of the concept. The counter-figure, you see, happens to be Woman. It's she who has to be made permanently immune to Hegel's charms. And to that end, she must be loved and guided to the serious ethics of marriage. This didn't make things any easier for our dear Kierkegaard, because getting married was a huge deal for him, and he finally gave up on it.

I've been rambling around in all this material so as to tell you that we've now reached the point where we can try to pin down Lacan's identification of philosophy, always bearing in mind that this identification is not addressed to the philosopher but to the counter-figure, the analyst. Which, by the way, is an important indication because it means that, in Lacan's view, the analyst himself is threatened by philosophy. But why should philosophy be such a threat to the analyst? Among other things, because the psychoanalysts are far too ignorant about philosophy to appreciate the danger it represents. Ironically, Lacan the anti-philosopher never stops insulting the analysts because they're ignorant about philosophy. "I told them to read the *Parmenides*, but how many of them have read it? Not a single one," and so on. And yet, the point is to extricate them from philosophy. The analysts ought to read philosophy but only to put it to the test under the ultimate law of the analytic discourse, and therefore to read it not to get *into* philosophy but to learn how to get *out of* it. I think there's one overwhelming reason for this injunction, namely that psychoanalysis is constantly threatened with being a hermeneutic of meaning. And it's clear that its innermost danger is philosophy: to be tempted to forget the psychoanalytic act in favor of the philosopher's hermeneutic position; to turn the treatment into pretentious chatter.

In the final analysis, there is a Lacanian anti-philosophy because something about philosophy endangers the analytic act. Clearly, Lacan's thesis is that philosophy endangers the act all the more to the extent that one is unable to identify philosophy. That's why it's very important to insult the analysts about their ignorance of philosophy.

Let's return now to the three statements I reminded you of at the beginning of this session. As things stand now, we can say that Lacan's anti-philosophy will knot these three statements together, meaning that philosophy will be identified by knotting together the triple definition of its relationship to mathematics, politics, and love. We must immediately ask what the principle of this knotting will be. As a first approximation, we could say that Lacan attributes to philosophy a religious recovery of meaning. It is by attributing to philosophy a function of meaning that, in its structure, is ultimately of a religious nature, that the three statements (being blocked by mathematics, plugging the hole of politics, and having love at the heart of its discourse—although we'll see that it's the inconvenient love of truth) will be put into circulation and knotted together. With regard to this issue, which I'll back up with evidence as I go along, there is, it must be said, a certain, quite explicit, Lacanian brand of Nietzscheism, which identifies religion as a powerful, and even in some respects consistently crucial, structure. And philosophy is not independent of this structural power. Metaphysics, traditional philosophy, is not independent of the religious logic of meaning, of the meaning of life, of the meaning of fate, of the meaning of sin. This leads us to what I'm always stressing when it comes to this business of anti-philosophy: the antinomy between meaning, or sense [*sens*], and truth. Let me remind you of the axiom I've established over the past two years which needs to be tested to see if it's valid for Lacan: essentially, an anti-philosophy always asserts the primacy of meaning over truth. That may even be its key operation.

In Nietzsche, for example, meaning, which is always an evaluation, the result of the evaluation of forces, is absolutely primordial, and truth itself is merely a certain typological register of meaning. Truth is only one of the possible figures among the great typological evaluations out of which vital difference is created. Roughly speaking, for Nietzsche, truth is the categorial type of the reactive force. And it is in the evaluation of the active force that the key to the question of truth, that which subordinates truth absolutely to the register of evaluation, hence to the register of meaning, can be found.

As regards Wittgenstein—I'm bringing this up again because it's rather oddly related to what we'll see with Lacan—"meaning" has two meanings, it has a double meaning. There's a first, very clear meaning: the meaning of the proposition. The proposition makes sense or produces meaning [*fait sens*] insofar as it describes a state of affairs the possibility of which is inscribed in the very substance of objects. This meaning is the propositional or linguistic meaning. Then there's a silent, archi-aesthetic or ethical—they're the same thing—meaning, which has to do with the act, that is, can in no way be written in the form of a proposition. It is this second meaning that is unsayable. One must remain silent about it: an imperative injunction that places meaning in the ethical order of the act. This meaning is the sense of the world, or the sense of the subject; they're one and the same. And this meaning radically trumps truth, which, for its part, is only the description of an existing state of affairs—something that happens, or that has happened. What is true are the natural sciences, the exact linguistic descriptions of existing states of affairs. And that's not very important compared with the meaning of the ethical act.

So let's bear in mind that this issue would obsess Lacan relentlessly. For Wittgenstein, truth is pure contingency: whether a state of affairs happens or not has no necessity whatsoever. And, as truth is the descriptive proposition of a state of affairs that happens, it turns out that being true is a contingent status of the proposition. Consequently, the primacy of meaning over truth—the anti-philosophical axiomatic—will ultimately be, in Wittgenstein's thinking, a certain form of primacy of necessity over contingency. Contingency is on the side of truth, while true necessity is on the side of the act, or, in other words, on the side of the sense of the world, or the sense of the subject, which amounts to the same thing.

At any rate, in both Nietzsche and Wittgenstein, despite their completely different itineraries, a manifest primacy of meaning over truth can unquestionably be observed, even and especially if meaning is real only as an act and is not accessible as a propositional or linguistic figure. In Nietzsche, the act expressed as "breaking the history of the world into two halves" is not of the order of a proposition either. What *is* of the order of a proposition is its announcement or its anticipated glory. It's Zarathustra, but Zarathustra, as he himself says, is his own forerunner. He thus belongs to the saying [le dire] that is prior to the act, which, for its part, is not of the order of a declaration or an announcement. For Nietzsche as for Wittgenstein, truth, as compared with the act that produces meaning, is a limited figure. With Nietzsche, it's a typological figure: the figure of the philosopher and the priest. With Wittgenstein, it's a scientific figure: the figure of natural science. The more profound and fundamental figure of the act is always located in the register of meaning.

Now how is this issue presented in Lacan? And how is it connected to anti-philosophy? Well, unfortunately for us, it's very complicated—extremely complicated. Once again, let's simplify things so that we can have an initial framework of analysis.

We could say that there's an early Lacan, for whom truth is clearly under the ideal of Galilean and mathematized science and where it moreover has a crucial causal function.[1] Truth—this is a very rough, but not false, statement—is the cause of the subject. And it is certainly true that, in this stage, meaning is partly dethroned. You can observe all the twists and turns of this issue by consulting the basic text of reference of this first stage, "Science and Truth," translated by Bruce Fink in *Écrits* (725–45).

Then there's a very noticeable shift that makes it possible to speak of a late Lacan, for whom, as I propose to show, truth is instead in a position of eclipse between supposed knowledge and transmissible knowledge. What becomes of meaning in all this? The tricky point is that, in this late Lacan, we can't get around the problem within the strict framework of the meaning/truth dichotomy. It doesn't work that way. Why? Because meaning must be examined in terms of its correlation with *knowledge*. Once again we find that triple figure, itself fragmentary—but we have no choice but to break things up, into truth/meaning/knowledge—in which the question of the identification of philosophy will be decided.

With this triple figure it is not possible to interrogate the function of meaning in terms of a simple classic anti-philosophical effect of destitution of truth. So what comes to the fore? Everything hinges on the fact that the real is partly definable on the basis of the absence of meaning, or sense. We will see how insistent and extremely difficult an issue this is. For if the real is definable on the basis of the absence of sense, then sense is involved in the definition of the real, even if it is in the form of absence: ab-sense.[2] We'll then have to ask: What is ab-sense? It's a lot of things. It's the absence that sense requires, which is even often internal to sense. It's the subtraction of, or from, sense. And it's something that is part of the classic function of lack in the early Lacan, something that is aligned with sense in the form of its withdrawal.

You can see clearly how everything hinges on the difference between ab-sense and non-sense here. From time to time I tell you with regard to Lacan: if we understand such and such a thing, we'll have understood everything. So I'm telling you once again: if we truly understand how ab-sense is different from non-sense, we'll have truly understood the real—which is no small feat, and is, moreover, according to Lacan himself, beyond all understanding. But, in fact, we'll have understood where to situate the primordial incomprehensibility of the real.

Let me give you a few guidelines taken from "L'Étourdit." A first statement that I find interesting is the following one, in which Lacan, once again, attempts to tell us what Freud's real contribution was—a statement there are countless versions of. Here, it's:

Freud tips us off to the fact that ab-sense denotes sex. (*AE*, 452)

Furthermore, we know that the real as the basic principle at the heart of the analytic discourse—the real as impossibility proper—is expressed as "There's no such thing as a sexual relationship." So what is this "sex" that is denoted by ab-sense? To pursue the question, Lacan invents the appropriate portmanteau word: "ab-sex sense." Ab-sense denotes sex, but ultimately sex as the real, or as nonrelationship, is an ab-sex sense. So we could say that ab-sense isn't non-sense, because it is ab-sex sense, meaning that ab-sense does indeed denote a real in a register that may, after all, be called the register of sense, even if it is sense as ab-sense. We're making progress . . . because sense as ab-sense is also sense as ab-sex, and therefore it is indeed real.

Don't think I'm losing my thread, the thread of knowledge and meaning! Because it may well be, then, (and this is all consistent) that the transmissible knowledge, the famous transmissible knowledge of which, as we know, the real is the impasse—if there *is* a knowledge and an integrally transmissible knowledge, and ultimately if it's a matheme—then, it must be a touch of the real, even if in impasse. And this transmissible knowledge must be correlated with ab-sense, that is, with ab-sex sense. Truth, for its part, is instead the veiling, or the unveiling, insofar as something remains concealed right from the start.

Very roughly, this could be put as follows: (1) The matheme is what is integrally transmissible. (2) Truth can only be half-said. So it's certainly not integrally transmissible. The logic is impeccable. It is therefore true that integrally transmissible knowledge is not essentially connected with truth, which, precisely because it's the gesture that both unveils and conceals, is essentially only half-sayable, capable of many things but definitely not of being integrally transmitted. We might then maintain that, if it's a question of knowledge here, such knowledge must be constitutively connected to that function of sense of the real that is ab-sense, which is the same thing as ab-sex sense. It is nonetheless very important to understand that ab-sex sense means real sense, that the real is the "there's-no-such-thing-as-a-sexual-relationship"; it's ab-sex itself. That's why, as far as this issue is concerned, I think that Lacan kept up a flirtation with Heidegger regarding truth or regarding the fact that there is an essential function of unveiling-veiling in truth, that truth is always in close proximity to the very thing it conceals, whereas nothing like that will be claimed about knowledge, which, as knowledge correlated with ab-sex sense, is capable of being integrally transmitted, of being a matheme.

Let me quote a passage from "L'Étourdit" that illustrates what we're talking about here:

> And I'm returning to sense to remind you how hard it is for
> philosophy—the latest to save its honor by being up-to-date where

the analyst is absent—to see what the analyst's everyday resource is: that nothing conceals as much as what reveals, that truth, *aletheia* = *Verborgenheit*. Thus, I'm not denying the fraternity of this saying [*dire*], since I'm only repeating it from the perspective of a practice that, being based on a different discourse, makes it indisputable. (*AE*, 451)

What is Lacan telling us here? He's telling us that philosophy has had a lot of trouble seeing, behind the question of sense, that truth is what conceals and is even the nothingness that conceals only insofar as it reveals. This is an instance of the flirtation he kept up with Heidegger, which I'm pointing out in passing and which was actually relatively late (1972): Heidegger was still philosophy, "the latest to save its honor by being up-to-date where the analyst is absent." It is in his daily practice that the analyst encounters the ab-sex of sense and experiences that truth is what conceals as much as what reveals. Heidegger was the only philosopher who was up-to-date about this— we should make a mental note of that, shouldn't we? With great difficulty, he saved the honor of philosophy. This is also a very Lacanian theme: for things that are the analyst's daily bread, philosophy has to make endless efforts just to obtain a little crumb of it. We work and struggle like crazy for things that any analyst sees in his daily practice. I'm not sure that's as true as all that. But whatever.

———— ✼ ————

Apart from the flirtation with Heidegger, you can see what the Lacanian stance is:

— First, the connection of knowledge with sense: if it's really knowledge, then it's in terms of the real that it's expressed as ab-sex, and the name of this connection is ab-sense.
— Second, the connection of sense with truth will be expressed in terms of withdrawal and unveiling.

– Finally, one must assume—even though this is a pretty risky assumption, but I'll make it here provisionally—that philosophy remains within the framework of sense and truth and that, by not including knowledge in the Lacanian sense in it, it fails to grasp ab-sense, that is to say, the real.

This is a very strained hypothesis in terms of what it implies about the identification of philosophy, but if it's correct, it becomes clear that Lacan's problem is not that of sense without truth. That's not what he actively opposes to philosophy. The problem is that philosophy is defined by the fact that it remains within the sense/truth relationship, whereas it's in terms of *knowledge* that the status of the real in this business can be expressed—the real that, under the constraint of the analytic situation, has the impossibility of the sexual relationship as its content. Hence, a key category that Lacan opposes, not to truth but to the sense/truth opposition as philosophy uses it, a category that is none other than the category of ab-sense. To the sense/truth confrontation in which philosophy supposedly only discovers the function of concealment and veiling (and even then, only when it has worked really hard, as Heidegger did), to this confinement of philosophy within the coupling of sense and truth, psychoanalysis, according to Lacan, opposes not a reversal of the hierarchy or primacy of either of the two terms but an ex-centering in terms of knowledge, i.e., of the real, under the category of ab-sense, which must be thought as being in no way identical to non-sense.

In my view, much of the rationality of the Lacanian apparatus, the reason it presents itself as an apparatus of thought and reason and not as one of irrational intuition, hinges on whether the category of ab-sense is rational or not. This is the testing program I would subject it to. You can easily see why: all forms of irrationalism produce a category of non-sense in one way or another. But in Lacan's case that's not the point, because everything hinges on the radical difference between non-sense and ab-sense, or, more precisely, between non-sense and ab-sex sense: ab-sense, insofar as it names the lack of sexual relationship, is ab-sex sense, which is not at all a form of non-sense.

This figure of rationality is crucial for the entire Lacanian apparatus, especially when it is known, as we'll see, that the analytic act consists in a production of transmissible knowledge of ab-sex sense and thus of ab-sense, which is ultimately based on absence. That the act brings to light what was absent, in terms of sex, is what is shown us by any analysis. This is precisely why analysis is archi-scientific. It was indeed under the ideal of science that Freud was able to tip us off, as Lacan writes, "to the fact that ab-sense denotes sex."

Lacanian anti-philosophy is not, then, a new version of an existential act that reveals sense to us—regardless of whether the sense is silent or sayable—and establishes its radical primacy over the limited and abstract space of truth. It is the act's keeping at bay the simple confrontation of sense and truth, in favor of the space of ab-sense or ab-sex sense, which can only be tested in terms of knowledge.

If I'm right—I've been talking a bit about something other than what I intended to talk to you about, but never mind—if I'm right, then you'll understand the extraordinary importance of the business about the pass. I'm going to say a word about it because it will allow us to get back to philosophy. What is the pass? It's a procedure that consists in establishing whether or not an analysis took place. Obviously, to the extent that one establishes that an analysis took place, one will be entitled to say that there was an analyst. But this is the direction it works in, not the other way around. You don't establish that there was an analyst in order to then say: since there was an analyst, an analysis took place. That's the procedure favored by the Chicago crowd, the Yankee International! By contrast, the aim of Lacan, who fought against Chicago right from the start, is to attempt to establish that an analysis took place and then, to the extent that an analysis took place, the analyst involved in this "taking place" will be said to be an Analyst of the School.[3] I'm not sure whether the analyst gives a damn about being recognized as such, but it means that it will have been declared by someone that an analysis took place, hence that there was an analyst.

So how can one test whether an analysis really took place? It will depend entirely on the idea of transmissibility. Someone will tell someone else what took place in an analysis, then that someone else will tell this to a third person. And, without going into technical detail, you can see what the principle is: someone tells someone else what took place and this someone else tells it to a third person, and the third person says: "Well, OK, then!" To verify transmissibility, there have to be two levels of transmission. This is very reasonable, because if someone tells someone else that something has taken place, it's not at all certain that there has been the slightest transmission. In order to determine whether there has really been any transmission, the second person has to tell a third person. And the third person, or persons, actually, who constitute a committee, say: "Right, in this case, an analysis took place!"

Two things about this procedure are of interest to me.

First of all, there's a certain empirical line of continuity with scientific procedures in the usual sense of the term. In science, when someone claims to have discovered something—even just a mathematical proof—how can it be ascertained that it really involved mathematics? The proof has to be shown to someone else or to several other people. And it will only be confirmed when these several other people have themselves been able to explain it to some other people. That's for sure. The three stages are always the stages of scientific verification because these are the stages that confirm transmissibility. When it comes to science, it's clear that there is a certain form of integral transmissibility, verified by the fact that the person who thinks he has discovered something will submit his discovery to the people called "referees" in the journals, who have to vouch for it before a final tribunal, usually the editorial board of a scientific journal, which tries, as far as possible, not to publish too much crap. All right. So this procedure is needed: the discovery has to "pass" and it always "passes" in three stages. That's why the pass is an empirical confirmation of the archi-scientific nature of the Lacanian conception of the act. The institutional form of the test of "an analysis took place" is based on the model of the transmissibility of a scientific discovery that serves as a test for its validation in the organized world of scientists.

Second of all, what is of even more interest to me is this: an analysis can only really take place if there's an analytic act, since in all thinking of the anti-philosophical type an ultimate primacy of the act can be observed. So if the proofs of "an analysis took place" are wholly of the order of tested transmissibility, that means there can be no confirmation of the act other than knowledge. For, in the pass, it's really a question of transmissible knowledge, and of it alone. So it would have to be maintained that the analytic act—as the real of analysis—can only be confirmed by the production of transmissible knowledge on which the act is based and which it validates.

You can see that we're very close here to a question that's essential for all anti-philosophies and has to do with whether or not the nature of the act is ineffable. Is there something that remains unsayable in the act? Does the act put a stop to all language protocols? Is the act essentially silent, as is the case for Wittgenstein, for Pascal ("Joy, tears of joy") and, in fact, for the whole anti-philosophical tradition? When it comes to this issue, Lacan's position will once again be quite surprising, innovative, or, at any rate, unique.

On the one hand, in effect, the act is the act—that is, it's not presentable as such in a proposition. That's for sure. In other words: it takes place in its place, which is the couch. The replacement of the divine [*le divin*] by the couch [*le divan*] has always struck me, because, with Wittgenstein, the place of the act is the divine.

Someone in the audience objects: *No, the* armchair *is the place of the act.*

The armchair then! Mind you, there are two places: the armchair and the couch. Does the act take place sitting up or lying down? There are two possible places or locations for it. Whatever the case may be, the act takes place in its place. Fine. In this sense, it must not, as a real act, be in the form of a proposition. And yet, the act can only be confirmed in the form of knowledge. We have something altogether new here, which can be summarized like this: the analytic act can only be confirmed as knowledge—not as truth, because I'll be damned if the pass makes it possible to verify any truth whatsoever! Knowledge, sure, as much as you like, but truth isn't involved—because, ultimately, it's knowledge that touches ab-sense. What's more, the pass produces absence, since over the course of the successive transmissions the original protagonist disappears. In the end, everything is judged in the absence of the interested party, in the absence of the person who is "passing" the pass. Fortunately, the analytic candidate is not a defendant, or else you could say: that's a perfect example of a court where they judge in the absence of any possibility for the defendant to defend himself. But he's not a defendant. He's a . . . He's a volunteer! And that's the whole problem: to what extent is he a volunteer, really a volunteer? But still . . . the fact remains that everything is judged in his absence. I think that this *in absentia* is virtually a theatrical metaphor for the fact that it's a question of ab-sense, i.e., ab-sex sense, something of which there can be integrally transmissible knowledge. And the verification of the transmission, which is the very procedure of the pass, makes the act depend on the singular connection between knowledge and sense as ab-sense. That's why it has to be judged in the absence of whatever person has experienced this absence.

But, you'll say, what about philosophy in all this? Well, philosophy is that which *doesn't pass*. This is something Lacan was deeply convinced of. I'd even go so far as to say that the detritus of a pass must be entirely philosophical—the waste material of a pass, if you look at it, which would moreover be very interesting. Show me the trash cans of a pass sometime—I think they'd be full of philosophy. That's what doesn't pass! And why doesn't the philosophical aspect of an analysis pass? Because it consists of everything that turned out to be hermeneutics, banal interpretation, various and sundry types of bullshit, disastrous totalization, self-awareness in an intense cogito [*cogito concentré*], absolute false knowledge, the triumphant authority of the master who never criticizes himself, and so on. What is all that? It's philosophy, ultimately! In that respect, the treatment can consist of pleasant philosophical bull sessions. But Lacan's hope was that that, at any rate, would not pass. Not for doctrinal reasons—not because the judges would say: "No, that's not it, that's very different from analysis"—but it wouldn't pass because, in its very essence, it doesn't pass into knowledge, because it remains trapped in the dichotomy of meaning and truth, at best. At best! It may be just a horrible load of meaning, but even at best it remains trapped in the coupling of meaning and truth, and because it's trapped in it, it doesn't pass. In the end, you could say that the pass procedure is the ultimate expression of anti-philosophy, its practical form of organization.

In Wittgenstein's case there was also the temptation to invent an anti-philosophical device to detect and sort the philosophical garbage. It was a grammatical device. You examined the sentences to see if they made sense or not. If they made sense, fine; they were scientific. If they didn't, they were philosophical. So you sorted, too. But it's not anywhere near as good as the pass device. The grammatical device is a poor, hit-or-miss device. And as for deciding whether something makes sense or not, everyone ends up getting confused. Whereas with the pass, that's not the case: in principle, philosophy quite simply doesn't pass. There's no need for outside criteria; it must not pass. So the pass is the ultimate organized form of anti-philosophy.

———∞———

Thus, we can ask ourselves the following question: Why was it in the field of psychoanalysis, and particularly in its Lacanian guise, that a serious anti-philosophical device, a philosophical garbage-sorting machine, was finally invented? I'm convinced, incidentally, that Lacan had a pretty machinelike notion of the pass. It was not supposed to depend on other people's expertise or good will. Even if the passers or the judges aren't particularly smart, even if they're actually idiots, it still works! That was the whole point. Because you can easily see that if the pass depended on people's expertise it would be all over for it. There'd be no test of transmissibility. Sure, a little competence is needed, naturally: you're not going to submit mathematical propositions to someone who's never done any either. But in principle, there's something stupid about the pass, because all that's required is seeing whether something passes or not. So it's a machinelike procedure, and that's why I'm speaking of a *device*. An anti-philosophical device, because, in my opinion, the waste material, the stuff that doesn't pass, is the blah blah blah, the brilliant interpretations, the brand-new concepts, the sophisticated psychological explanations, the analyst's postures and impostures, and all of that is philosophical.

———∞———

There's a crucial difference here between Lacan's anti-philosophy and that of the other anti-philosophers. I would call it a "historical" difference because it has to do with history, with the foundation of psychoanalysis, with the perennial need for a return to Freud. Why is the "return to Freud" a recurrent slogan in the history of psycho-analysis? It's true, you always have to return to Freud at one point or another, which is a sign that this is not like what happens in science. In science, you can study the history of science, but you don't need a slogan about the return to Euclid; that has long been assimilated. So why is it necessary to return to Freud? You'll say: because psychoanalysis isn't a science. OK, sure! But in the specific domain that concerns us, which is psychoanalysis as a production of knowledge, it's very important to ask why it's periodically necessary to return to its foundation. Well . . . it's necessary to return to it because the big difference between this anti-philosophy and the ones before it is that it's the first to be able to assert that its own act has taken place. That's a critical difference when compared with Nietzsche's act or even Wittgenstein's, which are programmatic. They spelled out the act's conditions, lines of demarcation, boundaries, and borders, but they couldn't say that it had taken place, whereas something of the analytic act *did* take place, as was proved by psychoanalysis' founder, Freud. He wrote five case histories and had all five of them "pass" before an eternal pass committee, namely, all psychoanalysts without exception. This doesn't mean that there shouldn't constantly be new places for new acts, but the proof is there, for all to see, that an analytic act took place. Therefore, the analytic act is not a pro-gram, and psychoanalysis is not a programmatic anti-philosophy. It's an anti-philosophy that can always invoke its act, at least in the dimension of the Freudian foundation: there, something did take place. In other words, there was analysis, for all time.

However, nothing is a match for this "having-taken-place." Maybe there's no analysis anymore. That's sort of what Lacan said at some point: there was some in Freud's time, and then, later, there wasn't any, in fact, until I, Lacan, came along. There wasn't any, or only very little, and in a completely confused way. But in any case, there was certainly some at the time Freud founded it. So the question becomes as follows: What difference does it make for an anti-philosophy to hold to the conviction that the act took place? What difference does it make in its inner disposition no longer to be a programmatic anti-philosophy? No longer to be the program of the act, the promise of the act, the examination of the context of the possibility of the act? I think this changes its relationship to knowledge. If the act took place, it must be confirmed in knowledge. If the act did *not* take place, or is unsure about its taking-place, then it is beyond any knowledge. The latter situation is patently obvious in the case of the other anti-philosophers, who are all, in one way or another, prophets and mystics. And therefore what is changed—but this is a major transformation, if it's true—is that, in reality, the act is no longer transcendent, as it inevitably was in all the previous anti-philosophies. In those anti-philosophies, from Pascal to Wittgenstein by way of Rousseau and Kierkegaard, there is always a touch of transcendence in the act, on account of the fact that the act, insofar as it's programmatic, is located outside the observable or identifiable forms of knowledge, hence in a position of yet-to-come, of future arrival. But if the act did take place, it is no longer transcendent, because it must be legible in knowledge itself, in the production of knowledge. It must pass, it must make itself recognized as such in the mighty historical pass. That's why I would say that Lacan developed the first *immanent* anti-philosophy and, as such, it is the last anti-philosophy. Because if it is real, then it attests to itself as knowledge.

As a result, though, we now have to deal with two very serious questions.

The first question is: what attests to the fact that the act took place, even if only once? This is basically the question: What is Freud? This question is internal to psychoanalysis; it's not a question of history. And you can see why. Because it's the question: What happened with Freud? Did something happen and what was it? This question in fact revolves around the act. To be sure, Freud came up with new theories, new hypotheses, of course he did, but he was neither the only one, nor the first, to do so. What we're talking about is much more serious. It's the act: What act, whose general name is Freud, took place? In particular, as regards the question that concerns us, what act with respect to philosophy? Or: What did Freud disrupt in philosophy? Did he, as Nietzsche would say, break the history of philosophy into two halves? So much for the first question. It is essential that the question of Freud, of the return to Freud, of who Freud was, of Freud's self-analysis, not be just a niche in the history of psychoanalysis, because, on the contrary, it is crucial for psychoanalysis itself. All the attacks on psychoanalysis amount, moreover, to saying that Freud was an impostor and that he didn't achieve anything—in the sense of the act. That's why psychoanalysis always requires that Freud be reexamined and why there will always be a need for the return to Freud.

The second question is: Is ab-sense actually what transmissible knowledge can be based on? Is ab-sense or ab-sex sense a rational category? Is it really what is transmissible in a triangulation with sense and truth? You can see the obvious connection between the two questions. Freud opened something up, that opening is the very existence of an act, and that act, which everyone knows has to do with sex in terms of its effects on thought, comes down to the fact that ab-sense denotes sex, such that a real point of the Subject is discovered, a real point on which transmissible knowledge can be based. So we'd finally have, as guaranteed by Freud, a genuine knowledge of the singular Subject.

With respect to this we can put philosophy on trial in completely new terms. First, philosophy is unaware of the register of ab-sense. It remains stuck in the opposition between sense and non-sense. Second, philosophy, being unaware of ab-sex, cannot reach a position of knowledge in the real. Third, all philosophy ever does is make sense and truth mirror images of each other, and that is its specular paralysis. The speculative is the specular.

This is why it blocks and is blocked. This is why it thinks it can get out of the conundrum through love, the love of truth.

——⊶⊷——

Do these implacable conclusions leave us philosophers speechless? That's what we shall see—next time.

Session 4

January 11, 1995

Someone takes the floor and asks a question that he summarizes as follows: *Psychoanalysis is on the side of the disjunction between meaning and truth on account of a knowledge based on a foundational event in the past: the advent of Freud. It's not a philosophy. Is it an anti-philosophy, or isn't it rather a religion, and more precisely a revealed religion, which simply heralds the coming of another savior?*

There are two aspects to your question—which is not really a question but a statement.

The first aspect is that every time anyone, including myself, claims that something, if not about knowledge then at least about the specific way knowledge is connected to truth, is based on the event, it's clear that the figure of Christianity—and especially Pauline Christianity, in that second foundation that's actually Saint Paul—crops up as if it were paradigmatic. This first point, which I think I touched on in *Being and Event* with regard to Pascal, is inescapable. No doubt I'll have to have it out publicly with Saint Paul someday. This persistence of the Christian paradigm can obviously be interpreted in two ways. You could say that it's the only true event and any other figure is an inferior copy of it. This amounts to saying that there is no event but the God event. Or you could simply say, and this is obvious, that something about the relationship between truth and event was brought to humanity's awareness in the first dimension in which things are often revealed: the dimension of a fable. In this case, it's the fable of Christ's resurrection. That doesn't diminish the formal significance of the paradigm, but neither does it require taking a stand on whether the miraculous event was real or not.

So we can deal with the second aspect of your question now. As regards psychoanalysis itself, there will in fact need to be an evental attribution, as there must be for anything that's an apparatus of truth, if there *is* an apparatus of truth. And the fact that there is this evental attribution will itself be judged according to the answer given to the first part of the question. If you think there's really only one unique event, an event that is the emergence of evental transcendence as such (this is indeed the status of Christ's coming, death, and resurrection), then any other event, whatever it may be, is only an inferior copy or an imitation of it. However, if you think there's nothing in these religious fables but the advent in fictional form of the possibility of a thinking of the event, then psychoanalysis shouldn't be particularly blamed for having originated in an event, since that's the case with *any* truth procedure. Remember, for example, that when Kant, in the Introduction to the *Critique of Pure Reason*, reflected on the existence of mathematics, he immediately interpreted it in terms of an event: it was due to "the happy inspiration of a single man,"[1] whose name, for Kant, was Thales.

Generally speaking, it could be argued that every truth procedure can be traced to an event, with the understanding that, if that's the case, we will have to acknowledge that there's an irreducible multiplicity of events, without any paradigmatic event of which the individual events would be replicas. In the final analysis, leaving aside for the moment the specific question of the Freudian foundation of psychoanalysis and its relationship to Lacanian anti-philosophy, the basic question is: Is there a paradigmatic event or not in the figure connecting the evental upsurge to truth procedures? Is there an event that, by its very nature, establishes once and for all what an event is—an event with a capital E? Christianity's great strength is to have placed this question at the heart of its apparatus, that is, to have announced that the Event had taken place. Of course, there could be other ones, but all the others, from then on, would be mere replicas or shadow images. For if there is an Event in the sense of the emergence in immanence of transcendence as such—in this particular case the emergence of a Man who is God—then any other truth event is a pale and pointless imitation. But if that *isn't* the case, if the Event with a capital E is only a fable, then there will be all sorts of proper names connected with all sorts of truth events: Aeschylus for the theater, Lenin for politics, Schoenberg for music, Cantor for mathematics, and so on. The multiplicity of truths is also the multiplicity of events to which a proper name is attached. The same is true of Freud for psychoanalysis.

⸎

Let's return now to our three-part question about Lacan's identification of philosophy: the philosopher as someone who is blocked by mathematics, plugs the hole of politics, and has love at the heart of his discourse. Today we're going to examine these Lacanian-style dictums one by one.

First of all, why, in Lacan's eyes, is the philosopher blocked by mathematics? This question of mathematics—clearly, I never stop harping on it—is extremely important in the anti-philosophical apparatus, and always has been. For instance, we've seen that in Wittgenstein's or Nietzsche's anti-philosophical apparatus—I'm reminding you of this because it's a framework that will not, in fact, be Lacan's—it is essential to be able to assume an ultimate identity between mathematics and logic, or between mathematics and a simple theory of signs. And then it will be shown that philosophers' predilection for mathematics, which they mistake for a form of thought, is nothing but an illusion with devastating consequences. In other words, in a consistent anti-philosophy there is always a certain thesis about mathematics, as a prolegomena to the discredit attaching to philosophy. This is the anti-Platonic side of every anti-philosophy, insofar as, from the very beginnings of philosophy, Plato defined a particular linkage between philosophy and mathematics. Since there's this particular linkage in Plato, the anti-philosophers' recurrent anti-Platonism will always have to take a stand on mathematics in order to take a stand against philosophy itself.

To be sure, Lacan's statement "the philosopher is blocked by mathematics" reminds us that it's impossible to take a stand on philosophy without taking a stand, one way or another, on mathematics. But we immediately see that Lacan's stand on this issue is very unusual. With Nietzsche and Wittgenstein, the identification of mathematics basically aims to disparage it. It aims to show that what philosophy claims to find in mathematics is *not* in it. Or that philosophy attributes a guarantee function to mathematics, which anti-philosophy will show that mathematics can't sustain. That's really the crux of the problem: anti-philosophy will prove or attempt to prove that mathematics is not a thought. That is its central thesis, which amounts, more or less, to saying that mathematics is only a grammar, a logic, or a logical grammar, let's say. And if mathematics is not a thought, then whatever aspect of thinking, and even of paradigmatic thinking, philosophy claims to find in it is completely illusory. Lacan's statement, it would seem, is the exact opposite of this. His fundamental gesture seems to be to identify mathematics as a thought, or even as the only possible science of the real. He will go so far as to state, at least in *Encore*, that what philosophy lacks is precisely the real thinking dimension of mathematics. You can see that this is the opposite of Nietzsche or Wittgenstein. It's not a question of saying that philosophy finds a thinking dimension in mathematics that doesn't really exist but of saying, on the contrary, that philosophy doesn't see in mathematics the thinking dimension of access to the real that *is* in it, and by which it remains blocked.

So it's Lacan himself who will base himself on mathematics, rather than blaming philosophy for doing so mistakenly. I explain this by the fact that Lacan's anti-philosophical act, unlike Nietzsche's archi-political act or Wittgenstein's archi-aesthetic one, is archi-scientific, i.e., dominated by the matheme. It's because his act is dominated by the matheme—which, don't forget, is nevertheless not mathematics but the impasse of the mathematizable—that the relationship to mathematics is the reverse of that of the contemporary anti-philosophical tradition.

Now we need to interpret "blocked." What is this fundamental dimension of mathematics that philosophers fail to grasp, that they remain blocked by? It's important to understand that, for Lacan, mathematics is a figure of what could be called "the bone of truth." Let's take "bone of truth" to mean that aspect of truth that is stripped of all meaning. To the extent that meaning is part of consciousness, mathematics is in exemplary fashion its stripping. Mathematics, as Lacan often repeats, is "science without consciousness."[2] This also means, as he points out in "L'Étourdit," that in mathematics, and I quote:

[T]he said [*le dit*] renews itself by using a saying [*un dire*] rather than any reality. (*AE*, 452)

This is what's integral to the discourse of mathematics: the fact that the said renews itself by using a saying rather than any reality.

Just as an aside, I want to say something that's still a bit esoteric for the time being but will become clear later on in this seminar. I think Lacan reached a genuine understanding, in his own opinion, of what mathematics was only by means of the dialectic of the saying and the said and not exactly by means of the dialectic of the signifier and the signified. There are complex overlappings between the two, but the identification of mathematics is really the fact that the said renews itself by means of a saying. The saying is, I wouldn't say an event, but at least an appearing. It's only insofar as there is the saying that it is said. And it is really only in the space of this connection between the saying and the said, and the specific way in which one can "use a saying" to transform, invent, or renew the said, that mathematics can be identified, in Lacan's view. Mathematics is related to the saying, not to any reality. I'll have a chance to show how this is different from a figure that would attempt to grasp mathematics strictly within the field of the signifier/signified correlation, as well as from a formalist thesis about mathematics, which would purport to reduce it to a crystal-clear said, an entirely and explicitly coded said.

But let's leave that for later.

What accusation will be made against philosophy? Because it *is* an accusation! A serious one! After mentioning Tristan Tzara in one of his final texts, Lacan says: "I rebel, so to speak, against philosophy" (*M*, 17). I have to find it for you—it's so wonderful! It's a text that dates from March 18, 1980, entitled "Monsieur A." Lacan had come across one of Tristan Tzara's titles, a Dadaist title: "Monsieur Aa, l'antiphilosophe" [Mr. Aa., the anti-philosopher]. Lacan remarks in passing that when he gave Tristan Tzara his essay "The Insistence of the Letter [in the Unconscious, or Reason Since Freud]" (*É*, 412–41), it had made no impression on him. "It left him indifferent," wrote Lacan—even though Tzara was an anti-philosopher! "I thought," Lacan laments, "that I'd said something that might be of interest to him. Well, no, not at all. You see how mistaken one can be!" The insistence of the letter was of no interest to the lettrist[3] Tzara, the anti-philosopher Tzara. But Tzara may have had good reason not to be particularly interested, as an anti-philosopher, in the insistence of the letter. He may have been perceptive . . . Lacan nevertheless comments on the lettrist whom the letter in its insistence left indifferent. Let me quote, with a few of my own remarks in passing:

> This Mr. Aa is an anti-philosopher. As I am. I rebel, so to speak, against philosophy. What is certain is that it's something that's finished [*there he goes, flirting with the thesis of the end of philosophy*], even if I expect some offshoots to sprout back from it [*he's being cautious nonetheless*]. Such regrowths often occur with things that are finished. Just look at this ultra-finished École [*all of this has a whiff of the dissolution about it*][4]: up until now there were lawyers in it who'd become analysts. Well, now, people become lawyers since they didn't become analysts [*this was the time when people were going from one trial to another after the dissolution*].

Note that to rebel against something you say is finished would only be like asininely kicking someone when they're down. Lacan, who's anything but an ass, is well aware that philosophy must not be so finished that there'd be no point in rebelling against it. And he rebels in particular against the fact that philosophy is blocked by mathematics, for a reason that's ultimately quite clear: in its relationship to mathematics, philosophy completely fails to grasp that the renewal of the said is rooted in the saying and thinks, instead, that it derives from meaning. Philosophy approaches mathematics by way of an implicit or explicit hermeneutics that's bogged down in the consciousness/reality dyad, whereas it needs to be grounded in the saying/said dyad in order not to be blocked by mathematics. In other words, philosophy, as usual, claims to give a meaning to truth. However, mathematics is free of meaning. It is a meaning-less saying that is realized as an absolute (integrally transmissible) said. And this is precisely what the philosopher fails to grasp. As the giver of meaning, philosophy's operation thus remains a religious operation vis-à-vis mathematics.

—∞∞∞—

I've had to repeatedly stress that the question of religion, the question of Christianity, is central to the anti-philosophical apparatus. There's always a clear connection between the extraordinary, unprecedented act that anti-philosophy opposes to the philosopher's abstract concept, and religion as the active donation of the meaning of life. Yet Lacan largely inverts this anti-philosophical disposition or, at any rate, he's more Nietzschean than Wittgensteinian or Rousseauian or Pascalian when it comes to this issue. And what's interesting and important is that he inverts the implicit relationship to religion at the same time as he inverts the position of mathematics. At the same time as Lacan says that philosophy fails to grasp the real—and meaning-less—essence of mathematics, he will not invoke meaning but inveigh against it as an ultimately religious figure. And so you could say—even though this is a bit forced, albeit still enlightening—that Lacanian anti-philosophy switches the positions of mathematics and religion with respect to the anti-philosophical tradition: mathematics comes to be in the position of what has essentially failed to be grasped (rather than fetishized) by philosophy, while, as Lacan sees it, there's a collusion between philosophy and religion with regard to meaning. Consider this key statement from the "Letter of Dissolution" of January 1980:

> The stability of religion stems from the fact that meaning is always religious [*the idea is explicit: meaning is always religious*]. (*T*, 130)

And Lacan goes on to say something no less interesting:

> Whence my obstinacy on the path of mathemes . . .

These two statements—"the stability of religion stems from the fact that meaning is always religious" and "my obstinacy on the path of mathemes"—sum up what I call the switching. Instead of opposing the silence of meaning in its Wittgensteinian archi-aesthetic dimension or its Nietzschean archi-political dimension to the formal emptiness of mathematical truth or of mathematical pseudo-truth, Lacan will oppose the path of the matheme to the irremediably religious nature of meaning. It is precisely in this respect that philosophy is accused of colluding with religion in the very way it deals with mathematics, because it stubbornly attempts to ground mathematics in the dimension of meaning, and, ultimately, meaning is always religious, while the paradigmatic value of mathematics lies in its being the unsurpassable model of a thought that has no meaning.

⸙

OK. But is this thesis any good? Is it true that philosophy's historical relationship to mathematics consists in arranging it religiously in the space of meaning? I'd like to take three examples: those of Plato, Descartes, and Hegel. In all three cases, as we shall see, some indisputable support for Lacan's thesis can be found, but, as I see it, so can some indisputable objections.

Let's consider the support first. Let's take Plato's *Meno*, a text that Lacan returned to time and again. You're familiar, I assume, with the classic scene where Socrates has a slave boy brought in to show that this slave can understand a geometry problem—the problem of doubling the area of a square—and, on that basis, to present the theory of recollection by saying that the slave can figure out this difficult problem even though he has never learned how to. So the idea underlying the problem must somehow already be virtually at work in the slave's "ignorant" mind. Here we have an indisputable relationship between philosophy and mathematics, since this experiment, this thought experiment—bringing in someone uneducated and showing how, without knowing it, he possesses knowledge, knowledge that will be able to be revealed—proves that there is always a self-antecedence of knowledge. And this self-antecedence of knowledge will be called "recollection," which—but I won't pursue this line of thinking—might well be Plato's name for the Freudian unconscious.

Does this theory give rise to a Lacanian anti-philosophical critique of Plato? Yes, without a doubt. Why? Because what's at issue is the coming to consciousness of this knowledge, whatever its initial locus. In other words, mathematics will be grounded in its coming to consciousness via a bit of reality. For, on closer inspection, it's actually the *drawing* that brings to the slave's mind the process of understanding the mathematical problem he's been given to solve. It's only by making the drawing, the diagrammatics of the problem, that the slave's mind awakens to the concepts involved. You could say that in this relationship between the coming to consciousness and the figural diagrammatics (the square and its diagonal will be drawn and will aid the conscious comprehension of the mathematical proposition), Plato demonstrates that mathematics can always be inscribed in the space of the consciousness/reality dyad, and that it's there that it will make sense [*faire sens*] to anybody, even someone uneducated like the slave boy. So in the *Meno* there is indeed a philosophical experiment in which mathematics is brought in only to prove that it makes sense to the mind once a way is found to restore it to the consciousness/reality dyad. This crucial experiment would support Lacan's accusation that the philosopher is blocked by mathematics because all he ever does is try to ground it where it is not, in the consciousness/reality dyad. So, in Lacan's view, Socrates's operation in the *Meno* ultimately amounts to a mystification, which will have consisted in bringing forth the consciousness/reality dyad by means of a dialectical trick that eliminates the connection between the saying and the said as the true essence of the mathematical method.

If we take the example of Descartes now, what is striking is that mathematics is used, in philosophy, as a methodic paradigm of something other than itself. You all know the famous passage: "Those long chains of utterly simple and easy reasonings, etc."[5] of which mathematics is the paradigm and model. The whole aim is to construct a metaphysics that's truly faithful to that paradigm. But it's clear that, here, mathematics is being treated as a method, or, more precisely, as a methodic paradigm, such that, when equipped with this paradigm, one can grasp properly metaphysical chains of reasoning, without Descartes's admitting, Lacan would say, that, in reality, mathematics cannot be paradigmatic for any signifying reality whatsoever, since it only renews its said from its saying. The connection between saying and said is all-important here, since, if mathematics only renews its said from its saying, that means it's not capable of being paradigmatic for a meaning or reality effect that is different from it. Therefore, the very idea of method in its Cartesian sense is a restoration of philosophy's relationship to mathematics in the space of meaning.

Finally, if we take the example of Hegel, who is on Lacan's mind in "L'Étourdit," and if, this time, we take the tremendous remark about infinitesimal calculus in Hegel's *Science of Logic*, then it's even clearer here, because Hegel's aim is to say (to grossly oversimplify) that mathematical infinity is an infinity that of course exists in and of itself but doesn't grasp its own intelligibility in the element of the for-itself. And that, after all, it's a blind infinity. You could really say that what Hegel contends is missing in the mathematical concept of infinity is, very precisely, the element of consciousness in the Hegelian sense of the term, namely, the element of internalization. This amounts to saying that, for Hegel, mathematical infinity is cut off from its own meaning. What he calls the speculative concept of infinity consists precisely of restoring to infinity the process of its meaning, a process to which mathematical inventiveness remains

blind. So here we find almost immediately the meaning/conscious-
ness or meaning/internalization dichotomy as that by which mathematics needs to be supplemented for it to be introduced into the
space of philosophy.

⸺⟐⸺

With these three examples, which I'm oversimplifying in the extreme without, I think, substantially misrepresenting them, you
can clearly see where the Lacanian thesis takes root. It's true that
there is, on philosophy's part, an operation on mathematics that
attempts both to deliver it over to meaning—to bring forth its
meaning—and to connect it to the consciousness/reality dyad. In
my opinion, however, you could also argue, if not the opposite,
then at least that the opposite is at least as true as its opposite. So
here we're at the heart of a line of contact between philosophy and
anti-philosophy.

What objection does Plato raise to mathematics in his analysis of
it in the *Republic*? He objects very precisely that it functions on the
basis of hypotheses that it doesn't justify. To this he will oppose the
philosophical dialectic, which instead appropriates the principles or
possibly *one* principle. But the one principle is what is intelligible
in itself and, at the same time, the source of intelligibility, and so it
is unconditioned, nonhypothetical, anhypothetical. OK, this is very
well known! Except, what is meant by: mathematics only begins
with hypotheses that it doesn't justify? It means that Plato understands perfectly well that mathematics originates in a pure saying.
This he knows; you can't say he failed to grasp it. Indeed, he says
that the process of mathematics is only guaranteed by a saying—
which, in contemporary terms, we call the axiomatic dimension of
mathematics, i.e., something is first said and then there's a chain of
reasoning that's faithful to this constitutive original saying. The said
stems intrinsically from a saying.

But, you'll object, that's precisely what Plato criticizes mathematics for. It's necessary, he says, to go back up to the principle that's in the intelligibility, and not just in the consequences, of its original saying. That's true. Except that it's quite a different thing to say that he objects to mathematics, quite a different thing to say that he failed to grasp the essence of mathematics. In fact, I'm utterly convinced that, even if Plato objected to it, he had a very sure intuition that, in mathematics, there is precisely an absence of the meaning originating in the primacy of the saying. He criticizes mathematical thought's limitation, but he's by no means "blocked" by the nature that Lacan accords this thought.

Someone asks: *But then how are the lengthy paradoxes of the One and the many in the* Parmenides *to be understood?*

But we can leave those paradoxes aside for the time being, because they don't involve or refer to mathematics at all.

The questioner insists: *OK, but their discourse does obey a logic.*

Careful! Logic and mathematics are not at all the same thing, even if, today, logics are formalized in a system that's similar to that of mathematics. Furthermore, our inquiry, for the time being, has to do with the letter of the texts, insofar as it constitutes a symptom for the conflict between philosophy and anti-philosophy. Our aim is very precise: it's to determine, on the basis of a word-for-word analysis of the texts, whether Lacan's thesis that philosophy is blocked by mathematics because its own discourse attempts to contaminate mathematics with meaning is justified or not. So I say: yes, in a certain sense, there are texts that allow for such an objection, but there are others that run counter to it. The fact that mathematics is based on a pure saying is something that Plato completely understands and that will in fact establish the difference between philosophy and mathematics for him. That's the essential thing. Plato's thesis doesn't seek to assimilate mathematics to something outside itself, to a hermeneutic of meaning. Plato says mathematics is wonderful, it should be studied for at least ten years, but we dialecticians have a different objective, a different ambition, a different aim, which replaces the rigorous consequences of a meaning-less saying with the power of thought of principles. There's a distinction in Plato between dialectic and mathematics that runs precisely between the dialectic of meaning and the prescription of the saying. Mathematics is governed by the prescription of the saying. In Plato, philosophy seeks the self-foundation of meaning, but in a position of separation from opinion, from immediate experience, and in this position of separation, mathematics is a model, a key source of support. That it then must be acknowledged that mathematics is incapable of making use of the dialectic of meaning is actually tantamount to acknowledging that mathematics is indeed something like the bone of thought, something that, because it provides absolute support for the renewal of its said from the saying, is unable to initiate or implement a real problematics of meaning and to answer the question: What is the true life? Even if, to understand the body of truth, you have to be very familiar with its bone.

—◆◆◆—

As regards Descartes, there is no question, as I said, that the methodic use of mathematics means that a formal disposition is taken from mathematics and is then used in operations of meaning production. Nevertheless, there is at least one point in Descartes's argument that proposes a completely different identification of mathematics: for him, mathematical statements have a special position in relation to the operation of doubt. Why? Because, in actual fact, mathematical statements are first and foremost things that cannot be doubted. We can't doubt mathematical statements, or mathematical truths, as he calls them. To doubt them, hyperbolic doubt will be needed, that is, not subjective doubt, simple negation, but a hyperbole of doubt that calls for totally extraordinary operators: the evil demon, the deceiving God—nothing short of the hypothesis of a bad Other, Lacan would say, an Other for whom our thinking is merely its mislaid toy. This is a theory that Descartes would, of course, later discard. But still, it requires nothing short of that. Which means that mathematical truths are such that, once they've been stated, they are binding on the subject—and this is the great subtlety of the thing—not as a result of any reality, because realities have long since been able to be doubted: ordinary doubt, with the help of a few rhetorical tricks, can eliminate the fact that there's something—an outside world, a world *tout court*, or, in a nutshell, anything in the guise of reality. But when it comes to mathematical truths, hyperbolic doubt is required. Here, mathematics lies in the gap between doubt and hyperbolic doubt. It is hyperbole, meaning that, between mathematics and subject in the Cartesian sense of the word there is a singular linkage that does not depend on reality. So it could certainly be argued that it's because mathematical truths, being of the order of the saying, are not based on any reality that doubt about reality doesn't affect them.

So it's not entirely true that Descartes grounds mathematics in consciousness and in meaning only by way of the method. It is just as true that he grounds it in this exceptional position that ties it to the subject in a figure from which reality is subtracted. This is at the same time compatible—and this was his stroke of genius—with the idea of its ontological contingency, because, as you know, mathematical truths are created by God. They therefore have no necessity, in terms of their being-itself. Descartes invented this amazing, and, at bottom, quite profoundly Lacanian, figure of truths—since that's what he calls them—that are not based on any guarantee of being, in the sense of necessity. These truths are dependent on pure divine freedom and are nevertheless binding on the subject. The fact that mathematics is identified as that which, since it derives from the event of the saying, is evental and contingent and which, nevertheless, since it doesn't derive from reality, is absolutely necessary—necessary under the authority of the saying—means that, in this regard, Descartes founded the distinct regime of mathematical discursivity.

Thus, in spite of the operation of appropriation that the idea of method represents, I don't think it can be maintained that there's a failure on Descartes's part to understand the true identity of mathematical discursivity. On the contrary, I would say that Descartes proposes a particularly radical thinking of mathematical truths, a thinking separate from the meaning/reality dyad or, in other words, separate from religion. In Descartes there is a profoundly nonreligious thinking of mathematical discursivity, precisely because mathematical truths are created (by God, in Descartes's terminology, but that doesn't have the slightest importance here).

⸙

Finally, to take my third example, that of Hegel, who was on Lacan's mind, it is a very interesting one inasmuch as, in note 1 on page 453 of "L'Étourdit," Lacan, as I already mentioned, after acknowledging that Hegel was knowledgeable about mathematics (indicated by the phrase "when I say 'blocked,' it's not ignorance, it's not 'not knowing' ") next writes that Hegel said more or less the same thing as Russell. He then goes on to say that, even though Hegel said the same thing as Russell, there's no blockage where the latter is concerned, while there is blockage where Hegel is concerned.

For Lacan, it's really the fact of being caught up in the strategy and operations of the philosophical discourse that obscures mathematics, regardless of what Hegel said about it—since, if what he said about it were said by Russell and in the context in which Russell said it, it would have been correct. And Russell in fact said that mathematics has no meaning. I told you a while back how we ought to consider this issue. It's true that Hegel attempted to show that the mathematical concept of infinity, because it's not subject to internalization, is an inferior concept as compared with the concept of infinity as philosophy was to use it. Only, here too, he'll fall back into that complex dialectical disposition that we've just seen with both Plato and Descartes. Hegel nonetheless says that, regarding infinity, mathematics is the first saying that is worth retaining. Which means: the first nontheological saying, i.e., the first rational saying in the very sense that Hegel means it. So, what should we take away from this? The inadequacy of the mathematical concept for the dialectic of meaning and internalization? Or the fact that this concept is inaugural, that it inaugurates, in the dimension of the saying, of the axiomatic, of the decision of thought, an absolutely new figure of infinity? Hegel acknowledges that mathematics is the historical emergence of truth-telling about infinity. Which, in a sense, is the historicized equivalent of what Plato says, in a nonhistorical way, in the sphere of the Idea, namely that something essential for thought is begun there, in the form of a saying. Furthermore—and this is an issue that's often very hard to understand in Hegel—his thesis is that mathematics will continue as a beginning. It is for all time the beginning of the truth-telling about infinity. Mathematics won't get bogged down in the speculative becoming of the concept. It will remain the inaugural figure of infinity and will refine the original saying that it is. This explains why, even today, the mathematics of infinity is inventing amazing things. Mathematics is the saying without internalization, to be sure, but it is nevertheless utterly alive and creative. It is therefore true for Hegel that mathematics, as such, will only renew its said from the saying and will never succumb to the internalization of its own meaning. This enables him to simultaneously glorify it, to let it be in its creative becoming, and to go beyond it toward the absolute Idea, within which it is constantly beginning the trajectory of infinity.

This is why I think it's totally wrong to claim that Hegel is blocked by mathematics. He merely maintains the detachment toward it of someone who has understood the value of beginning that it defines regarding the question of infinity, and who has the ability to let this value be while at the same time ignoring it. That detachment is under a very peculiar ideal—you could say, and I do say, an ultimately absolutely untenable ideal—but an ideal that I think is the crux of his thesis: Hegel is the thinker in the history of philosophy who has assigned as telos to philosophy to gradually become free of all its conditions, to go through them only in order to win its full independence. Henceforth, in the realm of pure thought, once it has reached the absolute Idea, philosophy will no longer need art, no longer need mathematics, no longer need politics, and no longer even need philosophy itself in its historical form. That is what is meant by art being "a thing of the past," and by mathematics continuing to refine its own saying. Philosophy will no longer need politics: that's what's meant by the end of history. So it will be free of all its conditions. Hegel dreamed of what I'd call a pure, unconditioned philosophy. One could naturally say—and this would be right—that the ideal of a pure philosophy is untenable, because, ultimately, philosophy is intrinsically always under evental conditions external to it. This is what *I* think about this specific issue; I'm not a Hegelian. But you can't say that Hegel misunderstood the intrinsic meaning of mathematics as inauguration by the saying of truths about infinity. You can't say that he was blocked by mathematics.

Last but not least, Lacan *un-divides* philosophy when it comes to the question of its relationship to mathematics. He un-divides it, that is to say, he fails to recognize what, in my view, is an essential aspect of philosophy, namely that it is always an immanent resistance to its own temptation, the temptation of the One. Lacan is well aware that philosophy's temptation is the temptation of the One—what

Heidegger calls the enframing of being by the One. But philosophy is not reducible to its immanent temptation; it is also the specific way by which it frees itself from that temptation. And as regards mathematics, I think that in Plato's *Meno*, in Descartes's *Rules for the Direction of the Mind*, and in Hegel's *Science of Logic*, both aspects are present. There is of course the specific way in which philosophy's primacy over mathematics is asserted, that is, in which the temptation of meaning is produced. In Plato's case it would be expressed as: substituting principles for axioms; in Descartes's case, organizing metaphysics methodically; and in Hegel's case, overcoming or subsuming the mathematical concept of infinity. It's true that this aspect is there, and it's ripe for Lacan's invective. But in every great philosophy there is also the immanent production of resistance to this. In Plato, it will be expressed as: the identification of mathematics as being under the law of the saying, or, in other words, the acknowledgment of both its constraint and its contingency; in Descartes: the position of mathematical truths in the order of the hyperbolic; and in Hegel: with regard to the question of infinity, mathematics is inaugural and remains so.

Let me make one comment: by disregarding this constitutive division of philosophy, by giving in to a—somewhat Heideggerian—uniform judgment on an inherent errancy of philosophy, it is Lacan who shows himself to be a bit, just a little bit, blocked by philosophy.

Lacanian anti-philosophy consists, in part, in un-dividing philosophy when it comes to this particular issue while actually basing itself on philosophy's division. This is a fundamental schema, and if we were to indicate its "conceptual figure," as Deleuze would say, it would be Lacan's relationship to Socrates. For Lacanian anti-philosophy, this relationship to Socrates, and to Socrates/Plato, consists at once and indivisibly, so to speak—we're talking about the origins of philosophy—in a process of destitution and identification. Socrates is the first philosopher but also the first analyst. Why?

Well, precisely because philosophy is conceived of as both undivided and as a possibility of using or exploiting its division. This is why Lacan is just a little blocked by philosophy, a tiny bit. Identifying with Plato's Socrates in order to disparage Plato, he experiences in his own way the syndrome of temptation and resistance to temptation that has haunted philosophy from its inception.

Now what about the philosopher plugging the hole of politics? Obviously, the first question is: In what sense is politics a hole? I think we can really get into the Borromean knot here and say that this business about the hole of politics can be formulated in terms of the imaginary, the real, and the symbolic.

Let's consider it first as an imaginary hole. This is the most well-known and obvious aspect: politics is a hole because it is undeniably linked to the group imaginary. Very specifically, it can be put like this: insofar as politics is located in the group imaginary, it is an imaginary hole in the real of Capital. The real of Capital is the real of universal dispersal, circulation, and absolute atomization. Furthermore, it's a certain regime of *jouissance*, hence of the real. So, in the granular consistency of this real, politics consists in making kinds of glues [*colles*]—kinds of School-glues [*Écolles*, pun on the word *école*, "school"]—which are actually times when the consistency is like a pierced or porous bone. It is about making imaginary pores in the dispersed, real consistency of Capital and surplus value. That's how politics is glued to meaning, and, insofar as it's glued to meaning, it makes an imaginary, or if you will, religious, hole in the real of Capital. That is politics as a Church effect. Lacan has several different names for it: glue effect (it glues the group together), Church effect, and meaning effect. But once again, I would put it in a more technical way: an imaginary hole in the real.

Let me remind you that when the École was dissolved in 1980, when the act of dissolution was experienced by everyone as a political act, Lacan wrote the following:

Demonstrating through acts [*Here's the act again! The act is the act of dissolution. And I should point out that the question of whether there can be another sort of act than an act of dissolution will be one of our final questions.*] that it is not of their doing that my École would be an Institution, the effect of a consolidated group, at the expense of the discourse effect expected from an experiment, when it is Freudian. One knows what price was paid for Freud's having permitted the psychoanalytic group to win out over discourse, to become a Church. The International [*the International is the Chicago people, right?*], since such is its name, is no more than the symptom of what Freud expected of it. But *it* is not what weighs in the balance. It's the Church, the true one, which supports Marxism insofar as it gives the Church new blood . . . of renewed meaning. Why not psychoanalysis, when it veers toward meaning? I am not saying that out of vain banter. The stability of religion stems from the fact that meaning is always religious. Whence my obstinacy on the path of mathemes . . . (*T*, 130; trans. slightly modified)

Politics makes a hole inasmuch as it sweeps up all discourse effect into the group effect, "the effect of a consolidated group, at the expense of the discourse effect," and as for Freud, he permitted "the psychoanalytic group to win out over discourse." So what is at stake here in terms of politics—the group as such—makes a hole when it makes glue [*colle*] or School-glue [*École*], in other words, precisely when the group wins out over discourse. This maxim, "it makes a hole when the group wins out over discourse," is a very important one. Why? Because we understand from it how philosophy can plug the hole. It will plug it by turning the fact that the group wins out over discourse into a discourse. This is what will be attributed to philosophy in terms of its relationship to politics: when the group wins out over discourse, you have a kind of imaginary hole in the real of Capital, and that's all you have. In this sense, we shouldn't think that political philosophy or philosophy dealing with politics only plugs something that's lacking. It's a much more complicated operation. In reality, when the group wins out over discourse, philosophy comes from behind—as it always does, doesn't it?—to restore legitimacy in the discourse based on the group's winning out over discourse. And philosophy will call this "politics." It's when philosophy calls "politics" the fact that the group wins out over discourse and turns this into a discourse that it's playing its role as hole-plugger of politics, whereas it should leave the hole open so that we can see in it that the group wins out over discourse and that, as a result, it's the imaginary breach or collapse of the pure glue effect.

In this connection, Lacan's relationship to Marx should be mentioned: it's in the text "Monsieur A" again, in which Lacan rebels against philosophy and in which he says:

> I paid tribute to Marx as the inventor of the symptom. [*He didn't pay tribute to Marx only as the inventor of the symptom. That's what he focuses on here, but as you know, he paid tribute to him as the inventor of surplus-enjoyment, hence of something that touches the real directly.*] This Marx is nevertheless the restorer of order, simply because he breathed the *dit*-mension[6] of meaning back into the proletariat. All it took for that was for him to say what the proletariat was as such. The Church learned a thing or two from this: that's what I told you on January 5 [*and he would come back to it later*]. Be aware that there's going to be a boom in religious meaning in a way you can't even begin to imagine [*indeed, we haven't been disappointed on that score since then*] because religion is the original refuge of meaning. (M, 18–19)

Actually, if you think about it, what Marx is being accused of here is having been a philosopher. He was a philosopher because he breathed meaning back into the proletariat, whereas the proletariat was a real hole. That's what the proletariat was: a real hole.

And it was this hole that Marx plugged up by breathing meaning back into it. Consequently, Marx allowed the proletariat as a group to win out over any possibility of a discourse. He could then be said to be the restorer of order—in Lacan's eyes—precisely because he silenced the proletariat. This is an interesting thesis since Marx is usually considered as someone who gave a voice, a political voice, to the proletariat. In Lacan's view, he silenced it precisely at the point where, once it was Marxized, the proletariat was no longer anything but a group. That's the Party position. The proletariat was a group, or a party, and the Party did, in fact, take precedence over discourse. And it turns out that, by a sort of retroaction, Marx was the philosopher who plugged the hole beforehand, by discursively allowing the group to win out over discourse, by launching . . . what? Well, *The Communist Manifesto*, or, in other words, by letting it be known that the group was the condition of discourse. But when it is assumed that the group is the condition of discourse and not that discourse is the condition of the group, then you have an effect of blockage of the real hole. There would have been something real if there had been a proletarian discursive discontinuity, so to speak, authorizing the group. Lacan constantly created groups, so the point is not whether or not there are any. The point is that the group must be prohibited, if possible, from authorizing discourse.

This thesis of Lacan's is very interesting because, at bottom, what was Lacan's dream about this issue? His dream? No, his project—let's say his project! Lacan presents this project in the passage I read you a moment ago: an "effect of a consolidated group, at the expense of . . . an experiment" must be prevented at all costs. The discourse effect expected from the Freudian experiment must win out over the group. But if the group wins out over discourse, both a (real) hole effect and a (philosophical) plugging-of-the-hole effect will necessarily occur.

We might, however, wonder what all of this means in actual fact. Indeed, everyone is constantly wondering about it! When Lacan says this, he is admitting: I failed, I failed. Then, of course, as a man who won't give up on this issue, he quickly starts over again. But he still says: I failed. I failed in what respect? I failed to make analytic discourse win out over the group, so I was like Marx; I did the same thing he did. I invented lots of things just as he did, but, in the end, I restored order. And as *I* realize that I restored order, I will dissolve my school just as Marx did when he dissolved the First International in 1871. Lacan constantly imitated Marx. Not only did he imitate him by inventing a discourse, but he also imitated him in politics: he dissolved the group that purported to be the condition of discourse.

This brings us to the concept of dissolution. In its generic sense, it's the moment when one tries to ensure that politics as a hole isn't plugged by philosophy. That's precisely what it is—the moment when one would have a chance to perceive—if only for an instant—the difference between discourse and group. In fact, even when Marx dissolved the First International, it was obviously in the hopes of making a possible identification of a discourse of the proletariat in terms of its difference from the group, in terms of a creative uncovering of the discourse as opposed to the group, an uncovering—an un-plugging— that the group's dissolution would make it possible to perceive.

The only problem is, isn't this the thesis of the existence of a pure discourse, this possibility of thinking the difference between discourse and group right at the time that the group disappears when it's being dissolved? "Pure discourse" would then mean a discourse that is visible and thinkable in terms of its strict difference from the group, i.e., in terms of the group's dispersal, and therefore a discourse freed from philosophy, if it's assumed that philosophy is always what legitimizes the group's predominance over discourse in politics. This, in my terms, would mean that philosophy is always what legitimizes the state. Political philosophy would be nothing but state philosophy, which is unfortunately too often the case. But in Lacan's terms, the fact that it's state philosophy means that it's the philosophy of the legitimation of the group's predominance over discourse. Assuming that dissolution is the operation that restores the productive relationship between discourse and group, it's not just because things aren't going well in the group. Basically, dissolution is an operation of uncovering of discourse by means of a dissolutive marginalization of the group. So this also means that the operation is directed against philosophy, whose subject matter is assumed, by Lacan and many others, to be the assertion of the group's predominance over discourse in politics—which actually means: the authority of the state.

So, with dissolution we have the clearest of the anti-philosophical operations. It's no coincidence that it was just when his psychoanalytic group was being dissolved that Lacan exclaimed: "I rebel against philosophy." It's a necessary correlation. I rebel against philosophy because it is always an operation that legitimizes the group's predominance over discourse, and that's why it plugs the hole of politics. And I, Lacan, want the hole to be seen. At a minimum, we should be able to see the hole. But philosophy, as the discourse of the group's predominance over discourse, as state discourse, makes it impossible to see the hole: we can't see anything anymore; it's plugged up. If I want to see the hole, what do I want to see in the hole? Well, the hole signifies discourse, and therefore ultimately the analytic discourse.

Someone asks a question: *Can it be said that Lacan treats philosophy as an ideology?*

No, that's not exactly right. If philosophy is state discourse—which, for me, once again, is its temptation but by no means its essence—then its real surpasses the real of the imaginary functions of ideology. With dissolution, as opposed to the state-based predominance of the group, you have an act that uncovers discourse. That's what's so extremely difficult, because the operation of uncovering of discourse is a political operation and not just the practice of the true (or scientific) discourse against ideology. It's a specific operation that Marx, Lenin, and Mao Zedong constantly struggled with. What's more, if you take a good look at it, revolutionary activity is always, to a great extent, a political operation of uncovering of discourse. And maybe it's always essentially a dissolutive operation. This operation introduces an extreme tension owing to the correlation between anti-philosophy—freeing the hole of politics from its plugging by philosophy—and the dissolutive conception of the group as the act of uncovering discourse.

The question of dissolution has haunted revolutionary politics since Marx's day: from the dissolution of the First International to Lenin's threat, in the middle of the transition from February to October 1917, to dissolve the party at any moment. This is well known: we've got the texts to prove it. Consider, for example, "The Crisis Has Matured," in which Lenin constantly says: "If that's the way it is, I'm going to quit. The Party's nothing at all; I'm going to quit, I'm going to dissolve it." And, in a way, the Cultural Revolution in China was nothing but a gigantic operation of dissolving the party. Dissolution persistently haunts the figure of the revolutionary act because there is always a question of the political uncovering of discourse. Lacan was the absolute heir to this. He was perfectly right to compare himself to Lenin in terms of his relationship to Marx. But this paves the way for an extreme tension, because this thesis indicates that politics can only be freed from the hold of philosophy—as anti-philosophy sees it—in the perspective of dissolution or of something akin to dissolution, since nothing can be opposed to philosophy's plugging of the hole except the uncovering of discourse.

So much for the hole of politics as an imaginary hole by means of which the group ensures its predominance, its glue effect, over the true discourse.

I also think that politics is a symbolic hole. I told you that it's an imaginary hole in the real of Capital. But it's also a symbolic hole in the imaginary consistency of discourse. As you can imagine, it will ultimately be a real hole in this symbolic order, too.

I'm just going to give a brief sketch of this issue. There's something very striking—including in the Lacanian conceptual framework— namely, the fact that, for Lacan, politics isn't a discourse. You've got the discourse of science, the discourse of the analyst, the discourse of the hysteric, and the discourse of the university but not the discourse of politics. Yet this point, which may seem to be just a simple state- ment of fact, is in my opinion an all-important point. How is it— actually, I'm going let you solve the problem for yourselves between now and next week—that politics, for Lacan, isn't a discourse?

---᠅᠅᠅---

It's not easy to make a connection between Lacan and Deleuze. But here it's possible to do so. Why isn't politics a thought for Deleuze? I'm not saying "a discourse" because that's not his vocabulary, but if you take *What Is Philosophy?* you can read in it that science is a thought, that art is a thought, that philosophy is a thought, but not politics. We know very well why, in Deleuze's view, psychoanalysis is not a thought: he explained this at length in *Anti-Oedipus*. But why can't politics be added to the list that includes art, science, and philosophy? I'll just leave you with this observation tonight: for Deleuze, politics isn't a system of thought. There's no political plane in the sense of the philosophical plane of immanence, the scientific plane of reference, or the artistic plane of composition as opposed to chaos. The equivalent in Lacan is that there's not strictly speak- ing any discourse of politics. And it's because there isn't any that, in fact, politics always makes a hole in the discourses. And more precisely in what, in these discourses, is based on imaginary consis- tency, or, in other words, is based on semblance.

Let's say that politics is a symbolic hole in semblance.

Session 5

January 18, 1995

As there's going to be a break lasting till early spring, we need to draw some conclusions now about the protocol we've been dealing with, which is based on a single question: How does the anti-philosopher Lacan identify philosophy? I showed that the answer to this question involved three mediations: philosophy's relationship to mathematics, its relationship to politics, and its relationship to love.

As far as mathematics is concerned, the results were split, as I showed with the examples of Plato, Descartes, and Hegel. I concluded that while recollection, method, and dialectical sublation, in Plato, Descartes, and Hegel respectively, illustrate Lacan's thesis of a shift from the relationship between the saying and the said in a matheme to the consciousness/reality dyad in the realm of meaning, it is nevertheless the case that the axiomatic method, hyperbolic doubt, and the inaugural advent of a thinking of infinity—or, more precisely, the hypothetical nature of the axiomatic method, the hyperbolic nature of doubt, and the irreducibly creative inaugural advent—represent identifications of mathematics as the pure authority of the saying, even if each such identification is preliminary to a declaration of its inadequacy.

The position I'll take with regard to Lacan, though at a remove from him, is that the great philosophical tradition is fundamentally divided in nature, precisely when it is under the condition of mathematics, because mathematics divides philosophy. A distinctive way in which philosophy is conditioned by mathematics is that it is ineluctably split between, on the one hand, an identification that subjects it to the test of meaning-lessness, and, on the other, a temptation of recollection of meaning, a suturing operation. This is in fact a variant of a general issue on which I'm strongly opposed to Heidegger: in my view, there is no historial unity to philosophy. Philosophy is a divided process. Its dividing line runs between the metaphysical temptation of the One and the dispositions that take their distance from it, that detach themselves from the One. In the test of mathematics, a test that philosophy has always had to undergo, there is a temptation of recollection of meaning, a hermeneutic temptation with regard to scientific intentionalities. But there is also an identification of mathematics that is resistant to interpretation and is even geared toward a thinking of truth as alien to meaning. Mathematics, in that case, teaches philosophers that all truth is meaning-less. A great philosophy always consists in the establishment of a divided process. This doesn't mean that it's not systematic; it is the system of the division itself. And it's not a dialectical division, a division open to a synthetic use. It is philosophical thought itself that is the process or the establishment of this division. It's just that mathematics is a particularly sensitive issue when it comes to establishing this division.

This can be put even more simply: philosophy is a procedure of separation from the religious, so you can always say the religious is in it, that's always possible: what is separated from is presupposed in the act of separation. This is what the positivist, scientistic, anti-metaphysical, etc. critiques all say. Fine. "Religious" is being taken here in its broadest sense as the establishment of a space in which truth is absorbed back into the space of meaning. But philosophy is not just the—ultimately ever-present—religious, since it is the separation from this presence of the religious, and this is why it's a living operation rather than a historically defined reiteration of the same gesture. Philosophy is that which, under conditions of constantly changing truths, always begins the separation from the religious anew. Ultimately, philosophy, even theological philosophy, has always asked what man would think and become if God weren't there, if God were to die. We can grant Lacan that the religious is intrinsic, but it should be added that philosophy is one of the sites where the separation from the insistence of religion begins anew. And so you can say that religion insists in philosophy, but only provided that you add that philosophy is constitutively a certain regime of disruption of that insistence.

—∞—

Next, I considered the question of the identification of philosophy, or metaphysics, as "plugging the hole of politics." I said in what sense politics could be identified as a hole. I suggested in this regard a structure related to the RSI (real/symbolic/imaginary) schema. Here are its components: (1) Politics can be regarded as an imaginary hole in the real. (2) It can be regarded as a symbolic hole in the imaginary. (3) It can be regarded as a real hole in the symbolic. Philosophy would then plug this triple hole all at once.

The first point: politics as an imaginary hole in the real. When faced with the real test of the absolute fragmentation that capitalism produces, politics, as an imaginary glue, keeps the community or the group together. This is what Lacan calls its Church effect or its School effect, which he also calls its glue effect. I'm not going to go back over this point since we dealt with it at length last time.

So let's begin with the second point this time: politics as the symbolic hole in the imaginary coherence of discourses. Politics is not, strictly speaking, a discourse; it's an interdiscourse, a practice, and insofar as it is operative, i.e., that there is a certain being of politics, it is precisely only in the sense that its functioning never coincides with any discursive imaginary coherence whatsoever. When it exists, politics is a functioning that is not reducible to the discursively presentable imaginary coalescences. Marxism expressed this in its own language: the political theory of revolution, communist theory, makes a hole in the dominant ideology. Lacan would end up saying—and I think this is a maxim by which the hole is in fact exhibited as a symbolic hole, as a hole in which one operates in an excentered and autonomous way as opposed to the cohesion of the imaginary discursive position—Lacan, then, would end up saying: "I expect nothing from individuals, and something from a functioning" (T,133). That was his final statement about politics. Consequently, the "functioning" produces effects that can't be recapitulated in the group's discursive imaginary. As measured against these effects, individuals, leading personalities, are relegated to their own nothingness.

It's an interesting thesis. Basically, for Lacan, politics, in its most general sense, is related to a symbolic authorization that functions on its own, without requiring any specific individuals to be connected to it in the position of necessary agents for the functioning to occur. And something can be expected from this functioning. What is it, this something? We have to come back to it ultimately: it's knowledge. In the sense that it makes a symbolic hole in imaginary discursivity and the subjective positions it involves, politics, for Lacan, is the functioning of knowledge. It's not knowledge per se but the possibility that some knowledge might function with a sort of indifference to the particularity of those using it. This also means that, in a sense, politics doesn't touch truth, at least not directly. Politics is, at best, what can be expected, in terms of knowledge, from a functioning.

Finally, politics can be a real hole in the symbolic, or in the law, simply because it can be in a position to decide life or death. It can decide death. And when it does decide it, we know that it always makes a hole in the law. So politics might also be in the position of this real hole in the symbolic. This is what, with Carl Schmitt, will be reformulated as: the purpose of real politics is to establish a state of exception outside the law.

All of this is quite a clear structural description. Lacan will then say: this triple hole is transversally seized and concealed by philosophy, which, in this instance, he calls metaphysics. How does metaphysics plug these holes? It does so with a discourse that is assumed to have no holes. And this supposedly hole-less discourse of philosophy is the discourse of ideal politics, good politics, or politics finally grounded in its concept. Indeed, we know that the discourse of ideal, good, or grounded politics is philosophical in origin. Beyond any possible doubt. Suffice it to say that it is, apparently, what motivated Plato. Plato has often been read as if everything, in his thinking, was dependent on the possibility of having a hole-less discourse on politics, a discourse in which everything is in its place. And it has been said that the construction of the "communist" City in the *Republic* is under the ideal of such a hole-less political discourse.

Lacan didn't care very much for the *Republic*.[1] He said it was like a well-run horse breeding stable. But he didn't conclude from this that Plato was appalling, totalitarian, etc., not at all! He concluded that, from one end of the dialogue to the other, Plato is pulling our leg. In other words, it was absolutely inconceivable that someone great like Plato—because for him, Plato was not just anyone—could have believed in such a horrible, depressing thing. So he thought the *Republic* was a fundamentally ironic dialogue. That's an interesting hypothesis, because that great edifice, in which each thing is in fact enigmatically put in its place, would actually be an ironic demonstration of the fact that politics is a hole. The best proof that Plato, as revised in this way by Lacan, gives of this is that if you try to plug the hole, you wind up with the depressing figure of a well-run horse breeding stable. That's irony in its purest form! It didn't prevent Lacan, elsewhere, from claiming that this is nevertheless what philosophers do: plug the hole of politics, even if, at the same time, he attributes an irony to Plato that would actually be a monumental irony in history—I mean, literally, an irony in the form of a monument.

Except, is philosophy really as blind as all that? The basic question returns here: Is philosophy blind to the objection raised to its own enterprise? I don't think so, even taking the extreme case of Plato's *Republic*. Sure, there's the great Platonic construction of the state: the distribution of places, the craftsmen and farmers linked in a one-to-one fashion with their tasks, and the philosopher guardians, selfless and ascetic, at the top. The least you can do, if you're attempting to plug the hole of politics, is be part of the plugging yourself. So it stands to reason that, at the top, philosophy, or more precisely the dialectic, is doing the plugging. That's exactly what Plato says: if you want a politics worthy of the Idea, then philosophers have to be in power. But you'll note that, in the dialogue, Socrates's interlocutors immediately sneer and say: "That'll be the day!" And that objection runs insistently throughout the whole dialogue. At the point of the real of politics, then, at the point of what happens, Plato is not at all in the element of reabsorption or blindness. He knows that there's a dangerous hole.

Three features of this dangerous hole can be mentioned, all of them essential for understanding the political construction in the *Republic*. First of all, the acknowledgment of multiplicity. Indeed, Plato's system consists in saying that there are *a number of* political forms. That's what the real is. There are tyrannies, there are democracies, there are oligarchies. And that's what there is. So in no way is there any blindness on Plato's part when it comes to the fact that there is politics. This "there is" is the "there is" of an irreducible multiplicity.

Second of all, at the very heart of his construction Plato acknowledges the extraordinary precariousness of politics. "Precariousness" clearly means that something is never filled, that no hole is plugged forever. Third of all, he admits the chancy nature of his construction.

As for the precariousness of the different political forms, it has a threefold meaning.

First, every political form is compelled to change into another. None of the real political forms among the multiplicity of political forms is stable. Each obeys a process of self-disidentification and transformation into another political form. The classic example, in Plato's eyes, is the inevitability of democracy's transformation into tyranny, but that's not the only one. In actual fact, any real form of politics suffers from a constitutive instability.

The second, even deeper, meaning of this precariousness is the fact that the "ideal" system proposed by Plato is itself precarious. Plato does not claim to be replacing the precariousness of the real political forms with a political form that would be freed from any precariousness. In one of his commentaries, admittedly a very strange but symbolically very striking one, he points out that, assuming his plan for the state were to come to pass, it, too, would be precarious; it, too, would eventually degenerate. It would inevitably turn into timocracy. The reason he gives for this—something psychoanalysts might consider!—is absolutely remarkable. It's that, at a given moment, there will be a repression, a denial, a forgetting: the forgetting of a number. In order for the system to work, the leaders must have the numbers clearly in mind, because the coding of the ideal political construction assumes that each thing is in its place in a harmonic, numbered way, through precoded proportion, distribution, and apportionment. So there is a system of basic numbers that govern the construction. But what Plato explains to us is that memory will fail: someday, one of the most important numbers will be forgotten, will be lost. And, for once, we can see the hole of politics very distinctly today: it's repression, in Freud's sense of the term. The number will disappear in the leaders' unconscious even though it's the very symbol of civic order. And what's a bit marginal, but remarkable, is the corrupting effect of that forgetting. Its empirical effect, its observable effect, will be that, in the educational curriculum, gymnastics will prevail over music. Something of the expressly military training will prevail over the generic element of intellectual and spiritual training. All of this is a sure sign that Plato is perfectly aware that any identification of politics must include its precariousness as an irreducible element. Even ideal politics—the politics that's supposed to plug the hole of politics, to use Lacan's phrase—is in fact, in this hole-to-come constituted by the retroaction of forgetting, a rupture of the subject's unity. This is because this business about the primacy of gymnastics over music means that something of the inner organization of the citizen-subjects will come undone and give way to a military dictatorship for which the predominance of foot racing, swordsmanship, and horse racing has prepared the ground.

Finally, there's a fundamental point, which is that the hole is inevitable in politics: Plato admits that the success of his project is ultimately a matter of chance. The ideal construction can only be real under iffy and unlikely conditions—atopical, excentered ones, what's more. For example, he stresses the fact that it is surely not in his own City that someone who's knowledgeable about this well-founded form of politics might achieve all, or part, of it. It will happen elsewhere, in some unknown place that is not his own place. And when Socrates's interlocutors say to him: "Your philosophers will never be in power," Socrates/Plato replies: "It might happen, it might happen." But that's all we'll learn about it. The truth is that there's no reason why it should happen, but no absolute reason why it shouldn't happen either. The real hole is still there; it hasn't been plugged. It's just that, within the construction, the hole has been given a series of different names. As we've just seen, the hole of politics is indeed identified by Plato and named in three different ways: multiplicity, precariousness, and chance.

So I'll conclude regarding philosophy's relationship to politics in more or less the same way I did regarding its relationship to mathematics: even at the height of its will to foundation—and God knows that's the case in Plato's *Republic*—philosophy identifies something in politics that can't be sutured but instead remains subjected to a sort of contingent hole that even the founding thought can't close up. Because, clearly, multiplicity, precariousness, and chance are, for the founding thought, its real. The rest is its discourse. But its real is the impasse of its discourse. And it can easily be argued that Plato has a thorough understanding of the impasse of his own political formalization, an understanding attested to by these three names: precariousness, multiplicity, and chance.

⸎

At this point, we can turn to Lacan and say: "All right! Philosophy plugs the hole of politics." (We don't really think so, but let's pretend we do.) What would *not* plugging it mean? What is the anti-philosophical political position? Is there an anti-philosophical politics, or a politics whose essence is not to plug the hole of politics? Does such a thing exist? When it comes to this issue, Lacanian theory is both radical and, frankly, difficult to grasp or understand, because it's presented, in my opinion, only in metaphors. This is why people are still fighting over Lacan's "political" teaching: it's transmitted in an essentially metaphorical way.

Take the question of the group. In what conditions is it not under the sway of imaginary coalescence? In the statutory texts that accompanied the dissolution of his own School in 1980, Lacan expressly says that this imaginary effect must be avoided: what I'm creating here, he says, must avoid the group effect. And I quote: "The Cause freudienne[2] must avoid the group effect that I condemn" (*M*, 18). It's all well and good to say so, but how can the group effect be avoided? You've got to admit that his proposal is disappointing on that score because, for one thing, it's already well known, and, for another, it's more metaphorical than rational. What does avoiding the group effect consist of? It consists of proposals of permutation, nonhierarchical stabilization, lability or changeability of everything, and putting an end to consistency as the duration of the group. On March 11, 1980 Lacan declared:

> The Cause freudienne is not a School but a Field. [*This is a metaphor* . . . *"Field" will be characterized by lability, permutation, instability. Then, with regard to what he is creating, there comes the wonderful phrase:*] From which it can be inferred that it [*the School that's a Field*] will only last temporarily.[3]

And finally, there's the abstract principle in which something like a quintessentially hyperdemocratic utopia can be noted:

> [T]he collaboration of anyone with anyone else in the Cause [*this time the metaphor will be that of swirling*] is what we should aim to achieve, but in the long term: that it should swirl this way. (*M*, 19)

That's all very well, but the truth is, what matters, the real principle, is dissolution. The Cause freudienne group will only last temporarily. But what is a temporary arrangement if not a recurrent resurgence that makes dissolution persist? Dissolution is an act in the sense that, from now on, it will persist. Ultimately, isn't this the old matrix of utopian democratism as such? What I mean by utopian democratism is a particulate, atomic, or quantum egalitarianism: nothing but swirlings and coalescings of anything with anything else, in their swirling motions that define a temporary arrangement, which will later break apart. It's similar to Lucretius's world: a collision of atoms that produces temporary figures destined to break apart owing to their immanent precariousness. So we might wonder whether, if that's the case, the situation isn't simply that there are nothing but holes. It's a radical process of detotalization, but does it constitute a politics? I see a kind of parallel between what Lacan identifies as political philosophy and his final statement about politics. On the one hand, in fact, the hole may have been plugged; each thing is in its place. But, on the other hand, the implicit norm is that there's no more place at all. That's truly what the field, the swirling, is: it's a space without place. A space that's essentially full of holes, made up of holes.

The problem is, it's of the essence of politics to deal with the question of places, in accordance with a variable principle of what a dis-placement is. The approach purporting to found an eternity of placement (the traditional Plato) is certainly extrinsic to any real politics. But so is an approach that claims there's nothing but the swirling of the nullified place, the omnipresent hole. If we accept that every politics proposes a displacement, then Lacan tells us nothing about politics, or, at any rate, he tells us nothing that hasn't already been said in the well-established variants of anarchist-leaning radical leftism. His most radical proposals, which are the ones dealing with dissolution, express, in actual fact, Lacan's true political vision, which I would call a tyrannical anarchism.

I'm saying "tyrannical" here without any value judgment. That's right, without any value judgment, because I'm not a Platonist when it comes to this issue. To be sure, Plato didn't like tyrants, but that was because, in ancient Greece as has often been the case elsewhere throughout space and time, they were the representatives of popular forces hostile to the aristocrats. That's why he didn't like them. Plato pretended not to like tyrants because they were bad men and thought only about their own desires. We know very well that, in reality, he didn't like them because the tyrannical movements, in classical Greek society, were the breeding ground for constitutional reforms in a space that was more open than that of the reign of a handful of patrician families. So I'm taking "tyrannical" in the sense of the act, of the ability to act on oneself in the space of the group. That is indeed how Lacan operates in the "Letter of Dissolution" [*T*, 129–31], where he assumes a perfectly tyrannical position, which he calls the *père-sévère* ["stern father," pun on the verb *persévérer*, "to persevere"] position. Lacan assumes the tyrannical position insofar as he is the one who, by withdrawing, ensures that everything falls apart and that he's the only one to have such power. And in addition, he's anarchistic—yes, profoundly so—because the ideal under which everything, including the tyrannical gesture of dissolution, occurs is that of the swirling motion without place. Except for his own place, after all, which is indestructible since it is solitary: "as alone as I have always been in my relation to the psychoanalytic cause" (*T*, 97). When you're alone, you can't leave your place: the place of solitude is the plus-one of all the other places. But this plus-one of all the others is the position of tyrannical anarchism. And this position is a classic, identified and identifiable one in the history of political forms and political philosophy. It's by no means a new position, particular to the analytic discourse.

—◦◦◦—

To conclude regarding this issue, at least for the time being, I would say that, on the one hand, Lacan fails to recognize that political philosophy identifies the political real as the impasse of its founding purpose, and, on the other hand, in the same way, that his own political gesture is not exempt from philosophy's identification of politics, that it is identifiable from the very standpoint of philosophy. It is not so unique that it wouldn't be identifiable in the process by which philosophy appropriates the identification of politics. Psychoanalysis, in this sense, remains silent about politics. Lacan didn't create anything new in terms of politics; he didn't introduce or establish anything new. Which would not, after all, constitute an objection if Lacan himself hadn't raised the objection to philosophy that it plugs the hole of politics.

Once again, there was nothing but dissolution. Thus, the analysts were disbanded and disbanded they remain! That's the situation of Lacanian psychoanalysis. They keep on disbanding. Because that is indeed the imperative that was bequeathed to them: "Disband!" But that imperative is better than many others. It's certainly better than: "Come together!" or "Love one another!"

So that was the path followed by Lacan in politics: dissolution goes on and will continue to go on because there was nothing new established other than that. And, since each of them thinks the dissolution doesn't apply to him personally, they restore things even while disbanding. Each individual analyst plugs the hole of politics! It's probably a more compact plugging than the one philosophy is capable of, because, when it comes to plugging the hole of politics, you've got to admit that the analysts, when they put their minds to it, are second to none.

One last thing I'd like to point out: Lacan thinks that Marx had already seen that philosophy served to plug the hole of politics. This is a Lacanian interpretation, let's say, of Marx's last thesis on Feuerbach: "Philosophers have hitherto only interpreted the world in various ways; the point is to change it." This can be understood as: philosophers have plugged the hole of politics with interpretations; the point is to unplug it, to open it back up. In *Radiophonie*, Lacan expresses this in a fine, Marxist anti-philosophical passage:

Question 5: What are the consequences [*of the fact that the discovery of the unconscious led to a second Copernican revolution*] as regards: a) science; b) philosophy; c) and particularly Marxism, or even communism? (*AE*, 431)

Answer: There is no clamor of being or nothingness [*here he means the philosophers: Sartre and all the rest of them!*]. . . that hasn't been stilled by what Marxism has shown by its actual revolution: that there's no progress to be expected from truth, nor any well-being, but only the shift from imaginary impotence to the impossible, which proves to be the real by being grounded only in logic: in other words, where I claim the unconscious is located, but not so as to say that the logic of this shift shouldn't hasten the act. (*AE*, 439)

In short, in Lacan's view, Marx showed that, instead of philosophical fantasies about the good state or the good society, it was the logic of Capital that had to be identified at the point of the real. Marx's actual revolution is a liquidation of philosophy. Should we say that Marx substituted a science or knowledge for the philosophical imaginary? No, says Lacan, because we must maintain that the "logic of this shift" must "hasten the act."

—— ❧ ——

So you can see that the anti-philosophical critique of philosophy or metaphysics as plugging the hole of politics basically means: the hole of politics is unpluggable. Marx had already understood this clearly. It's absolutely not a question of telling us what's good—the good state or good politics—and of making progress in anything whatsoever. All of that is only imaginary impotence. What there is, is a logic that captures a real and requires the hastening of the act. In Lacan's eyes, Marx is the one who invented the symptom, who invented a theory of *jouissance*. He's the one who made a radical break with the philosophical view of politics. For Lacan, Marx is the correlation of a logic with an act; that's the strongest point of subjectivation for Lacan in his relationship with Marx. It's the correlation of a logic with an act, not at all of knowledge [*connaissance*] with a project.

That distinction is still extremely relevant, in my opinion. The "classical" view of politics defines it as a combination of knowing what the situation is and carrying out sound projects. But that image was ruled out by Marx, as Lacan characterizes him: politics is not knowledge and a project but a logic, hence an occurrence of the real, which requires an act. If politics is knowledge and progress, then it's under the sway of meaning; it dispenses a meaning. If politics is logic and act, then it's free of meaning, which means free of progress in all its forms, free of the very idea of the representation of progress.

So much for politics as an imaginary hole in the real, a symbolic hole in the imaginary coherence of discourses, and a real hole in the symbolic or in the law.

Let's turn now to the last point, which I'm going to deal with pretty quickly: Why does Lacan say that love is at the heart of the philosophical discourse? First of all, what kind of love is it?

This is a very insistent question in the Lacanian corpus. There's a first form of it—focused on the problem of love for the master, its explanation by transference love—in the analysis of Plato's *Symposium* and of Socrates's relationship to Alcibiades. The key point there, but which I won't deal with right away, is that, for Lacan, there can be a *love* of knowledge [*savoir*] but never a *desire* for knowledge. This is what he states in the introduction to the German edition of his *Écrits*:

> I insist: It is love that is addressed to knowledge. Not desire: because, when it comes to "*Wisstrieb*," even if it has Freud's stamp of approval, you can go back and look: there's not the slightest bit of it. This is so much the case that it's even the basis for the chief passion of the speaking being—which is not love, or hatred, but ignorance. (*Scilicet* 5, 16; *AE*, 558)

As you know, for Lacan, the human being's three major passions are love, hatred, and ignorance. But, ultimately, the chief passion is ignorance. It is ignorance because there's no desire for knowledge. This very radical thesis has perhaps not been sufficiently noted. The key position of love actually stems from the fact that it is the real subjective correlation with knowledge; there is no other. There may be a love of knowledge, but that love is not based on any desire.

This thesis opens up an abyss, aside from the fact that it's not very easy to understand. But for the time being, let's just take it literally. There's no desire for knowledge. What there is may be love for knowledge. As far as desire is concerned, the human being's absolute passion is ignorance. There's such a lack of any desire for knowledge that ignorance, if I may put it this way, fills it up as passion. But there may be a love of knowledge. And what philosophy—according to Lacan—will graft onto that love of knowledge is the illusion of a love of truth. In his eyes, the major philosophical assumption is not only that there is a love of truth but that there *must* be a love of truth. The philosophical imperative—this is why it's at the heart of philosophy's discourse—would be: "You must love truth!" And maybe it's even more forceful than that, something like: "Love truth more than you love yourself."

Why, once again, is there an anti-philosophical accusation by Lacan? This will hinge less directly on the question of the love of truth than on what is loved in the love of truth. There are a lot of passages on this subject, but I'm going to use the following one, from Seminar XVII, *The Other Side of Psychoanalysis*, where Lacan asks: What is the love of truth? Locating himself within what he calls the discourse of the analyst, he will answer as follows:

> The love of truth is the love of this weakness whose veil we have lifted, it's the love of what truth hides, which is called castration. [*He adds:*] I should not need these reminders, which are in some way

so bookish. [*And then he'll beat up on his usual counter-figures, the analysts:*] It seems that it is the analysts, particularly they, who, because of these few taboo words with which their speech is soiled, never understand what truth is, namely, impotence.[4]

So there's something that the analysts, who are Lacan's whipping boys, don't understand in the least, namely that the love of truth is the love of weakness, the love of what truth hides—in other words, the love of castration, ultimately. This will also be expressed as: the love of truth is the love of an impotence. After all, it's clear what this means. It's obvious that, for Lacan, there can be no love of truth except as love of what is impotent with respect to the whole. What the love of truth loves in it is the fact that it's impossible to say it all, that it's always only half-said. It's this weakness, this impotence with respect to the All, that constitutes an object of love for the philosopher.

Furthermore, it's clear that castration is hovering in the background as a figure of the access to the symbolic, and that, ultimately, there is no truth effect except under that condition. The love of truth must be the love of that condition itself, hence also the love of that which impedes, cuts, limits. And from whatever angle it's approached, we understand very well that, if there is love of truth, it's the love of a weakness, of an impotence, of a barring [*barre*], of a limitation, of a half-saying, and so on.

Lacan will draw several conclusions from this: that, where the analysts are concerned, it's better not to love truth. There's no point at all in loving it when you're an analyst. However, loving *knowledge*—that, yes. You can see how this theme I mentioned at the outset is constantly in play; you can see the process by which the problem of the act comes into play as a result of the magnetism induced by the question of knowledge, while truth remains partly in shadow. Such is the anti-philosophical thesis. In contrast, the love of truth is at the heart of the philosophical discourse. But—and it's here that Lacan's case against philosophy finds its main argument—the philosopher purports to love truth as *power* and not as impotence. So we'd have to say that the Lacanian anti-philosophical statement doesn't have to do directly with the question of the love of truth in its counter-position to the love of knowledge, although that's one of its essential quibbles. It has to do with the fact that philosophy purports to promote and subjectivate the love of truth as power. And it is this pernicious illusion—which the analyst must avoid at all costs—that is at the heart of its discourse.

We'll stop here for today. Let's just say that the real Lacanian thesis is that, if you purport to love truth as power, if you reject the fact that all true love of truth is love of an impotence or a weakness, if you purport to love truth as power and not as weakness, then you'll be helpless in the face of ignorance. This is a very powerful dialectic: in terms of subjectivation, you can block the passion for ignorance, which is, so to speak, the normal state of the human being, in terms of truth, only if what you love in truth is weakness. That may seem paradoxical, but it isn't. The power of the love of truth, including its power to block ignorance, is precisely to be the love of a weakness, the love of a certain impotence. Ultimately, the love of truth is only powerful if it is the love of an impotence. Or else you have to have recourse to knowledge, to the love of knowledge, which, for its part, possesses real power. If you want neither one, neither the love of truth-weakness nor the love of knowledge-power, then the way is wide open for the passion for ignorance. At the point of the real, that passion can only be thwarted, Lacan tells us, by the love of knowledge as power or of truth as impotence. If you want the power of power rather than the power of weakness, then turn, not to philosophy, but to knowledge.

I'll leave you with that "Turn!"

Session 6

March 15, 1995

As you'll recall, there are three formal features of anti-philosophy: (1) The destitution of philosophy's theoretical pretension, a destitution that always takes the form of a discrediting and not centrally, or mainly, the form of a refutation. (2) The exposure of the true nature of the philosophical operation. Behind its presumed and discredited theoretical pretension there is a properly philosophical gesture that must be identified by anti-philosophy because it is usually concealed by philosophers, and is obscure or indiscernible. (3) The opposition of a new type of act—a radically different act that completes the destitution of philosophy—to the philosophical act thus reconstructed.

These general features can be found in a generic way in all the well-known anti-philosophies. In what way or in what forms are they found in Lacan? This is what we'll be concerned with in this first recap.

⸻

First of all, the destitution of philosophy's theoretical pretension means more specifically: the destitution of philosophy's pretension to be a theory of the real, whatever that presumed real may be. In Lacan's eyes, philosophy is incapable of producing a theory of the real, for no fewer than four reasons.

The first reason is that philosophy is dependent on the figure of the discourse of the master. On closer inspection, it should be said, instead, that philosophy claims to be exempt from the rotation of the discourses. The most important thing is not so much that philosophy is enunciated on the basis of the discourse of the master but that its inherent, constitutive claim is that it puts a stop to the rotation of the discourses. For Lacan, as you know, there are four discursive positions: the discourse of the hysteric, the discourse of the master, the discourse of the university, and the discourse of the analyst. You can find all this in Seminar XVII, *The Other Side of Psychoanalysis*. This is a dynamic theory, not a classificatory one. These discursive positions can only be truly intelligible if the quarter-turns by which they move relative to one another are understood. Yet philosophy claims to be a stopping point of the discursive disposition in general. This is another way of saying that, from within the Lacanian apparatus, philosophy claims to be foundational. Indeed, a discourse that supposedly founds itself, that is supposedly self-foundational, as is always the case with philosophy, would be a discourse that would bring the inevitable rotation of discursive configurations to a halt. Thus, this first defect of philosophy could be called the pretension to establish a stopping point that would make its own discourse self-sufficient.

This point can be formulated in a completely different way, as is so often the case with Lacan. It can be formulated as: philosophy claims that there is a metalanguage. This is the point where Lacan enters into complicity with Wittgenstein—the encounter between two anti-philosophical figures—by giving Wittgenstein credit for having denounced philosophy for its untenable pretension to be a metalanguage that supposedly towers over the rotation of the four discourses. The phrase Lacan uses to condemn this pretension is "philosophical crookedness." What is specifically crooked is its assumption that there is a metalanguage.

Incidentally, it would be interesting to ask whether all crooked-ness involves this assumption that a metalanguage exists. It's quite possible that it does, and, mind you, it would also be a way of say-ing that all crookedness is philosophical. That's a stronger statement than just saying that philosophy is crooked.

The second reason philosophy is incapable of producing a the-ory of the real is that it constitutively fails to recognize that, ulti-mately, the real is the ab-sense of the sexual relationship. It could be said that philosophy is built upon a foreclosure of that issue, which, from a logical or formal point of view, means that there is always a moment in philosophy when nonrelationship is forced into relationship. Philosophy is a discursive discipline within which it can be seen that a nonrelationship has been forcibly brought into relationship. This could also be expressed as: philosophy forces what is strictly ab-sense into sense. This is perfectly compatible with the fact there are philosophies of non-sense, of the absurd, etc. The spe-cifically philosophical way of affirming non-sense is still a forcing into sense of ab-sense, which, as I've said over and over, is utterly different from non-sense. The philosophical category of non-sense persists in being an operation of forcing of ab-sense into sense. It is there that the fantasy of totality originates. In Lacan's view, the (traditional) critique of the philosophical fantasy of totality, or of system, should instead be conceived of as an effect rather than a cause. The real cause lies in forcing nonrelationship into relation-ship, in forcing ab-sense into sense, in totalizing everything through a generalization of the relationship to sense.

The third reason is that philosophy doesn't want to know any-thing about *jouissance* and therefore anything about the Thing in the Lacanian sense either. Philosophy abhors the Thing of *jouis-sance*. This is moreover why—I'm adding an argument that I'm not sure is actually in Lacan (no one ever knows what Lacan said; no-body knows everything Lacan said!)—there are philosophies that prescribe the return to the Thing itself, compulsively, so to speak. As you know, one of Husserl's directives is to return to things themselves. And if this compulsion to return is interpreted from a Lacanian point of view, it could be said that philosophy is only driven by this compulsion because it doesn't want to know anything about the Thing. It is this "not wanting to know anything about it" that makes it compulsively declare the imperative of returning to things themselves.

Finally, the fourth reason is that, ever since Parmenides, philosophy has assumed the false axiom "Being thinks," whereas in Lacan's eyes—and this is a crucial point—there is thinking only where there is a local absence of being. It is only where being is absent that "it thinks" [ça pense].[1] And it's not a question here of opposing "being thinks" to "the subject thinks," because even if it's a matter of the supposed-being of a subject, it's only where there's an absence of such being that " 'it' thinks." Lacan's dictum is: "Where 'it' thinks, I am not; where I am, I do not think." This is the chief reason for his dismantling of Descartes's *cogito*. What, in his opinion, is inadmissible in the Cartesian construction, aside from the fact that it's not excentered as it ought to be, is obviously the move from the *cogito* to the *res cogitans*. In Lacan's view, it should not be inferred from the statement "I think" that the locus of thinking is the figure of the *res*, the thing. And here, too, philosophy fails in its purpose or goal, since it is mistaken about the topos of thinking. The *place* where 'it' thinks is ultimately completely concealed beneath the false axiom that where there is thinking there is being, beneath the Parmenidean axiom "Being and thinking are the same." That axiom leads philosophy irremediably into blindness about the topos of thinking.

So this sums up the first formal feature of anti-philosophy in its Lacanian mode—the destitution of philosophy's pretension to be a theory of the real. Philosophy remains dependent on the position of the discourse of the master, forces nonrelationship into relationship, doesn't want to know anything about *jouissance* and the Thing, and is mistaken about the topos of thinking.

———∽∞∾———

Now let's turn to the second feature, which is that philosophy's discursive appearance conceals some constitutive operations constituting a specific act that must be reconstructed. Philosophy itself is blind to these operations, even though they constitute its own act. There are three interdependent, interrelated, constitutive operations. Let me remind you what they are: a dethroning of mathematics, a plugging of the hole of politics, and a promotion of love, which is the way around it. We've already discussed all this at length.

———∽∞∾———

As for the third formal feature of Lacanian anti-philosophy, the one that's critical for us, it is that philosophy's formal operations are opposed by an unprecedented act, whose existence, as I mentioned, is attested to by the emergence of Freud's work and which is known as "the analytic act." Even before we get into its problems, which are labyrinthine, we can nonetheless say that this analytic act, whose eruptive emergence gave philosophy's operations a battering, actually has easily identifiable distinctive features that make it radically opposed to philosophy. Let me mention a few of them.

The operations of philosophy claim to ultimately afford fulfillment, or even bliss. This is true even of skeptical or nihilistic philosophies, and even, perhaps, especially of them. That's why the discussion in Plato about whether the philosopher is happy, happier than the tyrant, for example, is of major, not minor, importance. It is of the essence of philosophical activity to state that its outcome is the possibility of intellectual bliss and to examine its value. You could say that, from the standpoint of his act, the philosophical subject appears as a subject who's virtually fulfilled. You see, we're still dealing with the metaphor of plugging: the philosopher fills and is fulfilled. This point never changes. It is indifferent to the tone of the philosophy involved. This is also the case even and perhaps especially when the tone is negative or critical. In fact, it is always a question of establishing the conditions for a fulfilled subject.

By contrast, the analytic act, for the psychoanalyst himself, only arouses anxiety and uneasiness. That is its lot. In a text ["The Other is Missing"] that dates from January 24, 1980, Lacan suddenly said something that can be regarded as an axiom: "Yes, the psychoanalyst holds his act in *horror*" (*T*, 135). This is a statement that should be taken in the strongest sense. In other words, if the psychoanalyst *doesn't* hold it in horror, it's probably because his act is ineffective. A psychoanalyst who is happy with his act is a psychoanalyst beaten by the philosopher! He thought he was engaged in the analytic act, but he's engaged in the *philosophical* act: he's fulfilled, he has fulfilled himself.

This is also indicative of a difference of position as regards the act. The philosophical act, in the system of interrelated operations I mentioned that virtually bring a fulfilled subject to the fore, presents itself as a product of discourse. Discourse is something whose particular effect or possible product is this fulfilled subject in a constantly revised but absolutely persistent figure of bliss. The analytic act, by contrast, is not, strictly speaking, a product of discourse, although, in a way, it is entirely within that tension. The analytic act is an enunciative act, but it is also its reversal, disruption, or waste product. I'll come back to this all-important category of waste product. But, as a result, the relationship to the act—if indeed this notion means anything, although, after all, there is at least the relationship of its subject-support holding it in horror—is less a question of producing the act, Lacan will say, than of facing up to it. There is a confrontation between the psychoanalyst and his act, a facing up to the act that is a completely different regime from the philosophical conception, whose outcome or product or so the anti-philosopher says—is the figure of the fulfilled subject or of bliss. In the January 24, 1980 text again, Lacan sums up his objective, writing: "As for the act, I am giving them the chance to face up to it" (*T*, 135). "I am giving them the chance": giving whom the chance? The poor psychoanalysts, to whom you're always speaking when you're Lacan, because, in his struggle against the figure of the philosopher, they are Lacan's counter-figure. "I am giving them the chance to face up to it": that is ultimately what the analytic discourse is about, I mean what its function is. The analytic discourse is the offer of a chance to face up to the analytic act, to accept its horror, or, more precisely perhaps, to *bear* its horror, to bear and bear up under the horror of the act. So that's what analytic theory gives one the chance to do. If it is not this chance that's given to face up to the act, then it's only idle chatter. It is, at bottom, philosophy in disguise. Clearly, this idea of facing up to the act as the sole justification of the discourse—a discourse of transmission, of teaching, of education, of whatever you like—is a typically anti-philosophical idea. You could say that all anti-philosophy assumes (except that this isn't the analytic act per se but a different one) the idea that the discourse of theory—hence, what they do, because all these anti-philosophers write, teach, head up institutions—is worthless unless it gives one a chance to face up to the act. Nietzsche will say, for example, that, ultimately, the sole purpose of the whole genealogical theory, all the analytic subtlety of the system of active and reactive forces, the whole typology of the generic figures of thought and discourse, is to enable one to face up to the act, which is "to break the history of the world into two halves"—the act of Dionysian affirmation. That's the only thing that matters. Discourse is hardly anything compared with the absolute intensity of the act. In texts that I commented on in great detail last year, Wittgenstein explains that what matters in the end is to bear the ethical act the way one bears a burden. And here again we find the notion of facing up to the horror. For the ethical act is no laughing matter. When Wittgenstein decided to go off and teach in some grubby little Austrian village, he was definitely experiencing the horror of his act. And to bear it, as he advised everyone around him to do, to bear it as a burden, was for him the true purpose of any discursive formation. Between the analytic act as horror that the discourse allows one to face up to and the bliss of the fulfilled subject that philosophy—according to the anti-philosopher—assumes can be a product of its discourse, there is obviously a striking antinomy.

Another example of radical opposition between the analytic act and the operations of philosophy is the following: the philosophical operations claim to be coextensive with truth. Philosophy describes itself in a quasi-generic way as a search for truth. But it's clear that the analytic act is anything but a search for truth. It is neither a search for truth nor is it imaginable in the context of such a search. This suggests that the analytic act is in the gap between presumed knowledge and knowledge transmissible as mathemes, but not that it is the actual occasion of a search for truth. This may, at bottom, be an oversimplification, but it could be put this way: the difference between analytic act and philosophical activity is a rearrangement of the truth/knowledge /real triad, a triad that's found in both philosophy and psychoanalysis. This is why the boundary between the two has to be constantly redrawn. It could be said that philosophy claims to set out, as knowledge, a truth of the real. That's what the search for truth is all about: it's the possibility of setting out, as transmissible knowledge, a truth of the real. But as far as Lacan is concerned, his conception of analysis cannot be described in that way. Lacan rearranges the triad.

Consider what he says in *Radiophonie*:

Question 6: In what respect are knowledge and truth incompatible? (*AE*, 440)

The answer Lacan gives us is an explicit explanation of the triad:

For truth is situated by assuming that aspect of the real that acts as
a function in knowledge, which is added to it (to the real). (*AE*, 443)

For Lacan, as we see, the truth effect depends on the fact that, in
knowledge, a real acts as a function, it functions. The topos of truth
requires that something of the real acts as a function in knowledge. That's why psychoanalysis can in no way be understood as a
search for truth. It can be an activation of a truth effect provided
that a real acts as a function in knowledge, but it is in no way a
search for truth. Thus, its act cannot be reduced to what we said
the philosophical act's ambitions—according to both tradition and
anti-philosophy—must be.

This has a simple but very important consequence. There is a common way of talking about psychoanalysis—common but extremely
persistent, and persistent to the point of being a constant immanent
temptation of psychoanalytic self-presentation—which is that the
unconscious reveals the truth of the conscious mind. Those of you
here who have been trained as Lacanians are going to go ballistic
and say "No, that's obviously wrong!" But it's not as obvious as all
that. To hold the position that that's wrong is, to my mind, one of
the key issues in Lacan's teaching. Ultimately, this dictum "the unconscious reveals the truth of the conscious mind" is precisely what
the philosophical appropriation of psychoanalysis is. It's this dictum
and the countless specious versions of it that bring about the philo-
sophication of psychoanalysis, and that's why the crux of Lacanian
anti-philosophy is the refutation of that dictum.

You'll recall that I cited one of Lacan's last texts, in which he says:
"I rebel against philosophy." What need is there for the psychoanalyst
to rebel against philosophy after he has discredited it theoretically,
identified its act, and opposed to that act a completely different
one? What can explain this extremely vehement statement? Why did

the final Lacan still need to say he was rebelling against philosophy? Because philosophy always attempts to appropriate psychoanalysis, and this appropriation operates, so to speak, under the word "truth." What I mean by this is that if it's assumed that the unconscious is the locus of truth of the conscious mind, then psychoanalysis in no way disturbs philosophy, quite the contrary: it gives it a hand or a boost. Ridding psychoanalysis of this immanent temptation, where truth is concerned, to succumb to being appropriated by philosophy requires anti-philosophical resolve. And that anti-philosophical resolve, that anti-philosophical rebellion, signals—and I must stress this—a danger immanent to psychoanalysis, which is plainly the subversion of its act, a subversion indicated just as plainly by the fact that one is happy with one's act rather than holding it in horror. Ultimately, any happy person is an unwitting philosopher.

Someone comments: *That difference doesn't take into account the anthropology that can be developed around the work of Freud, who held that the key to social dynamics is related to sexual repression, on which he risked an anthropologization of the Freudian subject. So he already took the risk of an anthropologization of psychoanalysis, a risk related to the temptation of the philosophical appropriation you were talking about.*

Absolutely. To the question of whether that temptation can already be found in Freud's work, I'd answer in the affirmative. For if Freud's work is a real foundation, it, too, has to be exposed to the immanent temptation of philosophy. That said, it's a temptation that can also be found in Lacan's work—we'll have occasion to come back to this later. How anti-philosophy can really manage not to be affected, in any of its respects, by the temptation of philosophy that haunts it is also a question Lacan would ask himself, not under the threat of an anthropologization but rather of a logicization. However, regardless of whether it is anthropologization or logicization, the danger posed by philosophy is clear in Freud and Lacan. In both cases, what's at stake is a potential subversion of the act. But, for the time being, I just wanted to explain the rationale behind Lacan's need for an anti-philosophical rebellion by showing that once the truth/knowledge/real triad is rearranged a little, what amounts, in Lacan's eyes, to a philosophical corruption of psychoanalysis is introduced.

Regarding this question of the unconscious and truth, I'd like to remind you of two clear and important passages, one of which is in *Radiophonie* and the other of which is in the seminar . . . *ou pire*. They're important because they show clearly that it's a matter of being opposed to any philosophical appropriation of the unconscious, in the form of: the unconscious is the truth of the conscious mind. In *Radiophonie*, Lacan states:

> The unconscious, as we see, is only a metaphorical term to denote the knowledge that only sustains itself by presenting itself as impossible, so that in consequence it is confirmed as being real. (*AE*, 425)

Thus, the unconscious denotes a knowledge that's in the guise of the real because of its self-presentation as impossible. You'll note that truth isn't mentioned in the sentence, a sentence that's a definition of the unconscious. It is important to understand that truth is in no way identical to the knowledge in question here, and still much less, of course, to the knowledge of this knowledge. So where can truth in analysis be situated in relation to the unconscious? It is situated in the assumption that if knowledge presents itself as impossible then there is a function of the real involved in that knowledge. With respect to the unconscious, if knowledge presents itself as impossible, truth can be situated. We can clearly see that the whole anti-philosophical effort to avoid psychoanalysis' being appropriated consists in keeping truth at a distance from the unconscious by only situating it as a function of the real in knowledge. In the published version of the . . . *ou pire* seminar, we find the very characteristic phrase: "the unconscious insofar as it presents itself as knowledge" (*OP*, 7). The unconscious accedes to its own truth in the guise of knowledge. But in no case can it be maintained that the unconscious is truth. On that basis, the truly enormous and apparently unbridgeable gap between the conditions of the analytic act and those of philosophical activity can be reconstructed. It could be argued that, for Lacan, the triad of the real, truth, and knowledge is structured around three negations. First of all, there is no truth of the real, whereas philosophy could be defined as the knowledge of a truth of the real. There is truth only insofar as there is a function of the real in knowledge. But "truth of the real" is not, strictly speaking, something that can be said. Second of all, there is no knowledge of the real either. What there is, is a function of the real in knowledge that enables truth to be situated. Third of all, of course, there is no knowledge of truth either. At most, you could say—and this is a bit metaphorical—that there is truth of knowledge provided that a real is acting as a function within it, is functioning within it. Therefore, there is no truth of the real, or knowledge of the real, or knowledge of truth. Ultimately, there is the truth/knowledge/ real triad, which cannot be broken up, which cannot be divided into parts. There is only the triad. So truth is only able to be situated insofar as a function of the real can be identified in or attributed to knowledge. In the final analysis, philosophy is an arrangement of the triad into pairs, since it assumes that there is a truth of the real and that there can be knowledge of this truth. The arrangement into pairs, the pair [*pair*], and the father [*père*]. It's the terrible arrangement into *pères*. It's the arrangement of the triad into pairs in all its possible combinations: there will be truth of the real, knowledge of the real, knowledge of truth, and so on. And, on the contrary, one of the possible formulations of Lacanian anti-philosophy is: no arrangement of the truth/knowledge/real triad into pairs is valid. The unconscious is the ultimate impossibility of the arrangement into *pères*.

In the final analysis, philosophy, for Lacan, is an inadmissible dismantling of the triad, or a subversion of the three by the two. It is what no longer holds them together. We then have the effect of a theorem, which I won't prove for you today: if you subvert the three by the two, you get a false thinking of the One. This false (philosophical) thinking can be expressed as: "The One is," whereas the true thinking of the One can be expressed as: "There is some One [or Oneness]" [*il y a de l'Un*] or, as Lacan puts it more colloquially, "There's some One" [*y a d'l'Un*]. Here's another Lacanian homework problem that I'll leave you with: Prove that if you subvert the three by the two, in the sense I've just given a precise example of—the philosophical arrangement of the truth/knowledge/real triad into pairs—this assumes and requires a theory of the One of the type: The One is. Which, in Lacanian terms, would be yet another way of opposing the philosophical act and the analytic act to each other by saying: the analytic act is based on the notion "There's some One," while philosophical activity requires positing "The One is."

You'll note that if we take things the other way around, it could be said that if philosophy assumes that there is a truth of the real, it [philosophy] is knowledge of this truth. Therefore, if it's the arrangement of the triad into pairs, the Lacanian statements completely demolish it, since there's no truth of the real, there's no knowledge, strictly speaking, of the real, much less any knowledge of truth. So there's a breaking-up, a radical fragmentation of the constitutive statements of philosophy. This is how what I've always told you about genuine anti-philosophy—that its ultimate aim is to *destroy* philosophy—is accomplished. Anti-philosophy is not just a critique. If the analytic act exists, and insofar as it exists, philosophy is destroyed. Except, the analytic act has to exist and its horror has to be borne. And to bear its horror or to face up to it, the whole analytic discourse has to exist. At bottom, this very complex and probably very aleatory system of the conditions of the analytic act results in the dismemberment of philosophy, a dismemberment from which it constantly revives, the way the body of Dionysus, torn to pieces by the Titans, was put back together.

Along this path, the description of the analytic act—the analytic act conceived of as the key to Lacanian anti-philosophy—will gradually become clearer.

Let's think about this: the real is not something there is truth about, nor is it something that is known. Indeed, if you assume that the real is something that's known, or that the real is something there is truth about, you're arranging the triad into pairs. If the real can only be situated in the truth/knowledge/real triad, then there has to be a correlation between the real and the act. To put it more simply, it's important to understand that in Lacan's conception of the real, the real is never something we know [connaît], either in the sense of truth or in the sense of knowledge [savoir], assuming that "knowing" [connaissance] is taken here as a non-specific word that subsumes both of them.[2] For anti-philosophy, however, that word makes no sense precisely because it purports to subsume both of them. What is certain is therefore that the real is not something we know. But neither is it something that we *don't* know. This is a very subtle point that we'll have to come back to, because it's very tempting to say that the real is something we don't know. Yet the real for Lacan is not something that is clearly inaccessible to knowing, as in a theory of the constitutive unknowability of the real or of its ineffability, as is the case for Kant's thing-in-itself, or Wittgenstein's mystical element, or the Skeptics' truth, to mention three references.

So our question is as follows: When it comes to the real, what is opposed to knowing [le connaître]? If the real is not what is known or what we know, what is the access to the real, whatever it may be? How is it that thought can gain access to it? And in what way, it being understood that that way is surely not a cognitive one? Lacan will tread a very fine line here between the philosophical and the anti-philosophical. He has to exempt the real from knowing without ending up with a theory of the ineffable or the unknowable. So he'll have to state that the real is neither knowable nor unknowable. Here, we're at the heart of hearts of his anti-philosophy. Consider what he says in *Radiophonie*:

> Thus the real differs from reality. This is not to say that it's unknowable, but that there's no question of knowing about it, only of demonstrating it. (*AE*, 408)

Let's examine this dictum closely. Let's start with what is simplest: we'll call "reality" what it's possible to know [*connaître*]. Hence, "knowing" will be associated with "reality" and therefore with a strong imaginary quality. This is the point where Lacan is vulnerable, in a way, to the accusation of Kantianism. Let's assume that reality is phenomenal: it is what can be known, and the real is the unknowable. This is Kantian then. Kant is the philosophical borderline of anti-philosophy. This borderline has since been called "critical philosophy," and what Lacan will do is avoid this Kantian solution. Lacan is not a critic. To be sure, the real differs from reality, which attaches its regime to knowing. But Lacan immediately says: I don't mean to say the real is unknowable. I'm not a Kantian. I don't oppose an unknowable real to a knowable reality. So the real is not unknowable, but "there's no question of knowing about it, only of demonstrating it." Although the real, as distinct from reality, is exempted from the knowable, which is the essence of reality, the real nevertheless does not end up being the absolute unknowable but is instead exposed to being demonstrated.

Before we turn to this enigmatic "demonstrate," I'd like to stress this point, which will take us to the act and the real. It is essential to understand that the real in the Lacanian sense of the term is in a position of radical exteriority to knowing, including to that particular form of knowing that is "not knowing." The unknowable is only ever a category of the knowable, a form of the knowable: it is its opposite, but in the same regime, just as non-sense, as we've seen, is a (philosophical) category of sense, which ab-sense isn't. To say, then, that the real is unknowable would in fact be to say that the real belongs to the same regime as reality, because it is open to the question of knowing, even if only to fail in relation to it. "Real" thus denotes something so alien to knowing that it can't be thought of as unknowable either. This notion that the real, what is real, is extrinsic to both knowing and not-knowing is a crucial, generic, key anti-philosophical notion. What is truly real is indifferent to knowing but cannot be stated, ascribed to, or symbolized in terms of the negation of knowing either. In other words, the real is indifferent to knowing as such, which encompasses not-knowing.

It still has to be demonstrated that knowable and unknowable do not cover the whole field of what exists, since the real is precisely what is absent from both the knowable and the unknowable, and yet it imposes itself on existence. So a point of access to the real will have to be found that is apparently supernumerary to the All in its analytic sense, namely, A and not-A, or being and not-being, or knowable and not-knowable. In short, an anti-philosophical thesis regarding the real is that the apparatus of knowing, when added to that of the unknowable, is not exhaustive. The real is the remainder of the disjunction between the knowable and the unknowable. Here we take the measure of the anti-dialectical dimension of every anti-philosophy: the point of the access to the real cannot be reached negatively. As compared with knowable reality, no negation procedure provides any access to the real. Something completely different from negation will be required. Regarding this issue of the anti-dialectical, which is at work in every anti-philosophy, I'd like to give you a few reference points in the history of anti-philosophy so that we can get to the originality of Lacan's solution. Because, to my mind, as compared with the previous dispositions of anti-philosophy, there's something uniquely Lacanian about the specific way in which the real is given as absence from both the knowable and the unknowable.

——⚬∞⚬——

The references I intend to give are of unequal weight, for reasons that have to do with preparing the ground for Lacan. I will stress Kierkegaard in particular, far more than Pascal and Rousseau.

For Pascal, the God of every rational philosophy, regardless of whether one reaches a conclusion of atheism or one "proves" God's existence, remains at a distance from the divine real, which escapes the rationalist opposition between the knowable and the unknowable. This is because in Pascal's apologetics the whole point is precisely to understand that, under the name of God—the name of the real—something must be absolutely beyond the regime of knowing, even if it is in the guise of the we-do-not-know. This is clearly the real meaning of the Pascalian opposition between the God of Abraham, Isaac, and Jacob, the God felt by the heart, and what Pascal calls "the God of the philosophers and scholars." This God of the philosophers is the God exposed to knowing, to the proof of existence, if for no other reason than to say that he cannot be known or that he doesn't exist. It doesn't matter: this God is the God of Descartes, who proved his existence, but he's the same as the God of any speculative atheism. In either case, the real God fails to be grasped, is absent. His presence can only be accessed in a unique way, which exempts him from the opposition between knowing and the unknowable.

How is this presented in Rousseau? Here, I'll just give you the references; you can reread the texts for yourselves. The complete anti-philosophical proclamation is set out in Book 4 of *Émile, or On Education*, which has to do with the age of reason and the emotions (from age fifteen to twenty), especially in Chapter 2, on religious education, in the famous "Profession of Faith of the Savoyard Vicar." It's no accident that we find these references in a treatise on education: in it, Rousseau put forward exactly what an anti-philosophical education might be. Once again, you'll find the three crucial points that lead to this supplementation of knowing and not-knowing by the real. First of all, there's the discrediting of philosophers' rational knowing, which is truly a running anti-philosophical theme from Pascal to Lacan. In "The Profession of Faith of the Savoyard Vicar":

> General and abstract ideas are the source of men's greatest errors [*this is still the criminalization of philosophy, which is not just false but dangerous*]. The jargon of metaphysics has never led us to discover a single truth, and it has filled philosophy with absurdities of which one is ashamed as soon as one has stripped them of their big words.[3]

Systematic philosophy, once again under the name of metaphysics, is both dangerous—"the greatest errors"—and impotent: there's nothing, not a single truth, that can be credited to speculative thought. This is because the locus of the act by which one gains access to a truth is not reason; it's what Rousseau calls "conscience":

> Too often reason deceives. We have acquired only too much right to challenge it. [*This is counterposed to the traditional scheme: imagination deceives us. Here, the destitution of reason has to be invoked.*] But conscience never deceives us. (250)

Under the name of "conscience" we have that which, as an exception to knowing and reason, provides undeniable access to the real: "Conscience never deceives us." That "never" is crucial. Indeed, we're as far as possible from any idea that it would have to do with the question "What do we know and what don't we know?" The knowing/not knowing opposition is irrelevant. Reason deceives us and conscience never does. Finally, there's the last point, the definition of the act: "The acts of the conscience are not judgments but feelings" (446; trans. slightly modified).

There is the dethronement of philosophy under the theme of general and abstract knowing, and the definition of the conscience as a site beyond the opposition between the knowable and the unknowable. Thus, he finally arrives at the definition of the act through which access to the real opens up. And this act is not in the form of judgment but in that of feeling. Ultimately, the feeling/judgment opposition will be, in Rousseau's terms, that which provides access to the real/truth opposition, which exists to some extent in Lacan, even though that's not his vocabulary. Feeling, as an act of conscience, and conscience as a place that never deceives, are the point of the real itself, entirely heteronomous to the cognitive regime of reason, which makes us conform to reality, of course, but ultimately in an errancy that is semblance.

I mention all this so that you'll note that in both Pascal and Rousseau—in classical anti-philosophy, shall we say—there is always a name for the place of the real. What I mean by "place of the real" is the place that is beyond the opposition between the knowable and the unknowable. There will also always be a name for the act, which, in this place, opens up access to the real. In Rousseau's case, the place is conscience, and the act, in this place, appears as feeling. This is a theme you can find everywhere in anti-philosophy: the idea that there's a subjective experience that never deceives. Since the real escapes the opposition between the knowable and the unknowable, something in the register of affect is what never deceives: the God felt by the heart, Pascal will say; feeling, not judgment, Rousseau says; and, finally, anxiety, Lacan will say. In anti-philosophy it is never reason that never deceives; it's something else, and it has a variety of names.

Last but not least, let's see what Kierkegaard has to say. He's a very important source for Lacan, especially as concerns the question of repetition, but it goes well beyond that. Once again, in Kierkegaard, we find the three points that I just dealt with in Rousseau. First, a sarcastic process of discrediting the regime of knowing, as philosophy—especially that of Hegel—claims to establish it. Second, an identification of the place where the real is something other than the knowable. Third, an act that identifies this place. As regards philosophy, let me just cite a passage from "Diapsalmata," at the beginning of *Either/Or*, which is a story I like a lot:

> What the philosophers say about reality [*this is still the same anti-philosophical terminology*] is often just as disappointing as it is when one reads on a sign you see in a secondhand shop: Pressing Done Here. If a person were to bring his clothes to be pressed, he would be duped, for the sign is merely for sale.[4]

Philosophy is a second-hand shop in which you find, among other things, "Here's how to live." And if you were to bring your life into it, you'd be duped, because it would turn out to be like everything else: some discourse for sale. This is a very nice story that really expresses what Kierkegaard felt about philosophy. As for the true life, Kierkegaard adds: "it does not depend so much on deliberation as on the baptism of the will" (2, 169). You could say that, for the anti-philosopher, knowing, in the philosophical sense of the term, is what is incapable of baptizing any will whatsoever.

I don't want to go into the very intricate details of Kierkegaard's thinking here, but what needs to be understood is that subjectivation in the instant, or the sudden summoning of the subject as such, overwhelmingly opposes existence to knowing. It is existence, itself coming to exist in the sudden summoning of the subject, that escapes the opposition between knowing and not-knowing. And this, Kierkegaard will call the ethical realm, which is opposed to any cognitive realm. To refresh your memory about this notion, read what's in *Concluding Unscientific Postscript to Philosophical Fragments*. *Philosophical Fragments* is a short book, but the *Postscript* is enormous. All of Chapter 3 of the second section of the second part entitled "Actual Subjectivity, Ethical Subjectivity; The Subjective Thinker" will give you everything you need in terms of the painstaking construction of a place of the real that escapes the opposition between knowing and not-knowing and is different from selling discursive promises.

I'm going to read you three excerpts that I'll sum up in a maxim so that you can get a good sense of the tone of the material that prepares the ground for Lacan. Kierkegaard's basic thesis is as follows: knowledge of reality is, immediately and solely, a knowledge of possibilities, not of the real. This is his own particular way of saying that the real is not involved. Any figure of the relation to reality in a cognitive mode is always, also and solely, an apprehension of possibility.

[*First fragment*] All knowledge about reality is possibility. The only reality concerning which an existing person has more than knowledge about is his own reality, that he exists; and this reality is his absolute interest. The demand of abstraction upon him is that he become disinterested in order to obtain something to know; the requirement of the ethical upon him is to be infinitely interested in existing.[5]

Whence, a little further on, the maxim I suggested that you bear in mind:

[*Second fragment*] The real subjectivity is not the knowing subjectivity, because with knowledge one is in the medium of possibility, but is the ethical existing subjectivity. Surely an abstract thinker exists, but his existing is rather like a satire on him. To demon-strate his existence on the grounds that he is thinking is a strange contradiction, because to the degree that he thinks abstractly he abstracts to the same degree precisely from his existing. (1, 316; trans. slightly modified)

Note the anti-Cartesian sarcasm. If this quibble is examined closely, you can see that it is closely related to the Lacanian decentering of the cogito. Let me read you that sentence again: "To demonstrate his existence on the grounds that he is thinking is a strange contra-diction, because to the degree that he thinks abstractly he abstracts to the same degree precisely from his existing." What we have here is the assertion that where I think abstractly I am not. Kierkegaard calls that "existence." And a little further on, he draws the following conclusion from his critique of the Cartesian cogito:

[*Third fragment*] To conclude existence from thinking is, then, a contradiction, because thinking does just the opposite and takes existence away from reality and thinks it by annulling it, by trans-posing it into possibility. (1, 317; trans. slightly modified)

For Kierkegaard, the fundamental condition of knowing is that existence be taken away. In so doing, reality is transposed or trans-figured into possibility. Reality as a correlate of knowing is only ever a possibility. This is the Kierkegaardian equivalent of what we find in Lacan, namely, the imaginary nature of reality, as opposed to the real. In Kierkegaard, what occupies the position that Lacan ascribes to the imaginary is the possible. If, as a consequence, I want to restore the real, I'll have to remove myself from knowing, for the correlate of the very operation of knowing is only possibility, and therefore semblance.

What will this act ultimately be whereby I remove myself from both knowing and the unknowable, which only have to do with possibility? It will be the act whereby the existent gives himself his own real. Once it has been established that the place is the ethical realm, this act will be called by Kierkegaard "the choice," which means deciding about existence. Later on, I will stress the very close proximity between Kierkegaard's "deciding about existence" and Lacan's "demonstrating the real." In any event, what emerges there as an instance of the real is, at the place of the act, in the form of a decision about existence, which is the choice, although it immediately turns out—and this is what will need to be reexamined with regard to Lacan—that its essence is in no way the choosing of this or that but actually choosing to choose. Let me give you the key reference, namely, the whole chapter of the second part of *Either/Or* (sometimes also translated [in French] as *L'Alternative*), which is entitled "The Balance Between the Esthetic and the Ethical in the Development of the Personality." This chapter, entirely devoted to the imbalance between the two, is a theory of the act. It is perhaps one of the most fully elaborated and significant texts about what the anti-philosophical theory of the act might be.

Allow me just a moment to emphasize what Kierkegaard is trying to tell us in a remarkably concise way, namely that there is only a real, or an existence released from the antinomy between knowing and not-knowing, when there is an act that is not determined by that of which it is the act. This is what Kierkegaard calls the absolute choice, the choosing to choose. For instance, he says:

> Rather than designating the choice between good and evil, my Either/Or designates the choice by which one chooses good and evil or rules them out. Here the question is under what qualifications one will view all existence and personally live. (*Either/Or* 2, 169)

It's at this juncture that we'll find what never deceives. If we can manage to get to it, then it never deceives. Kierkegaard will express it this way:

As soon as a person can be brought to stand at the crossroads in such a way that there is no way out for him except to choose, he will choose the right thing. (168)

If you're at the point of choosing to choose, then it never deceives. Is it possible to think—by giving a few twists to the vocabulary and thought, of course—that the aim of analytic treatment is to bring a person to stand at such a crossroads? To bring him to the point where there's no way out for him except to choose? You'll say: choose what? It doesn't matter, no, it doesn't matter! What matters is that there be no way out except to choose, that's all. You're going to object: but then, are we *forced* to choose? No. There's no way out except to choose means: you've come to the point where you have to choose to choose. That's what the act is: being at the point where there is nothing but the possibility of choosing. And *that* never deceives.

So then, where Lacan is concerned, is something about the connection between the real and the act the same sort of thing? This involves two questions. (1) Does the act presuppose a point of the act? This is explicit in Kierkegaard. But what about in Lacan? Does the process of analysis, and ultimately the analytic act, have the meaning of a "bringing the Subject to a point"? (2) Is there something that does not deceive, in the sense that Kierkegaard, Rousseau, Pascal, and ultimately all the anti-philosophers claim, namely that, once we've come to the point of the act, we can neither deceive ourselves nor be deceived?

In speaking about the act in *Radiophonie*, Lacan says: "the act effect that occurs as the waste product of a correct symbolization" (*AE*, 423). Can the correct symbolization—and what *is* the correct symbolization anyway?—be regarded as that which leads to the point where there is no way out except to choose, even if "choose" isn't the right word here? A choice that, retrospectively, makes the correct symbolization not what has produced the choice but rather what is required for one to be at the point of the choice, for there to be no way out except to choose—as a result of which the analytic act itself can always be called the waste product, the disjecta of this symbolization, something that drops off from this symbolization. At that moment, it will remain to be asked whether the waste product of this correct symbolization is really what never deceives. You can see that there is apparently one condition nevertheless, namely that the symbolization be correct. The act does not deceive provided and assuming that the symbolization is correct.

These are the questions we'll try to work through next time.

Session 7

April 5, 1995

L et's go back to the extremely complex issue of the Lacanian anti-philosophical framework. Last time I told you, in essence, that the dismantling of philosophy, a constituent part of Lacan's apparatus, results from three negative statements: there is no truth of the real; nor is there, strictly speaking, any knowledge of the real; and there is no knowledge of truth. And yet, Lacan maintains, the operations of philosophy, whatever the philosophical orientation concerned, are all dependent on the thesis that there can be knowledge of the truth of the real. In addition to the subjective figure of the philosopher, the discourse of the master, crookedness, and metalanguage, philosophy seems to Lacan to be dependent on a thesis about the possibility of knowledge of the truth of the real—a thesis that is dismantled by the three negative statements I just mentioned.

Lacan will assemble the triad of knowledge, truth, and the real in a completely different way. As you'll recall, in *Radiophonie* he says:

> For truth is situated by assuming that aspect of the real that acts as a function in knowledge, which is added to it (to the real). (*AE*, 443)

It is this maxim that reconnects the three terms of the triad. The second focal point of this process is that the way the function of the real in knowledge is revealed hinges on the analytic act, two basic features of which I mentioned earlier. First, the analytic act is an act that the psychoanalyst himself holds in horror. This means that it's an act the enduring or tolerating of which is a serious matter in and of itself. Second, and as a result, the most important thing is what Lacan calls "facing up to" the analytic act. It could be said that the ultimate aim of all his teaching—and there is no other, in my opinion—is, as he himself says, to give the analysts a chance to face up to their act.

The whole theoretical construction, all the analytic subtlety, the whole conceptual revision, the whole topology, the whole theory of the analytic instance, everything that can be said about the act itself—all this actually has only one aim, one purpose: to give the analysts a chance, a little better chance, to face up to the act. That is why, to my mind, if the analytic act is not taken into consideration Lacan's theoretical apparatus can easily be shown to be weak. This has been shown many times, but it's only relevant in terms of a philosophical, not an anti-philosophical, approach to the question. For it is perfectly legitimate that, in Lacan's space of thought, it should ultimately be only a matter of having a chance to face up to the act and that everything should hinge on that. And on that basis we can begin the process that concerns us here, which is what I call the process of *characterizing* the analytic act.

What is the singularity of the analytic act as an irreducible anti-philosophical act? I said that it was on this act that the revelation of the function of the real in knowledge depends. Since the function of the real in knowledge cannot be revealed from the standpoint of a knowledge of this knowledge, it must be from the standpoint of the act that it is revealed.

From the outset, I also said that this act can only be confirmed if an apparatus of knowledge verifies the cut that it makes. So an apparatus of transmissible knowledge must exist for the act to be confirmed, with the further understanding that the revelation of the function of the real is contingent on the act.

Finally, since all integrally transmissible knowledge is a matheme, it could be said—and this is the problem, with all its intricacies, that we'll be concerned with—that in Lacanian anti-philosophy everything ultimately hinges on the enigmatic relationship between the act and the matheme. It is owing to this enigmatic relationship between the act and the matheme that the truth/knowledge/real triad can legitimately be assembled anti-philosophically, the herme-neutic temptation can thereby be avoided, and the interlocutors who count (not the philosophers but the analysts) can be given a little chance to face up to their act.

Let me make a somewhat empirical digression here. Much of the dispute among Lacanians after Lacan's death, and even during his lifetime, had to do with the problem of the relationship between clinical practice and theory. One whole faction of Lacanians was accused of logicism or theoreticism, or of being too far removed from, or ignorant about, clinical practice, while, conversely, a whole other faction was accused of clinical empiricism or of giving way on crucial points of the theoretical apparatus. Ultimately, the "You're not a clinician," on the one hand, and the "You're giving way on the theory," on the other, is the basic backdrop to this dispute. In this way, it's a replay of a well-known dispute, internal to the commu-nist revolutionary movement, about the problem of the relations between theory and practice.

What we should think about this issue is simple, namely that this disjunction undermines the whole edifice. In no way can the Lacanian edifice be examined on the basis of such a disjunction. What I mean by this is not that there might be a synthesis or a fusion, or a clinical application of the theory, or a point where the two would be one and the same—no, that's not it. It's that the very use of this distinction undermines the whole edifice. Indeed, the analytic act, assuming it is confirmed at the heart of clinical practice, can only be productive, in the double sense of its process and its transmission, if it is based on the desire for the matheme. Act and matheme cannot be grasped in a divided figure that would refer, in its turn, to the opposition between clinical practice and theory. It is therefore very important to understand that at the heart of the act there is the desire for the matheme, and that, conversely, the matheme itself is only intelligible from the standpoint of the act.

Looking ahead, I would say this: what I call the desire for the matheme, which is a provisional category, is that without which the analyst cannot bear his own act. Without the matheme, the horror of his act wins out. Without the matheme, the analyst cannot bear the degradation that makes him end up in the position of an abject remainder. Consequently, we shouldn't say that there is the act, on the one hand, and the matheme, on the other, let alone clinical practice and theory, precisely because the question of the matheme is involved in the process whereby a chance is given to the act.

Let's make a detour. I reminded you of Kierkegaard's statement:

> As soon as a person can be brought to stand at the crossroads in such a way that there is no way out for him except to choose, he will choose the right thing. (*Either/Or*, 168)

You can see that what's called the absolute choice is a disposition in which the access to the real, which exists only in the guise of the act, is also such that it cannot deceive. The whole problem is to have been brought to this "crossroads" where there is no way out except to choose.

As far as this matter is concerned, there's a constraint, which is none other than the harsh constraint of freedom. Even though Kierkegaard speaks about an absolute choice, the choice is constrained: a person will choose the right thing provided he has been brought to the point where there is no way out except to choose. Thus, this choice qua absolute choice, which Kierkegaard calls "choosing to choose," does not deceive provided that it's constrained, since there's no other way out. The subject must be brought to it with his back to the wall and must not be able to do anything except choose. Then, the absolute choice will not deceive. This "bringing the person to the crossroads" is what I call a constraint mechanism.

In other words, when you make the question of the real dependent on that of the act—and this is a basic principle of every anti-philosophy—the whole issue is what mechanism brings a person to the act, in what constraining figure the act makes a cut. If you've got the constraining dispositions of the mechanism in which the act makes a cut, then the act has no need of any external norm. The fact that it doesn't deceive means that it is its own norm, that it is self-normed. This is one of anti-philosophy's fundamental notions: there is a self-normed act, an act that is no longer referred, in terms of its truth value, to an external norm but which, intrinsically, does not deceive, since this "not deceiving" presupposes that the act is embedded in a system of constraints in which its absoluteness is indisputable.

How will all this be presented in Lacan? Our point of departure will be a commentary on the second part of a sentence that I already singled out:

> Thus the real differs from reality. This is not to say that it's unknowable, but that there's no question of knowing about it, only of demonstrating it. (*AE*, 408)

As far as the real is concerned, it is only a question of demonstrating it. Here, "demonstrating" is what stands in opposition to the knowing/not knowing pair. It's not a question of knowing, nor is it a question of the unknowable. It is a question of demonstrating, of de-monstrating. But what does this de-monstration involve? It is this demonstration that will include both the constraint and the lack of any other way out. Other than what? We shall see. At any rate, let's just say: the lack of any way out other than . . . the right one. The demonstration will necessarily include all of this, and it will also necessarily include the impossibility of deception. It is precisely for this reason that it will be a demonstration or, in other words, something that makes it possible to ascertain that no deception is possible.

This gives us a provisional definition of the analytic treatment: an analytic treatment is the demonstration of a Subject's real. A demonstration in which, at the same time, the act makes a real cut. There must be a constraint such that no other way out can be meaningful, but, at the same time, the act is not reducible to this constraint; rather, it makes a cut in it. You bring someone to the choice. He has no way out except to choose. But this doesn't mean that the fact that he has no way out justifies the choice. The choice remains an absolute choice. Shifting from Kierkegaard to Lacan, let's agree to say that the analytic treatment is the space in which a real is demonstrated, adding that the act makes a real cut in this demonstration itself. The demonstration constituted by the treatment is both the constraint and its cutting edge. We could also say that the treatment is a constraining formalization in which the act makes a real cut.

But what does "demonstration" mean exactly? "Demonstration" means that the real is not what is shown or monstrated [*ce qui se montre*] but what is de-monstrated [*ce qui se dé-montre*], hence that it's the undoing of the showing. This also means, approximating formalism, that that to which a Subject's real, insofar as it is demonstrated, can be linked is writing. This is because a Subject's real is precisely not of the order of monstration; it is what is de-monstrated, and this de-monstrating links it to writing. Only writing as such de-monstrates without monstrating. This writing cannot be a symbolization of the real since the real cannot be symbolized, which is tantamount to saying that it escapes the question of knowledge. In the demonstration there will be a diverted monstration, a diversion of monstration due to the impasse of a formalization, of a possible linkage with writing, of which the real will naturally never be what is monstrated in it but what is demonstrated in it—in other words, a breakdown or an impasse, or, to use Kierkegaard's terminology, a lack of a way out, no way out. In short, "demonstration" means that, in the very space where the real will insist, there must be the impasse of a symbolization, but this symbolization must contain the constraint that creates the impasse. Otherwise, it would be useless or would go on indefinitely. So something must come to be symbolized under conditions of constraint such that, on the verge of the impasse of this symbolization, only the real can emerge, but this time in the guise of the act.

The constraint effect, which we are going to focus on now, is that effect without which the direction of the treatment would be nothing but endless hermeneutics. But if the treatment is not endless hermeneutics it's precisely because the regime of symbolization it establishes is such that it is forced into a no-way-out situation. And this constraint effect will be the demonstrative promotion of an impossibility of symbolization. Let me quote Lacan:

> In psychoanalysis the point is to raise impotence [*the formalization that accounts for impotence*] to logical impossibility [*the impasse of the formalization that conveys the real*]. (*AE*, 551)[1]

All I'll say is this: raising impotence to logical impossibility is the equivalent of what Kierkegaard calls bringing a person to the crossroads. It doesn't include the act itself, but it's the mechanism through which the no-way-out situation is created.

To digress for a moment, some people have this simplistic idea that you go into analysis because you have no way out and you'll be given one. "Not at all!" says Lacan. "You go into analysis because you *do* have a way out, and I'm going to take it away from you, I'm going to construct, from within, your own personal no-way-out point where the conjoining with your real will occur." In this respect, Lacan is in complete agreement with Kierkegaard. Naturally, Kierkegaard won't say: the point is to free people. No! The point is to force them to choose, but in order to force them to choose, you have to set up a phenomenal system of constraints. In Lacan's eyes, however, the process of constraint in the analytic treatment is precisely defined by the following dictum: to raise impotence, which accounts for the fantasy, to logical impossibility, which embodies the real. In other words, everything that tends toward the act or constitutes its edge of possibility is recapitulated in the transformation of an impotence into an impossibility. It could then be more accurately said that you go into analysis because, in one way or another, you're impotent in every sense of the term, and you leave it because you've been pushed up against the wall of impossibility, where there's no way out except to choose.

We're going to examine this dictum closely—and don't think we're losing track of the relationship between act and matheme!

The impotence must first of all—this is an essential task of the analytic process—be situated. Its locus needs to be constructed and the signifier of the impotence isolated. Isolating, separating, sectioning off the signifier of the impotence is of the utmost importance. We know, since this is a point of doctrine, that impotence is embodied by the phallus as an imaginary function. Thus, initially, to be able to raise the impotence to impossibility, what will be required is a whole effort of situating, of constructing a signifying topology of the impotence itself, which, says Lacan, is marked or embodied by the phallus as an imaginary function. This will be the beginning of the process. Then, once the signifier of the impotence has been isolated, which amounts to a sort of revealing of the fantasy, it will have to be raised to impossibility.

Before we go over the steps of this process in detail, let's ask ourselves about the emergence of the act. Let's assume that what is called "bringing someone to the crossroads" in Kierkegaard is called "raising impotence to impossibility" here. When your back is up against the wall of impossibility, it is *hic Rhodus, hic salta*,[2] as the Latinist Marx was fond of saying: it is here that you have to leap into the real. In other words, only the act can confirm you now as a Subject. There are two steps: isolating the signifier of the impotence by successive interpretive operations and interruptions, and then raising that impotence to the point of its logical impossibility. These two steps bring forth the no-way-out situation. At that point, the act will reveal the real as the waste product of this whole operation of symbolization, and this justifies the quote I already gave you, which I'll give you again: "the act effect that occurs as the waste product of a correct symbolization" (*AE*, 423).

We thus have a definition of what, in Lacan's eyes, a correct symbolization is: it is an effective raising of impotence to impossibility, and nothing more. To say that the act effect will occur as a waste product of the correct symbolization means that this effect, in psychoanalysis, is the ultimate waste product, the product as something abject and as the abjection of the whole correct symbolization, which is itself thinkable as the raising of a situated impotence to a logical impossibility.

Five points sum up this process by which is determined what an analytic treatment should be: a clinical practice whereby every philosophy is required to degrade itself.

1. The demonstration of the real is a kind of process, and it is the process of the treatment, if it exists at all. An analytic treatment will have taken place only if a real has been de-monstrated in it. This process is regulated, and the regulation can be called "the direction of the treatment." I would further argue, and this isn't a Lacanian formulation, that this process only operates, where the analyst is concerned, as the desire for the matheme. Free association and free-floating attention, for example, can only be understood in terms of the desire for the matheme. Why? Because even if they seem to be the opposite, they are really nothing but rules whose purpose is to construct the space of the constraint.

2. The de-monstration of the real, as a process, is a sort of formal constraint whose name is "correct symbolization." This suffices to make us understand that it is never a hermeneutics of meaning. From that point of view, the word "interpretation" in psychoanalysis—and Lacan explains this point—is ambiguous. It can be kept, but it needs to be reconstructed. If what is meant by "interpretation" is something that amounts to a hermeneutics of meaning, then the word is inappropriate, because what's really involved is an appropriate and constraining formalization and not at all the uncovering of a hidden meaning.

3. The first stage—this isn't chronological; it's accumulated sediment layers—requires that the impotence be situated, given that the demand for analysis is basically always to ward off some form of impotence, ultimately the inability to love, of which sexual impotence is only one variant. But it could be called the inability to live, the inability to exist. That's where the demand comes from, but the impotence has to be situated in such a way that the formalization

procedure can apply to or inform it, and that's not at all easy at the beginning. The starting point is to set in motion something that will put a stop to the wandering of the impotence. We can more-over (I'm the one saying this) call the wandering of the impotence "suffering." It's not so much a question of the impotence itself, for if it were only the impotence itself we could deal with it, and, what's more, we always do deal with it. We're always impotent in one way or another. It's the *wandering* of the impotence that is devastating. So the first stage of the direction of the treatment involves, at the very least, putting a stop to the wandering of the impotence, which means that it must be pinned down. Only insofar as it is pinned down, secured within the framework of fantasy that assigns it to the imaginary function of the phallus, can its formal raising to logical impossibility begin. To be sure, in the first stage, you'll stop the wan-dering of the impotence, but if you go no farther than that, it will start to wander again, that's all! So, next, it has to be connected to logical impossibility.

4. The second stage is therefore to raise the impotence to log-ical impossibility. This raising of the situated impotence, the impo-tence whose wandering is temporarily halted in the process of the treatment, is an absolutely crucial stage. It's also the most danger-ous one because it introduces the imminence of a conjunction with the real. It does not introduce the conjunction with the real per se, which falls under the category of the act, but the *imminence* of a conjunction with the real, which can only occur, in fact, through the de-monstration of the logical no-way-out situation, hence of logi-cal impossibility. This is the moment when one changes terrains or operations: what was situation, situating, stopping, really becomes formalization. The fact is, there's a complete break here with the ambiguities of interpretation. Here is where all the art of the ana-lyst lies: in supporting, or being the supporter of, the raising of impotence to impossibility through twists and turns that are always

unique, once the operation of situating has been accomplished. The first stage, that of localizing the impotence, is usually monotonous owing to its repetition effects. This is when the same sad stories about the different registers of impotence and despair are always heard. By contrast, the second stage, the specific way in which the impotence, pinpointed in a signifying way, will be raised to logical impossibility is a true art of singularity. It's an individual formalization. There's no such thing as a standard formalization. Localization is a lot more standard than formalization. Basically, knowing what's involved (the "diagnosis") isn't difficult, but raising it to logical impossibility is really a very complex operation.

5. Assuming that we have a correct, appropriate symbolization, hence a raising to the impossibility that a logical no-way-out situation represents, then we have a cutting edge, which, at the very point of impossibility—albeit there is only impossibility if there is an impasse of formalization—brings forth the real in the enunciative dimension of the act.

Let's sum up: situating, formal raising, and establishing a cutting edge are the main phases of the direction of the treatment, which denotes both the construction of a constraint and the boundary effect of an act.

I would say that the anti-philosophical singularity of psychoanalysis, in Lacan's conception of it, lies in aligning the construction of the constraint with the raising of impotence to impossibility. That is specific, unique. Is psychoanalysis capable of changing impotence into impossibility? I think caution is advised . . . But, in any case, that's what it's all about. Once impotence—the impotence that's the source of the demand in its broadest sense—is changed into the impossibility of being, the conjunction of a Subject with his real occurs at the moment of the act.

So what, in all of this, doesn't deceive?

If we adhere to Rousseau's or Kierkegaard's paradigm, it would appear that this "not deceiving" should be detectable in the system of constraints that construct the edge of the act. Lacan's formal position is that anxiety is that which does not deceive. See *Seminar XI: The Four Fundamental Concepts of Psychoanalysis*: "For analysis, anxiety is a crucial term of reference for in effect anxiety is that which does not deceive" (*F*, 41).

In the treatment process, with which we're concerned at the moment, what does anxiety correspond to? Be sure that you understand the problem we're going to be dealing with, because it's a pretty difficult but very important problem. When we discussed Kierkegaard, we saw that he said: it is the act itself that does not deceive. If you choose because you're forced to choose, then you'll choose the right thing. If you have no choice but to choose, you'll choose the right thing. However, if you're at a point where you could manage all right other than by choosing, then even if you do choose there's no guarantee that you'll choose the right thing. Let's assume that the choice, in Kierkegaard's sense of the word, is equivalent to the act. The thesis is that the act does not deceive, provided that it is really on the edge of a constraint, that it's really in the element of there being no way out but the act. This is an extremely important point because, in the final analysis, philosophy and anti-philosophy both share the question of truth, one way or another. What anti-philosophy maintains is that there is an absolutely nonphilosophical act, whether it's the voice of conscience, or Kierkegaard's existential choice, or the analytic act, which, as it happens, is precisely the act that does not deceive. It is the guarantee of truth or judgment. And philosophy is mistaken in believing that the guarantee of truth is of the order of knowledge of truth. This is the key debate between philosophy and anti-philosophy.

So, when Lacan says that anxiety does not deceive, we must determine what the relationship is between anxiety and the act, insofar as it would seem that anxiety and the act are not the same thing: we're not dealing with the same topology as Kierkegaard. So we need to situate anxiety in relation to the act.

To give ourselves some help, we should note that anxiety is actually one of Kierkegaard's categories, too. How convenient for us! He wrote *The Concept of Anxiety*. So what does he say about anxiety? For him, anxiety is related to sin. Anxiety is precisely the inner seat of sin. Now, to connect this with Lacan and the analytic treatment, we can assume that sin is impotence. This point is unproblematic. The first hypothesis would be as follows: anxiety is the inner sign that one is getting close to a situation of impotence, a situation of sin. This is moreover almost exactly what Kierkegaard says: anxiety is the surest psychological approximation of sin. Even so, it's not the presence of sin per se, because, in order to experience the real of sin—sin as the original mark, original sin (we're dealing with Christianity), hence sin as a mark of origin—a qualitative leap is required, even where anxiety is concerned. It is only in this qualitative leap, in a choice, actually, that there's the presence of sin. So anxiety would be the experienced possibility of the real of sin, but not the givenness of this real. And here again we find what I spoke to you about last time: the fundamental opposition in Kierkegaard between the possible and the real. Anxiety doesn't afford us the real of sin, which remains in the realm of the act, but we could say that it is the certain immanent boundary of sin: its surest approximation. For Kierkegaard, anxiety is therefore not directly related to the act. It is an affect of the *possibility* of the act. It doesn't deceive us about sin. It is trustworthy. When we're anxious, we experience, in an absolutely certain way, the radical possibility of sin, but we don't have the presence of the original mark, whose real is this sin. We could thus say once again, in the terms that I've been trying to suggest to you this evening, that, for Kierkegaard, anxiety is clearly on the side of the constraint rather than on the side of the act. It is the equivalent of a subjective formalism whose real, which remains inaccessible, is sin. It is indeed sin that makes us anxious, but it is not there; all we have is the inner experiencing of its possibility.

So, what will Lacan say about anxiety? How will this question of anxiety, which, for him, does not deceive, be set out in relation to the constraint and to the act? As many of you know, Lacan links anxiety to an excess of the real. There is a blockage of symbolization because every symbolization presupposes a lack, and the lack is blocked. Anxiety occurs when the function of absence that enables me to symbolize—the symbol actually occupies the place of the absence of the thing, the way the word "flower" brings forth "the one absent from every bouquet"[3]—when this absence, then, is eroded or undermined by anxiety, as if the real were spreading throughout. Lacan gives a wonderful definition of it: "Anxiety is the lack of the lack" (F, xi). It's clear why anxiety does not deceive: it's linked not just to the real but to the real in excess, to the real that paralyzes the symbolic function in the order of the lack. Is anxiety the real itself, in the sense of the act, though? No, it's not that either! It is not a matter of conveying anxiety as such in the direction of the treatment. The aim of the treatment is still for the act to take place.

I will therefore argue that anxiety remains, for Lacan, as it does for Kierkegaard, on the side of the constraint. Let me remind you that I call "constraint" the formalization that constructs the impasse in which the real is summoned as logical impossibility. Anxiety will be on that side, too, and this means that the direction of the treatment is a calculation of anxiety. Anxiety is that which does not deceive, provided there is a calculable figure of it in the space of the constraint. This is what Lacan explicitly says, once again in *Seminar XI*:

> In experience, it is necessary to channel it [anxiety] and, if I may say so, to dispense it in small doses so as not to be overwhelmed by it. [*And he adds something that's of particular interest to us:*] This is

a difficulty related to that of conjoining the subject with the real. (*F*, 41; trans. modified)

So we could say that the dosing out of anxiety, what I call its calculation, goes hand in hand with the question of the correct symbolization. In other words, the construction of the constraint, within the space of the treatment, is simultaneously, and through a complicated entanglement, the correct symbolization, the raising of impotence to impossibility to the point of there being no way out, and a calculation of anxiety that, as Lacan says, is related to the conjoining of the subject with the real.

Understanding this is both of the utmost importance and difficult, because constructing the constraint, and therefore the condition of possibility of the act, will involve an intertwining of the *impatience* for the formalization and the *patience* required by the dosing out of anxiety. Indeed, if you want to understand the full dialectic of this whole thing it is important to see that anxiety is a blockage of symbolization. That is what its definition tells us directly: if anxiety is the lack of the lack on account of the excess of the real, it is precisely because it constantly produces a paralysis of the operations of symbolization, and that is moreover precisely its affect. Conversely, the constraint procedure is a procedure of correct symbolization, whence the paradox: that which does not deceive is not the symbolization but its blockage by anxiety. Thus, there has to be a joint operation of symbolization—because there won't be any real except as a waste product of this symbolization—and control, or what Lacan calls the dosing out, of that sort of counter-symbolization that is anxiety, because it is also that which does not deceive us.

All of this can be summed up in two maxims that are virtually two imperatives. The first of these is to raise impotence to impossibility under the ideal of the matheme—because it's a matter of logical formalization—which then acts as a boundary for the real. This is the formal dimension of the constraint, what Lacan calls "the correct symbolization." And the second is to dispense anxiety in doses, which implies that a counter-symbolization acts as a guide, since it is that which does not deceive in the process of symbolization.

Dispensing anxiety in doses doesn't occur in the guise of taking little spoonfuls of it to weigh and mete out. So where does the dosing out of anxiety occur? Well, it occurs in the symbolization, because there's nothing else: the procedure indeed consists in raising impotence to impossibility, by and through a symbolization. The dosing out of anxiety will occur in a unique feature of the symbolization, which is its duration, its pace, its time. This time will be regulated by the dosing out of anxiety, which will mean that anxiety is that which does not deceive us about the symbolization itself, as regards the immanent organization of its duration.

There is a rush to formalize. The formalization is not regulated as to its timing. This is why there has been a lot of talk in psychoanalysis about premature interpretations, whose subjective impact is disastrous. But the crux of the matter is that if you stick strictly to formalization, there is a rush to formalize, precisely because it's a logical elevation and you're caught up in the haste inherent in logical time.[4] I would simply say that an analytic treatment is the specific way in which logical time is constrained by the time of anxiety.

So what about the act in all this? Well, I would propose the following statement: the act, as an edge effect, always occurs at the point where the rush to formalize and the restraint of the affect, in this case anxiety, converge. I'm using "restraint" here in the sense that, in restraint there is the idea of something that, in not deceiving us, restrains, in its very timing, the rush to formalize. The act is situated at that focal point where the rush to formalize and the restraint of the affect construct a convenient—if I may put it that way—no-way-out situation, one that may indeed rush into the figure of the act.

In terms of the psychoanalyst, it can be formulated this way: the desire for the matheme, which I think is inherent in the possibility of the correct symbolization, occurs as frustrated desire. Frustrated by what? Frustrated by that which does not deceive. This is really what psychoanalysis is all about, and the psychoanalyst along with it: the desire for the matheme, the desire for transmissible knowledge, frustrated by that which does not deceive, but which, here, is a kind of affect. And this frustration is to my mind the whole point of the ethics of analysis: "Don't give way on your desire!"—right! Except that, as the desire for the matheme (or "the desire for the interpretation," as it used to be called), it is in fact frustrated. Thus, the imperative can also be formulated as "Don't give way on that which frustrates your desire either, don't give way on the fact that the act will only be confirmed or proven provided that the rush to formalize and the dosing out of anxiety have been able to intersect."

That's why, next time, we'll examine all this from a different angle, namely, the famous problem of the ethics of psychoanalysis.

Session 8

May 31, 1995

I'd like to draw your attention to a remarkable book, which will merit our special consideration: Jean-Claude Milner's *L'Oeuvre claire*, subtitled *Lacan, la science, la philosophie* [Seuil, 1995]. I will be discussing the book with him on June 14, and this dialogue, scheduled for the last day of our meetings, can be given the meaning of a sort of critical supplement. So this will lend a provisionally conclusive character to my remarks today.

—◦◦◦—

The real cannot be known, Lacan tells us; rather, it must be demonstrated. Why is this crucial? Because it is obviously at the heart of this de-monstration that the irreducible singularity of the analytic act lies. To put it another way, we must always remember that it is the act that exempts psychoanalysis from any educational purpose. Even though Lacanian theory appears under the sign of discourse, it is in fact remote, of course, from the discourse of the university, but even more profoundly remote from any educational purpose. And this is moreover one of the features of anti-philosophy. Indeed, it could be shown that Lacan's conviction—a conviction it's easy to share—is that there is an educational impulse in philosophy. After all, the Platonic system, considered to be foundational, can be seen as an educational system. To this educational purpose of philosophy, even if "education" is taken in as lofty a sense as possible, is opposed the fact that psychoanalysis, if only in terms of its discourse, is a break with respect to any educational purpose. Lacan says as much, in the strongest terms, in a text ["Allocution sur l'enseignement"] that was his closing address at the 1970 Congress of the École freudienne de Paris. He says: "What saves me from teaching is the act" (*AE*, 303).

Needless to say, if Lacan claims that the act saves him from teaching it's because he felt threatened by it. He had to be saved from it. As usual with Lacan, we get ambiguities, gray areas, and their foregrounding. Thus, Lacan is well aware that there is something, not just about psychoanalysis but about his position vis-à-vis psychoanalysis, that, at any given moment, borders on the discourse of the university. But he is ultimately saved from it by the act. So, this anti-philosophical disposition connected to the act—the act involved or required in the demonstration of the real—is exactly counterposed to what Lacan regards as philosophy's constitutive weaknesses. This will be a way for us to summarize what has already been said.

To begin with, the first weakness is that the philosopher is blocked by mathematics, whereas the aim of the analytic process is to raise impotence to logical impossibility. Such raising to logical impossibility is necessarily under the ideal of formalization. This is the issue of the matheme, and it is counterposed to the mathematical blockage that obfuscates philosophical education.

The second issue is that philosophy succumbs to the love of truth, whereas the analytic process eliminates that love by bringing in the dimension of truth's weakness, a dimension whose theoretical name is in actual fact castration. So if there's a love of truth, it must ultimately appear as a love of castration, whereas philosophy acts as if there could be a love of truth as plenitude. In this regard it is, in its very love, an imposture.

Finally, the third weakness is that philosophy plugs the hole of politics. Psychoanalysis will expose the imaginary aspect of that concealing, the imaginary aspect of that plugging, and implicitly propose a theory of the collective, of something that, beyond the compulsion to dissolve, would finally be worthy of the name School of Psychoanalysis.

⸙

I'd like to dwell on that last point for a moment. Ultimately, what did Lacan end up thinking as regards the theory of the collective, the theory of the organization, the theory of the group? The most important thing seems to me to be that Lacan's final thesis was that there is nothing really relevant for a group except for the short period of its activity—and of its explicit activity, its empirical ability to produce transmissible knowledge, to produce a matheme. Consequently—and this point is crucial—Lacan's ultimate thinking was that there is no inherent legitimacy in the duration of a group of any kind. In particular, he thought that the project of doing something was semblance. Because, here, a distinction must obviously be made between the *project* of doing something, which is already a plugging of the hole, and the *actual* doing of something, which is immanently attestable and seems to justify the group's sticking together temporarily. In "Monsieur A," the following directive is his final word on the subject. Let me quote:

> [S]tick together for as long as it takes to do something, and then dissolve your group and do something else. (*M*, 17)

The problem is that a group's ability to move from one thing to another could be called "politics," in a somewhat generic sense, or could be called, more precisely, "political organization." It could be shown that "politics" cannot simply mean that people stick together for as long as it takes to do something. *That* might be a movement, or whatever you want to call it: a group, or a grouping, or an assembly, or a gathering. But it can't be an organization in the political sense of the term because a political organization is in fact only required insofar as there's a need to switch from one thing to another. If politics is defined that way, then we could say that Lacan's final thesis is that, as regards the real, there is no politics. What I mean is that there's no politics other than the politics whose hole is plugged by philosophy. I'd even say—this isn't something Lacan said—that what he fundamentally thought is that there's no politics at all; there's only political philosophy. And organizations that think they're political are in reality *philosophical* organizations. This was the conclusion Lacan drew at the time with regard to the Cause freudienne when he said that it should only last temporarily [*ne durera que par le temporaire*]. It would seem that, since then, in many schools of psychoanalysis, they've opted instead to stall for time by lasting [*temporiser par la durée*]. Could it be that they've wanted at all costs to be involved in politics? Or even philosophy?

—∞—

Ultimately, as you can see, the analytic act, in the threefold order of mathematics, love, and politics, authorizes the elimination of philosophy's founding pretension. To judge an anti-philosophy is always to judge its act and the ethics of that act. Here, it's a question of the analytic act, whose locus is the singularity of a psychoanalytic treatment, a treatment involving two people, the analyst and the analysand, and whose test is a Subject's real.

I said that an anxiety-dispensing procedure in the treatment goes hand in hand with the correct-symbolization procedure. As anxiety is, moreover, a blockage of the symbolization, it will be necessary, in the analytic process, to manage the correct symbolization, which is the point of impasse of the real, and at the same time to dose out its blockage, so to speak, with anxiety, which remains that which does not deceive.

So you can see the extreme tension that's involved: that which does not deceive is not the symbolization; it's the counter-symbolization phase. The analytic process, understood almost as an experimental setup, the analytic experiment as preparation for the act, is an absolutely unique, irreducible, methodical experiment. It's not some kind of inspired charlatanism. It is really a methodical procedure. What takes place in it is of the order of thinkability. Ultimately, this thinkability—and here I'm talking about the treatment itself—is that of a regulated counter-symbolization as the sign of that which does not deceive, and, naturally, of a correct symbolization taken to its point of impasse, which is its real point. Taken, that is, to its limit, because a correct symbolization does not just consist in producing symbolizations. If the symbolization must be taken to its point of impasse, because it's only there that the conjoining with the real is possible, this means that the symbolization must be taken as far as it can go. But at the same time there must be some control over the counter-symbolization insofar as it is the sign of that which does not deceive, even the sign of that which does not deceive as regards the symbolization. This means that the analytic act will necessarily be at the point of convergence of the rush to formalize, which seeks the extremity or the end point of the formalization, and of something like a restraint of the affect, of the affect that does not deceive. Because anxiety must be meted out in doses, or else you'll tip over into an excess of the real. And tipping over into the excess of the real will take the form of acting out. In actual fact, the act, in the analytic sense, is the exact opposite of acting out, which is of the order of the symptom. The act is precisely that of which there can be no acting out. The restraint of the affect also serves to ensure that the act is not destroyed for good by any acting out.

In all this, the desire for the matheme, for pure knowledge, is the analyst's, the Lacanian analyst's, desire. And the desire for the matheme is the desire for the correct symbolization to go all the way to the end, because it's only at that end that, having been put into impasse by its real, it can produce the matheme. Thus, the analyst's desire is the desire for the matheme; but it can only occur as frustrated desire. That's the formulation I proposed to you. It can only occur as frustrated desire because otherwise the analyst would be dealing, unilaterally, with the rush to formalize. And as the restraint of the affect, of anxiety, would be lacking, he would deceive himself, or be deceived. Deceived by whom? By the analysand—who is there for precisely that purpose! And this frustration—the fact that the desire for the matheme can only occur as frustrated desire—is the whole point of the ethics of analysis. The imperative is: "Don't give way on the frustrated nature of your desire." Which, in this case, is the same thing as the famous "Don't give way on your desire," because the analyst's desire is in essence a frustrated desire if it is really the desire of a true analyst, insofar as, under his direction, the treatment produces an indisputable and transmissible effect of the real. The frustration of the analyst's desire could be said to be based on the conflict between mastery and anxiety. I think the analyst is an anxious master. He isn't the one who feels anxiety, although he, too, may be. I say "anxious master" in the sense of the master who takes upon himself the restraint of the affect in its articulation as the counter-symbolization to the correct symbolization. Under those conditions, he is finally equal to his act.

—◦◦◦—

It is at this point, to my mind—at this point that's called the ethics of psychoanalysis, the direction of the treatment—yes, it's there that Lacan's anti-philosophy founders on something. That's my diagnosis, because the problem is: what apparatus of thought represents the frustration in question? In what apparatus of thought can this frustration be represented? I'm sure you've noticed that for the time being I've done no more than describe it. What apparatus of thought represents the specific way in which the desire for the matheme is bound up with the dosing out of anxiety? How are the correct symbolization, of which the act is the waste product, and the regulated counter-symbolization, which alone, in fact, determines something like the time of the conjoining of the subject with the real, coordinated? Because, if you think about it, the correct symbolization itself does not determine any time. The matheme is essentially time-less. The reason there is a time is not that there's a desire for the matheme; it's that this desire is frustrated. Therefore, the time is necessarily the time of the dosing out of anxiety. The time of the treatment is not the time of the symbolization; it is the time of the counter-symbolization. So it must be acknowledged that what determines the time—and you can see why we're inexorably approaching the thorny question of the time of the treatment, of the time, be it long or short, of the session—what determines the time, the time here being that of the conjoining of the subject with his real, has to do with the negative procedures of the dosing out of anxiety.

At this point, to which Lacan leads us, we expect a new thinking of the treatment as such. That is, if I may say so, something like new rules. Why? Because if analysis is a thought—"thought" meaning something that is neither theory nor practice but something in which theory and practice are indistinguishable from each other—the space of this thought is the act involved in the analytic process. And we know very well that it was Freud who demonstrated that such an act had occurred in history, that an act had taken place. But, with Lacan, we have a profound shift, upheaval, reworking of the issues, terminology, and connections in the general scope of things. You've really got to understand that! The truth is, it bears little resemblance to Freud. Ultimately, it is strangely silent about thought—about thought in the sense I just mentioned of thought being the process itself. There is a reflection by Lacan on organization. There are frequent reflections by Lacan on the pass procedure—I talked about this—and on which mechanism makes it possible to confirm that an analysis took place. There are stunning individual analyses. But Lacan never wrote: *What Is To Be Done?* I say this because on a number of occasions he compares himself to Lenin. He says he's the Lenin to Freud's Marx. I can easily see how Lacan wrote all the rest of Lenin's work. For example, he wrote: *Chicago Imperialism: The Highest Stage of the Perversion of Psychoanalysis.* He wrote: *State* [i.e., the symbolic] *and Revolution* [i.e., the real]. He wrote about ideology, I mean about the imaginary. He wrote: "How Should We Organize Ourselves?" He also wrote: "The Party Should Be Dissolved,"[1] which is what Lenin thought in September 1917: the party is crap, it should be dissolved. Lacan wrote all of this, but not *What Is To Be Done?* His successors are well aware of this, because they don't know what to do. They know how to organize themselves, they know how to read, they know how to study, they probably also know how to analyze, obviously—I'm not insulting the analysts here—they know all of that. But "What is to be done?" in a Lacanian sense, well, *that* nobody knows. Underlying Lacanianism, and after Lacanianism, to tell the truth, there's a mystery about the treatment, which everyone is disconcerted by. Everyone just cobbles things together as best they can: a little long, a little short, a little Freud. But what is to be done? I mean: what *else* is to be done? Yes, what else is to be done, because "to be done" always means: "what else is to be done?" In an anti-philosophical disposition, this should have become Lacan's central question. A big deal was made over the issue of short, ultra-short, or even nonexistent sessions . . . I'd be thrilled if there were a Lacanian theory of the nonexistent session, the short session, the ultra-short session—but there isn't! There just isn't. In fact, nothing in Lacan either sets out or founds anything at all when it comes to such questions. And there are even a few texts here and there that suggest that people should just do whatever they feel like, actually. Sure, but come on! Can you really say such a thing? When the apparatus of thought is the one I've just attempted to discuss, can you say such a thing when it comes to the question "What is to be done?" In my view, this is, objectively, an irreducible weakness of Lacan's legacy. There's no doubt about it. And especially in terms of its organizational destiny. Because there isn't anything, in the order of thinkability, that could be called a Lacanian direction of the treatment. You'll object: it's the return to Freud. No, it isn't! The return to Freud is not sufficient. Lenin is not the return to Marx! Because there is indeed a point where the newness of the thought must be attested to in the singularity of the preparation for the act. Otherwise, there's nothing to hold the group together around the analytic activity, that is, around the place of the act. We are well aware that there will never be any rules for the act. But that doesn't mean there are no rules for the *place* of the act. And the term "analytic discourse," or "discourse of the analyst," which Lacan sometimes uses almost as a synonym of psychoanalysis, is nonetheless ambiguous when it comes to this issue. Because "analytic discourse," in the sense we can understand it in the legacy of Lacan's thinking, doesn't give us the full answer to the question "What is to be done?" And therefore not exactly to the question "What is to be thought?" either, assuming "to be thought" is taken in its strictest sense, i.e., where theory and practice are indistinguishable from each other.

―――∞∞∞―――

The feeling I have, which will round out my analysis of anti-philosophy, is this: anti-philosophy is always based on a proclamation of the act's irreducibility, and, in the name of the act, condemns philosophy for its founding pretension to spread the glue of meaning all over. Well, I have the feeling that this is always accompanied by a relative uncertainty, in thought, as to the place of the act. And this is so for one basic reason: the conviction, held by all anti-philosophers, that if they venture into determining theoretically the place of the act, they'll be led back to philosophy, and then they'll be back where they started. After all, anti-philosophy begins with a cut or a hole made or diagnosed in the body of philosophy. That's why it always sets itself up as the philosopher's master. Regardless of whether the anti-philosopher teaches that the philosopher doesn't want to know anything about *jouissance* (Lacan), or that he abstracts existence (Kierkegaard), or that he knows nothing of the real God (Pascal), or that he's the enemy of feeling and of the voice of the heart (Rousseau), and so on, there nonetheless always comes a moment when the anti-philosopher, implementing the preparation for the act's irreducibility, that is, organizing the theory of his own mastery, is in his turn threatened with a philosophical overthrow, because the dominant protocol of legitimation of his act, and in particular the determination of the place of that act, also end up being a matter of discursive argumentation and of the concept, that is to say, they end up being, quite simply, philosophical.

Yes, everything hinges on the question of the place of the act, of what I'd call the preparation for it: What regulates the preparation by which the act attains its impossible necessity? It's the question "What is to be done?" And you're obviously not going to answer the question "What is to be done?" with: "The analytic act!" How dumb would that be?! "What is to be done?" means: what determination in thought should I maintain as to the place of the act? Or in Lacanian terms: What presents the frustrated desire of the analyst as best as possible, with no guarantees but as best as possible? What new rules can at least regulate the relationship between the symbolization and the counter-symbolization? What is to be done if I'm a Lacanian analyst? What is to be done other than what everyone since Freud has always done? But to decide about that issue is ultimately to answer the question: *What is to be thought?* However, that's too risky for an anti-philosopher. It's too philosophical. It's the issue in which the danger of philosophy crops up again.

It is well known, for example, that, for Pascal, the act is the question of conversion. Before there can be any thinking, you have to convert, you have to believe. We know that the thinkable framework of this conversion is the framework of the wager. The wager is the time of the act truly grasped in its place, because the wager is a logical argument, the proposition of a reckoning of chances that is obviously not the act of conversion itself but that articulates its place. We can clearly see the connection between the act and its place in the space of the proposition of the wager. But . . . but why wager? That's always the question Pascal comes up against. The libertine might answer: "*I* don't wager! I have no desire to wager! I don't even give a damn about your reckoning of chances!" So, it's clear that the question "What is to be done?" comes up here. In other words, what is to be done to make him want to wager? It's not enough to see that, once he wagers, he'll wager on God. He first has to wager. And in that regard, it's the question of the process, the question of the place, of the preparation for the act. And with Pascal, there's nothing, or nothing but a very minimal argumentative philosophy concerning the point that wagering on God is more advantageous than not wagering. It's very weak! That's as far as it goes. In the final analysis, there is no legitimation possible, in thought, of the decisive place of the Pascalian act—conversion—the place that's the figure of the wager. Because the question as to how you can bring someone around to wagering cannot be inferred from the wager itself and inevitably reverts to the methods of philosophical persuasion.

You can see how this question is the same as the one that I'm asking in connection with the direction of the treatment. Of course, there has to be a place of the analytic act. But what, ultimately, is that place, in terms of its novelty? You can easily see the problem, the point where the threat of a return of philosophy emerges. If Pascal had pursued the question "Why wager?" an answer would have been possible, namely, showing that the libertine is unhappy. That would be the only solution. Except, the thesis that the libertine is unhappy, unhappier than the wise man, is a foundational thesis of *philosophy*. It is Plato's thesis exactly: the bad man is unhappy. That's why it works for Socrates: he can tell the people who have a choice between becoming hedonistic tyrants or philosophical wise men: "My side's the right side! I'm going to demonstrate to you that, on one side, there's happiness, and on the other, there's unhappiness." So if you want to prove that the libertine is unhappy, you're in philosophy up to your eyeballs! And Pascal, a man of the utmost logical rigor, won't go down that road. He won't show that he and he alone for whom this wager is intended, the inveterate libertine, is unhappy and that he'd become happy by converting. As a result, we have no idea how he can go about bringing the libertine around to the wager. So there's no Pascalian "What is to be done?" either.

Someone interrupts: *Nor is there a Socratic "What is to be done?" when Callicles refuses to speak. There's a stumbling block there, too.*

Careful! Your comparison doesn't hold up! There *is* a Socratic "What is to be done?" because, unlike Pascal's libertine, Callicles [in the *Gorgias*] is by no means Socrates's interlocutor, the person he wants to bring around to the philosophical determination of the Idea. And so when Callicles, or, more important, Thrasymachus [in the *Republic*], refuse to speak, it's no problem for Socrates to leave them to their sorry fate, because we know that what matters are the young people who are at stake between them—that is, between the sophists and Socrates. And those who are at stake between them and Socrates clearly get what's going on: they see that at some point Callicles and Thrasymachus will have to shut up and that Socrates, who has remained master of the terrain, will show that happiness is on his side. And that's that! The situation is not at all comparable.

Pascal wants to convert the libertine, while Socrates has absolutely no intention of winning the sophists over. He just wants to show the young people that you can shut the sophists up and get down to business.

Another objection: *I think there's a place of the act for Lacan: it's a situation that holds together, that's consistent, even at the point of the cut.*

If you're saying that the act is the cut in the consistent space of a topology, I fully understand, but in that case it's a formal thinking of the act, which says nothing about the "What is to be done?" as regards the process by which we must conduct ourselves to create consistency in such a way that the Subject is faced with the lack of any way out except a cut. It says nothing about the "What is to be done?" Cutting a knot is a terminal operation of the treatment, but to say as much gets us nowhere in terms of the new rules of the process, which compels this cut while at the same time dosing out the affect that does not deceive about the state of the process itself.

The questioner persists: *What about interpretation?*

Interpretation is so far from being an answer to our question that Lacan's rule would more likely be—not that he says this either—to interpret as little as possible. That's moreover why one is always tempted—Lacanian analysts are tempted—to end the session at precisely the point when an interpretation would seem to be clearly required. Hence, short sessions. But Lacan never proposed anything that amounts to the thinkability of a rule about this issue. Even today it can still be argued that it doesn't matter whether the session is short or not, whether it's five minutes or an hour. But come on! It's not true that it doesn't matter! The question "What is to be done?" definitely matters. I have no idea how to answer that question. But I do have an idea about what the lack of any answer in an anti-philosophical apparatus means. I have an idea about Lacan's silence when it came to the actual forms, the rules of action, that would give meaning to this "ethics of psychoanalysis"—a term he coined—if that term is understood, as it should be, as relating to a new conception of the direction of the treatment. It is well known that the Chicago International had a regulatory and objectivistic ethics that regulated the treatment as if it were a technical process, with a system of quantified conditions. And it is well known that Lacan rightly thought that an ethics like that amounted to a radical forgetting of what was at stake in the analytic act. But he never opposed anything other than either very piecemeal or overly general ideas to that regulatory, objectivistic, technicized process, which he considered had become a mechanism of adaptation to the dominant social order.

Someone comments: *But there's nonetheless a signifier, as far as I'm concerned: the analyst plays the saint! For me, that's an answer to the question "What is to be done?"*[2]

You're referring to the analyst's position, to a sort of subjective paradigm. But what we're talking about under the heading of the question "What is to be done?" is not exactly that. It's the question of the composition of the process itself, of the rules of the process, which is an issue Freud dealt with time and again, and in the most precise way.

The questioner persists: *Playing the saint: it's better not to, at the outset. In other words, at first, the analyst positions himself elsewhere. So that clearly indicates what must be done . . .*

No, that doesn't indicate what must be done! All it does is describe the overall trajectory of the treatment. From the position of the subject-supposed-to-know, which is very similar to a position of mastery, and fostering transference at the beginning, the analyst must accept to end up as "waste material," with the status of an abject piece of trash, in a position of dis-being comparable, in fact, to certain ascetic figures of sainthood. That's the description of a subjective ideal, but it doesn't say anything about what the new norm of the actual process of the treatment might be. It doesn't say! Why aren't there any rules? Is Lacan's conception of the treatment that it has no rules? I don't think so. Nothing suggests that that's what he thought. It's surprising that he provided so many rules and regulations when it came to questions about the group, about what an analyst is, what the operating conditions of the organization should be, etc., but said nothing, or next to nothing, about the treatment itself. For me, this is an extraordinary paradox—unless we assume that the treatment's the same as it has always been. But if that's the case, then he didn't answer the question "What else must be done?" What you said is absolutely right, but then it's possible to think: it's always been like that. That's what Freudian analysis, where it existed at all, was. So, from this point of view, Lacan would not constitute an advance in thinking. Because if the name "Lacan" denotes nothing more than a reinterpretation of the Freudian system of treatment, a justified return to Freud, then it doesn't constitute an advance in thinking, in the sense in which we're talking about thinking here. Lacan, in that case, is not Freud's Lenin. If, however, Lacan is the name of an advance in thinking, it must be a revolution in the revolution, as they say. And *I* think that that is in fact the case. But what I note is that Lacan doesn't say in what sense, in terms of the direction of the treatment, he really *is* proposing a revolution in the Freudian revolution. On this specific issue, he doesn't say. And that's what constitutes the stumbling block in his own system.

Someone else strenuously objects: *But Lacan did write a very long text on the direction of the treatment . . .*

But there's nothing about the direction of the treatment in the text "The Direction of the Treatment [and the Principles of its Power]"! (*É*, 489–542)

Protests in the audience.

There's nothing! Lacan spoke time and again about the direction of the treatment, about the fact that all his thinking came from clinical practice, but who, on reading the text "The Direction of the Treatment," can consider himself a Lacanian in unity with the others on the question of the treatment? No one . . .

   The objector, more adamantly: *But maybe he wasn't seeking any such unity. I even think that Lacan considered a potential unifying thinking as something dangerous. That's how I've read him. This is a very important point. He is even somewhat suspicious of unifying thinking. And he says so in a number of his seminars. He's even quite close to the wager of Pascal that you were talking about. He says the treatment's a lost cause. But that it's really the only chance we have of getting better. That shows that there's an approach, in Lacan, to a direction of the treatment that may seem the opposite of a rule but is, for me at any rate, a guarantee, or, how should I put it, a kind of guarantee, actually, because it's not a unifying thinking.*

   To me, a thinking that is not unifying is not even a thinking, if by thinking, once again, is meant something that unifies theory and practice in an effective process. And how can you call yourself Freud's Lenin if you don't propose a new figure of the unity of action, if only in the treatment? What's the point of founding a School? Obviously, many Lacanians, or people who say they are, derive some benefit from making everyone think the total fog they've been left in regarding the problem of the direction of the treatment is precisely what the master's real teaching was. He did in fact seem to teach that there's nothing specific to be taught about this issue. Yet, when Lacan wanted to say things about all sorts of issues, he said them. So we can wonder, retrospectively, what it means for Lacan to have been so reticent about the locus of thought, about practical procedures, about what, in politics, is called "the working style." Of course, the Chicago crowd had defined rules that could be considered totally bureaucratized. He essentially condemned the theoretical revisionism this moralizing bureaucratization reflected. But, once again, there's a striking contrast between all the detail he went into about questions of organization and the paucity of what was said about the process of the treatment as such. It's not true that he didn't care about anything that had to do with practice. When it came to deviations, to the nature of organizations, he could be very strict about rules—and how! But what about the treatment? He was immediately attacked from all sides on the issue of the length of the sessions. But mum was the word on that, as on all the issues, practically speaking, that were related to the understanding of the process of the treatment.

My hypothesis is that the frustrated desire, which I was talking about as the place of the ethics of psychoanalysis, includes, if you want to give a thinkable local assignment of it, a theory of time. There you go. A theory of time, that is, of the time of the act. Because, in the final analysis, that's what it's all about. I already suggested as much to you: what determines the time is not the correct formalization and its impasse but the other aspect—the counter-symbolization that's organically linked to the dosing out of anxiety. It is therefore the dimension of the *affect* that determines the time. Obviously, this is not something separable; it's even completely intertwined with the process of interpretation, but it's in that dimension that the time is determined. A theory of time that is precisely not a theory of logical time.[3]

We should take very seriously the fact that the final Lacan was so preoccupied with space. It's very striking: the final Lacan's whole investment of thought was in space, including the theory of the act, which, in the guise of a cut in nonorientable surfaces, seeks its spatial paradigm. And, once again, the anti-philosophical spirit rears its head. For it could be shown that, in any given anti-philosophy, the unprecedented nature of the act is always characterized as not being subject to time. Or, more precisely, as being something like the nontemporal guarantee of time. That's the reason Hegel, for whom time is the being-there of the concept, is the mortal enemy of all the anti-philosophers, for whom the act is the *intemporal* essence of time.

Lacan often compared his topology to Kant's transcendental aesthetic. He said that his topology was a revision, a reworking at once aesthetic and critical, of the transcendental aesthetic of time, i.e., of the Kantian theory of space and time. Here, there's an anti-philosophical aesthetic that I'd simply say is a spatial metaphor of eternity, or something like that. Lacan is opposed to philosophy, contemporary philosophy in particular, because it supposedly always maintains the constitutive dimension of time. If you take his topology, how does it basically present the act? It presents it as a sudden, atemporal cut in a paradoxical configuration of space. But you can't derive any theory of time from such a view because the sudden cut is by no means a temporalization of the paradoxical spatial figure. It is, rather, its undoing. That's all. I think that topology, the topological objective of the final Lacan, produces the thinking of a paradoxical general space—neither Kantian nor Euclidean, let's say—such that no domain is preserved inasmuch as its truth lies elsewhere. That's what the figure of a complete spatialization is: it's that there is a spatiality such that any domain established in would require that another domain be established for the truth of the former to be able to be half-said in it.

Let me cite a specific passage in *Radiophonie* where Lacan tries to explain why he did topology:

> I only constructed the topology that sets up a border between truth and knowledge in order to show that this border is everywhere [*then he adds*:] and establishes a domain only if we start to love its beyond. (*AE*, 441)

To love its beyond . . . That's the prescription: that every place is also its outside-place [*hors-lieu*][4]. To subjectivate a domain of thought is to love in it the fact that every place is only ever the torsion of its outside-place, just as every point is out-of-line [*hors-ligne*]. This is indeed consistent with the final ethics of Lacan's silence: the silence of the period when all he did was show knots, that is, when there was nothing more to do than show the space of the outside-place, which was the final, complete spatialization. This could be called generalized topology, like a transcendental aesthetic without time. Lacanian anti-philosophy, in an almost silent tension, maintains that a cut in the spatial torsion will dispense with all rules of time. That is its desire, its desire as regards the place of the act. It is quite true that philosophy has always opposed to this the imperative of the "long detour," which is Plato's term.

In the end, there's a balance struck here. Allow me a moment to show that, ultimately, with Lacan, there is an "I hereby found" aspect. I hereby found, he says, "as alone as I have always been," I hereby found. His "I hereby found" seems philosophical to me, philosophical because it promises a time: "I hereby found" heralds a new time. It is philosophical because, even without thematizing it, founding introduces a time that tolerates the long detour—even if very quickly thereafter Lacan *didn't* actually tolerate it. Founding as such is always on the side of the long time; it is on the side of philosophy.

Then comes an "I hereby dissolve." And the "I hereby dissolve" is anti-philosophical. I've told you why: the "I hereby dissolve" attempts to dispense with temporal sedimentation. It is the act itself. Dissolution is the sudden cut in the twisted spatial configuration. It's the moment when Lacan publicly exemplified the act. This was really the epitome of the anti-philosophical disposition. But there was no guarantee that the attempt to dispense with temporal sedimentation would work, either. The basis of the "I hereby dissolve" is, once again, an "I hereby found."

So, perhaps this final spatialization, with that sudden cut that dispenses with every temporal esthetic, may simply be the moment when anti-philosophy borders on philosophy, or is faced with the test, with the danger, it represents. The danger I was talking about a little while ago, the danger involved in thinking the time of the treatment—not just the time of deciding whether the session should last five minutes or an hour but the time of constructing the symbolization and the counter-symbolization. This question of the time of the treatment is ultimately the basic danger of having to think time, because there is no modern anti-philosophical theory of it. Perhaps there is only a modern anti-philosophical theory of space. For example, on January 26, 1981, in the text called "First Letter of the Forum," Lacan begins this way: "A month ago I cut my ties with everything."[5] And on March 11, 1981, in what is actually his last attestable text, he begins this way: "My greatest strength is knowing what it means to wait."[6]

"A month ago I cut my ties with everything" is an anti-philosophical salvo, and "My greatest strength is knowing what it means to wait" is a good definition of philosophy. Between the two, without being a Lenin to Freud, stands Lacan.

In conclusion, let us say that, as regards any edge effect, there is cutting and waiting. That is the question: cutting and waiting. Or maybe cutting and/or waiting. I think that it is in this linkage—cutting and/or waiting—that we can find the current status of the legacy of a thinking.

Thank you.

Session 9

June 15, 1995

There is no doubt that a careful analysis of Jean-Claude Milner's book, whose importance I already mentioned to you, is perfectly fitting as a conclusion or—even better—as a supplement to our whole undertaking this year.

To emphasize the importance of today's talk again, I'd like to present the results of my reading of *L'Oeuvre claire* in four points, after which the control of operations will revert to the book's author.

First of all, what's striking about this book is its status. Very early on, Jean-Claude Milner points out the paradox that, in his view, the book in question is not, strictly speaking, a book about Lacan. To that effect, he makes the following very remarkable claim: all the books about Lacan are excellent! So adding one more, which could only be excellent, is unnecessary. But what can be the intent, then, of this book, which is not about Lacan and therefore runs the risk of not being automatically excellent? To my mind, it should be read on the basis of its title: *L'Oeuvre claire* [The Clear Work]. It should be read as a book producing clarity on a point of thought to which the textual signifier "Lacan" happens to be attached. But since this conjunction is just a conjunction, it's not exactly Lacan who is discussed in the book. Starting with a configuration of thought whose center of gravity is science, the author attempts to show how what can be understood or extracted—I think it's more of an extraction—from this configuration of thought and its evolution, or even, ultimately, its dissolution, functions in the Lacanian text. Of course, *L'Oeuvre claire* is a deliberately polemical title because it implies that there's a lot of obscurity surrounding what is at stake when it comes to Lacan. And, in that sense, this book is a book of the Enlightenment. This is what gives it its exceptional status as compared with everything else that's been written to date about Lacan.

My second comment has to do with the figure of science. We could say that the Lacanian extraction—let's call it that—is explicitly intended for placing this figure under a special light that will allow it to be X-rayed, as it were. Lacan is an operator: he is what makes a spectral cut of sorts possible in the contemporary figure of science. What then strikes Jean-Claude Milner about this X-rayed figure of the scientific configuration is the radical theme of contingency. Jean-Claude Milner is a great philosopher of contingency. What he means by his scientism—a word whose lost nobility he has gone against the grain of by restoring—is that a sort of confrontation between thinking and radical contingency unfolds within it. At bottom, it could be argued that when Jean-Claude Milner talks about the excellence of all the books about Lacan, what he actually means is that these books are only excellent for Greeks, because they're only about necessity. But we're not Greek. Lacan can no more be thought under the sign of necessity than can anything today. Let's say, as we are no longer Greek, that any figure of necessity is a pious figure. This is why the excellence of all the books about Lacan is the dubious excellence of piety, while the risk taken by Milner is that of exactitude.

My third comment concerns the theory of the work as a whole [*l'oeuvre*].[1] Jean-Claude Milner maintains that, within the Lacanian corpus, we can confine ourselves solely to the *Écrits*. In his opinion, nothing that is only in the Seminars is essential for understanding Lacan's work. Hence my interest. I have long been struck by the fact that there is a recurrent question about what the work of an anti-philosopher is. Having to decide between what has been published and what has not, what is posthumous, what is oral, what has a connected or disconnected form, what is aphoristic or architectonic, raises a number of very crucial questions. Anti-philosophy can be identified by the fact that, since it is dependent on its act, whatever form the work is in is not essential to it. It would seem that every text by Lacan is an intervention linked to specific circumstances. In the end, *we* always have to decide what is meant by "the work of Lacan." Milner's decision, which is entirely consistent with his general approach, is that the work of Lacan, in terms of what matters to him in it, is precisely all the writings [*écrits*] in the strictest sense of the term: those written, revised, and published by Lacan himself. Any other decision will have to produce its own justification. Nothing about this is given; everything must be decided.

My final comment has to do with the periodization Milner proposes, the construction of which is absolutely remarkable. Milner distinguishes a first classicism in Lacan, which is a hyperstructural axiomatics. This is followed by a second classicism, based on the matheme, which is a sort of final deconstruction of the first classicism: literality itself tends to vanish. The details of the demonstration of this distinction between two sequences of thought are very convincing.

One guideline Milner suggests for understanding the periodization is the status of the Lacanian doctrine regarding mathematics. And this is actually the question of the way in which Lacan was under the paradigm of the Bourbaki group. Thus, in his own way, Jean-Claude Milner clearly establishes that, as regards Lacanian anti-philosophy, mathematics is its condition, although he also shows in the most precise way that "matheme" can by no means be reduced to "mathematics."

In sum, there is a mathematical condition in the work of Lacan, but this condition, which is a paradigm that forms *and* breaks apart, is not exactly a state of mathematics, in the sense of a body of theorems, proofs, and innovations. Rather, it is mathematics apprehended as a thought project in a broad sense—in this case, Bourbakian mathematics as a signifier of the power of literality. When Jean-Claude Milner, in his deconstruction of Lacan at the end of his book, announces that, perhaps, mathematics' new destiny will go beyond literality or include cuts that will no longer be within the paradigm of literality, he shows how a change in this condition affected the Lacanian apparatus of thought. So the following assumption should be made: There is a paradigm function of mathematics that is less in its proof process than in what could be called the configurations of thought it activates. It is something like the prescription of literality at one moment and, at another, geometricality, or the prescription of spatiality in a torsion form. Mathematics would function as a generic condition, for thought, of an activation point grafted onto singular configurations. According to Milner, Lacan was a privileged witness of these variations because he had to undergo a paradigm shift.

Finally, where does psychoanalysis fit into all this? Jean-Claude Milner holds that there can be psychoanalysis provided a subject is thinkable, without our needing to be situated outside-liminality, liminality being the contingent condition of thought at any given moment. There was a thinkable subject under the structural condition of literality, and there was a thinkable subject under the condition of spatial torsion. It is the "there is no outside-liminality" that is constitutive. Psychoanalysis goes through various liminal configurations. This is also precisely the point to which Jean-Claude Milner assigns anti-philosophy. In his book, he shows that philosophy, which tackled this dilemma on its own account, made use, in an essential way, of outside-liminality, of "originary" necessity, of the historical transcendental not subject to contingent variation. It claimed to escape contingency. Lacan, however, and psychoanalysis along with him, firmly hold that there is no outside-liminality. And it is to this, in the end, that the hypothesis of the collective unconscious comes down. The unconscious is nothing but the statement, made from the subject's point of view, "There is no outside-liminality."

Now, let's let Jean-Claude Milner take over.

———⁂———

Jean-Claude Milner: I want to thank Alain Badiou, who published *L'Oeuvre claire* in "L'Ordre philosophique," the series he edits with Barbara Cassin, for inviting me to come speak about it in his seminar. The question he's asking me could be divided into two as follows: Why this book rather than no book at all, and why this book now, rather than at some other time? Let me answer the second one: Why this book now? It's because I realized that something similar to what happened with Freud was happening, among French-speaking intellectuals, with Lacan, namely, the evacuation of any thought that could be connected with the name Lacan. I'm obviously not talking about what's happening in the psychoanalytic movement; it's abundantly clear that a work of thought is going on there, particularly in the École de la Cause freudienne. I'm not adding anything to that. I'm talking about what is happening, outside the psychoanalytic movement, in what has variously been called the republic of letters, intellectual life, knowledge professionals, and so on.

Lacan had been very much present, and then he disappeared. In much the same way, Freud, before him, had disappeared. As we know, Lacan made sure that something resembling thought and something known as "Freud" could continue to be connected to each other. So it's easy to understand what my own intention was: for a variety of reasons, in a variety of ways, my aim was to ensure that something resembling thought could be connected to the name "Lacan."

In other words, I could sum up my project with a slogan, similar to the one Foucault wanted to borrow from Breton, Char, and Éluard: "Slow—roadwork ahead" [*ralentir travaux*].² "Slow—thought ahead," I would say. There is thought in Lacan's work; that's what I wanted to prove or show. Compared with that objective, establishing what that thought consisted in was really of secondary importance. It was secondary in a very precise sense: I only attempted to present the workings of Lacan's thought in order to prove that there is thought in his work.

You can understand why, in my eyes, my book is not a book *about* Lacan. Books about Lacan—and this is their very definition—take something called Lacan's thought for granted. But I hold that, in so doing, there is a risk of overlooking a question: Can it be proved that there is thought of some sort in Lacan's work? And if it can't be proved, can it at least be shown?

Such a question arises for people other than Lacan. It may even take on a dramatic character. We have a few examples of this near at hand. Take Marx: books elucidating his thought keep coming out, but they are powerless against the certainty that has developed over the past few years that there's not a shred of thought in Marx's work. So a lot of time can be spent explaining his theory, but if it hasn't been proved beforehand that there is thought in Marx's work nothing will have been achieved. It can only be proved if the question has been raised. But, at the same time, another one will have been raised: How can it be proved that there is thought? What are the criteria?

This is a frequently encountered problem that is usually not resolved. Yet, it's of the utmost importance. In many cases, far more numerous than is usually supposed, the solution depends on a pure and simple principle of authority. We accept as axiomatic that there is thought in a given writer's work because trustworthy people have accepted as much. These trustworthy people are assumed to be credible, often because we accept that there is thought in their work, too. In other words, we get caught up in a circle, which I wouldn't necessarily say is a vicious one: it's the very circle of every cultural tradition. We accept without proof that there is thought in Plato's or Kant's work because we've been told as much. We're free to replicate the proof for ourselves, but whether we realize it or not, that takes us back to the question of criteria.

Here's another, completely different case. For a long time the proof of Marx, if I may put it that way, was simply sensorial: the eruptive eventality of revolutions and the existence of states identifying as Marxist were sufficient evidence that thought existed. It should be noted that this evidence was probative for Marxists and anti-Marxists alike: they might disagree about the judgment to be made about Marx's thought, but their assessment (whether positive or negative) depended on the sensorial evidence. One could speak of a proof by effects here. Now that the sensorial evidence is fading away, or let's say more precisely that it is becoming less evident, as it were, the question of thought in Marx's work is becoming really serious again.

Now, in Lacan's case, the evidence was no less sensorial. All things considered, it was bound up with the fond memory some people, who had been direct witnesses to the force of his speech, had of him. As these witnesses become scarcer and their memory grows hazy, the sensorial evidence will fade away, unless it is passed down by some authority. Ultimately, two proofs are at work, in actual fact: the authority, for one thing, and the sensorial evidence for another, with the understanding that, over time, the authority will gradually tend to replace the evidence.

How can it be proved that there is thought in Lacan's work? How can it be proved without appealing to some authority? I made a number of decisions about this issue that are obviously decisions about method. First of all, I assumed that there is thought in a discursive ensemble only to the extent that there are one or more propositions.

A proposition is a minimal element, ideally a discursive atom. In terms of its expression in language, it tends to be coextensive with a sentence. This sentence may or may not be explicitly present in the discursive ensemble referred to. To that end, I constantly used single quotes; in my method, they serve to isolate a proposition. Propositions are thereby distinguished from citations, which are enclosed in double quotes. It sometimes happens that the propositions overlap with the citations, but that's not always the case. My method therefore consisted in setting the following agenda for myself: to isolate propositions, giving them the form of sentences—and, I would add, the simplest sentences possible.

Second of all, I noted, through simple observation, that one of the easiest ways of generating proposition-sentences comes down, quite simply, to the *more geometrico*. So I used a presentation in axioms, theorems, lemmas, and so forth. I don't mean by this that the geometric method is the only effective mode of proof. There are conclusive proofs that don't obey Euclidean rules; there are Euclidean proofs that are not conclusive. Lacan himself never submitted to Euclid, and yet I concluded, after studying him [Lacan], that he had proposed proofs. The *more geometrico* was clearly foreign to him; by subjecting him to it I was therefore allowing myself to do a certain violence to him. But such violence was part and parcel of my project.

Indeed—and here I'm coming to a third point—assuming one has managed to formulate propositions that are coextensive with sentences, they must also be independent of the discursive context in which the investigator has discovered them. In other words, they must retain their properties whatever the context—in the double sense of the word: the textual surroundings and the circumstances. This is what I call the forcible movement method, which involves taking a proposition and removing it from its natural environment. If it retains its propositional properties, then it can be considered a proposition in thought. By using the *more geometrico*, I put Lacan to this test.

To that end, I had to decide on the discursive ensemble to which the test was to apply. So a hypothesis came into the picture. I couldn't prove it; what is even more, I asserted that it wasn't a logical proof but the combination of convergent pieces of evidence. This hypothesis is empirical in that there's nothing logically impossible about the opposite hypothesis. I assumed that, one day, Lacan deliberately decided to put his written interventions, or at least some of them, in the work form. By that I mean a very specific form, whose history Foucault, among others, had begun to write. For us moderns, the work connects an author and an ensemble of published texts. This ensemble is intended to form a unit by itself. The sole author is usually regarded as necessary for this single unit, but he is never regarded as sufficient. Added to this there must be a principle of unity internal to the ensemble of texts. Publication, too, is necessary, even if it's posthumous. I thus pointed out that Saussure's *Course in General Linguistics* became a work retrospectively, whereas it was originally a compilation of his lectures edited by three of his students. I could also have mentioned Hegel's *Aesthetics* and many other such texts. Far from refuting the notion of the work, these examples prove that the work form is strong enough to compel recognition on its own.

The work is not identical to the book, but the fact remains that the book provides the most faithful material image of it: the name and title on the cover, very similar to a tombstone, embody, as it were, the imaginary representation that comes closest to what a work is in our ideology. Nineteenth-century philology contrasted the work form with textual ensembles that were unaware of any such thing when they were originally created. Were the *Iliad* and the *Odyssey* works? The question would have been meaningless for the rhapsodists who put them together. Are the Gospels works? The question would have been meaningless for their redactors. The activity of what has been called criticism consisted in refining ever more the arguments and counterarguments, now for, now against, without always being aware of the anachronism that undermined the enterprise right from the start. In contrast, the twentieth century problematized the work form, even for textual ensembles that, at first sight, were supposed to be connected with it. Is *In Search of Lost Time* a work? It would be interesting to assume that it isn't. And what about *Finnegans Wake* or André Breton's *Mad Love*? Or his *Nadja*? And so on.

Freud interpreted his own dream about the botanical monograph by identifying in it his anxiety about his own book—the *Traumdeutung*—which was taking him too long to write. My view is that that dream signaled a decision: Freud chose the work form rather than the monograph form, which is used in academic science. However, modern science is opposed to modern *culture* in that the former is indifferent to the work form while the latter has made it its foundation. Freud wanted to make a name for himself in science, but he in fact failed. He decided, strategically, to accept to make a detour through culture. This is how I interpret his invocation to Acheron, which opens the *Traumdeutung*. Since the Olympian gods of science had turned a deaf ear to him, Freud would instead address the kingdom of the dead: culture.

Lacan came up against similar deafness on the part of the institutional psychoanalysts, the people he called "the Beatitudes" in 1956. He made a detour through the world of culture, whose deathlike nature—the exquisite corpse[3]—the surrealists had taught him about and which he himself associated with the trash can. The term *poubellication* [a portmanteau word composed of *poubelle* ("trash can") and *publication* ("publication")] meant "the work form" at the very time, in 1966, when he became resigned to it, not without an ulterior motive, and published his *Écrits*.

Acknowledging Lacan's choice of the work form, I isolated in him what constituted a work: it was the *Écrits*, supplemented by the later

texts, which Lacan could only publish by linking them to the undeniable existence of the *Écrits*. These texts essentially comprise the
Scilicet articles and Seminar XX [*Encore*]. I grouped them all together
under the name *Scripta*. I gave reasons for believing that there's no
need to wait for the complete publication of the *Seminars* to examine
the question of his thought. The publication of the *Seminars* is of
course of the utmost importance, but we already have available to us
what Lacan wanted to present as a work. In short, my intention was
to provide material proof that there was thought in Lacan's work
and to do so on the basis of the discursive materiality of the *Scripta*.

Did this oblige me to further clarify the work form and in particular to reconstitute what might be called an art of writing? I don't
think it did. That kind of research is legitimate, but it didn't concern me. Obviously, a situation might have arisen where, in order to
prove that thought existed, I couldn't avoid commenting in detail on
the texts. But I did that as little as possible.

Once you've shown that there is thought in Lacan's work, it's
naturally better to explain what it is. Otherwise, the affirmation of
its existence leads nowhere. But going further than that, revealing
some admiration or a reservation or even just a difference of opinion, amounts to personal thinking. I made a point of refraining from
that. Showing that there is thought in Lacan's work and doing so
with concrete proof is totally independent of what I personally think
or don't think. That's why I stressed the fact that there should not
be a shred of personal thinking in *L'Oeuvre claire*, and if there was,
it would be a defect. To put it another way, showing that there is
thought in Lacan's work is done through the medium of persons—my
own person, in this case—but the point is, it's a question of mediums.

You might think that in refraining from any personal thinking
I was merely imposing on myself a restraint similar to the restraints
historians or biblical scholars impose on themselves. But the stakes
were higher. They were related to my conception of thought: it's

thought that I regard as impersonal, and it's because it's a matter of thought that impersonality is so crucial. At some point I spoke about discursive materialism. This, to my mind, is opposed to a widespread kind of nonsense that I called discursive personalism. I opted for discursive materialism with regard to Lacan. I don't rule out the possibility, quite the contrary, that it may also be applicable to other textual ensembles connected with other names. However, in the specific case of thought and Lacan, it seemed to me that there was a particularly urgent need for it.

On one of the detours I had to take to show that there was thought—in the form of propositions—I encountered the question of science. What strikes me as most important is this: in the Lacanian system of propositions, science is the *name* of the meeting point of contingency and infinity. In other words, science is the *name* of the identity between the predicate "contingent" and the predicate "infinite." To borrow one of Lacan's formulations, science enables us to understand how the predicate "contingent" represents the subject for the predicate "infinite,"[4] but also how the predicate "infinite" represents the subject for the predicate "contingent." The foreclosure of the subject, which Lacan speaks about in connection with modern science, is also a purification—in both senses of the word: the foreclosed subject is purified or purged by science, insofar as it only emerges in the relation "to represent for," established between contingent and infinite.

Now, science has two sources in Lacan's work: Freud, on the one hand, whose scientism Lacan repeatedly stressed; and Koyré, on the other hand, supplemented by Kojève. At first glance, nothing could be further apart than these two approaches. Koyré, as both a historian of science and an epistemologist, categorically rejected the empiricism and the empiriocriticism to which Freud, on the contrary, was committed. By defining Galileo in terms of mathematization, Koyré wiped out in one fell swoop all the approaches that linked Galileo to experimentation. Far from bringing about the revolution that enabled the move from Aristotle to Galileo, said Koyré, this experimentation depended on a decision that was prior to all experimentation, namely that mathematics, reserved by the Aristotelians to the eternal and the immutable, was applicable to the sublunary world of corruption and change. Whence it followed that the cosmological ensemble of celestial bodies need not be separated from the cosmological ensemble of earthly bodies. There is only one ensemble, called the universe. Let me pause here to point out that nineteenth-century scientism, and Freud along with it, reasoned completely differently from the way Koyré did. Experimentation was central; mathematization, subsidiary. The latter's role was to guarantee the exactitude and precision of experimental observations. Badiou and I, and many other people, were trained to accept three theses as self-evident: (a) the intrinsic superiority of any rationalist epistemology over any empiricist epistemology; (b) the descriptive and explanatory superiority of any historicization of the sciences derived from rationalist epistemology over any historicization derived from empiricist epistemology; and (c) the integrative nature of these superiorities, i.e., everything correct put forward by empiricist epistemology and history can be preserved and consolidated by the rationalist ones.

We've been so well trained to take propositions (a)–(c) for granted that we can no longer see the violence hidden within them. In particular, we no longer perceive how violent Lacan's appropriation of Freud was: contrary to all the historiographic evidence, he claimed that the science to which Freud referred was none other than the science Koyré spoke about. The gulf separating Freud from Koyré was deemed to be null and void. When Lacan acknowledges Koyré as "my guide" [É, 727], the correction made to Freud needs to be taken into account. What he means is: Koyré guides me through a dark forest, and this dark forest—this tangled mess, Lacan would also say—is Freud's theories.

That said, all the detail Koyré went into, the painstaking history of mathematized physics, the move from Galileo to Kepler, from Kepler to Descartes, from Descartes to Newton—all this research was important, of course. Lacan was familiar with it and commented on it occasionally, but, ultimately, it was irrelevant compared with the essential thing: the discovery that the universe of mathematized physics was both infinite and contingent; that the collision between the contingent and the infinite wasn't experimentation but mathematization; that it was the universe's contingency that allowed it to be mathematized and that it was its mathematization that allowed it to be called infinite, even though the mathematicians didn't have a clear mathematical concept of what infinity was.

If science is the name of the equivalence between the predicate "X is contingent" and the predicate "X is infinite," I conclude, conversely, that any collision between infinity and contingency is connected with science. Now, according to Lacan, his own approach depends entirely on what he calls his hypothesis, referring explicitly to Newton. Let me remind you what it is (it can be found in *Seminar XX* [*Encore*], page 142): " . . . the individual who is affected by the unconscious is the same individual who constitutes what I call the subject of a signifier." Let's unpack this. The individual is a speaking body. In his existence and in his body, he is inhabited by contingency. The unconscious stamps the mark of infinity on him. The phrase "the subject of a signifier" can be read in terms of the relation "the signifier is that which represents a subject for another signifier" [*F*, 207]. If, hypothetically, the individual so defined is the same individual as the subject of a signifier, we get what I stated above: the subject is that which the signifier "contingent" represents for the signifier "infinite." The crux of the hypothesis is the assertion "they are the same." But only modern science enables us to understand this "sameness."

Lacan's hypothesis seems to me to be no less than the hypothesis of psychoanalysis itself. This hypothesis turns out to tie infinity and contingency together, and, by the same token, it ties the questions of science and psychoanalysis together. Here, too, the problem I'm concerned with is not what psychoanalysis says—what it says in detail. The problem I'm concerned with is that it exists, with a number of features. I contend that it exists, or, more precisely, I contend that Lacan's hypothesis, what he himself calls his hypothesis, comes down to claiming that psychoanalysis exists. One of its features that strikes me is that it has something to do with the connection, in the guise of the unconscious, between infinity and contingency. More precisely, I contend that Lacan's hypothesis comes down to positing this connection. If there is an unconscious, it is because the embodied and speaking individual is affected by the infiniteness of the universe. He is affected in his body; he is affected in his speaking, if only because language (to use the notion running from Humboldt to Chomsky) is the collision between the finite and the infinite. *Lalangue*, as a refracting crystal, is all the more so.[5] Yet, the body, affected by infinity, is also affected, in one or more of its sites, by contingency.

The privileged sites of contingency are related to sexuation, sexuation being the ultimate mark of contingency on the individual. The throw of the dice that divides subjects into genders or sexes (it doesn't matter which here) cannot be abolished by the chance nature of social representations.[6] If the unconscious is the mark of infinity on the individual (who is the same individual as the subject), if sexuation is the mark of contingency, if modernity, owing to science, is based on the collision between infinity and contingency, then everything conspires to steer the modern disposition toward a discourse that connects individual, subject, unconscious, and sexuation. That discourse is psychoanalysis.

The emergence of sexuality with Freud and of the sexual with Lacan focused a chain of propositions on itself. I attempted to isolate these propositions and their intersections. Ultimately, they can be combined with each other again and a single proposition can be arrived at. I am stating that proposition here before you: *There is psychoanalysis.*

I didn't state this in *L'Oeuvre claire*. In the same way, in a properly-played game of [French] charades the word to be guessed ("my whole") isn't given. Rather, the game allows it to be figured out with the help of the different clues, or parts, i.e., "My first is a . . . ," "my second is a . . . ," and so on. In *L'Oeuvre claire* I gave the parts; today I'm spelling out what the "whole" was.

※

Alain Badiou: Thank you so much. There's enough food for thought in what you said for one of those unforgettable discussions that go on until dawn. But I'll just ask Jean-Claude Milner three questions, whose arrangement, though not their proof, is Borromean.

The first is an overtly sophistic question. You mentioned that the whole point, for you, was to attempt an impersonal proof of the statement "There is thought in Lacan's work." The question I would ask you is as follows: Is the assertion that an impersonal proof can be produced of *there is thought*—in Lacan's work, in this case—a thesis about *thought* or a thesis about the *there is*? Because, from the philosopher's point of view, they are two different options. If we assume that there can be an impersonal proof that there is thought—in Lacan's work, in this case—and that this is a thesis about *thought*, then that establishes a connection between thought and impersonal proof. I would call it the Mallarméan thesis. If, on the other hand, we consider that the emphasis should be placed on the *there is*—thought, in this case, and, what's more, in Lacan's work—but that the real issue is that an impersonal proof can be given of the fact that there is something—thought in Lacan's work, in this case—then the connection is established between impersonal proof and "there is." This is what I'd call the Heideggerian thesis.

At bottom, my question is very simple: Is the hypothesis of a possible impersonal proof of *There is thought* in Lacan's work a connection between impersonality and thought? In other words, does it concern the fate of thought, considered as something separate from the fate of being, or does it concern the fate of being, as something assumed ultimately to be subsuming the fate of thought?

You know as well as I that the dominant view today is that there's no thought at all. And the practical essence of this view—*there isn't any*—is that it's dangerous (totalitarian) for there to be thought. Your undertaking regarding Lacan is absolutely relevant to the contingency of our situation: you are taking a stand by asserting that there is thought, at any rate in Lacan's work—a view that runs counter to the dominant view that there isn't any. But as soon as you give an impersonal proof of this point, if it has to do with *thought* it's not the same thing as if it has to do with *there is*.

My second question has to do with science as the name of the equivalence between contingency and infinity. My question in this case is a very precise, specific one: Is this, in your opinion, a thesis about Lacan? Should we understand that, for Lacan, science is nothing but the name of the equivalence between contingency and infinity? Or is it a thesis shared by Lacan?

You'll note that I'm carefully avoiding making you leave the terrain of impersonality. I'm not asking you: Is this *your* thesis? There is, however, something I can call *my* thesis with regard to this issue. As it happens, I give the name *truth* to the equivalence between contingency and infinity. So I'm interested in knowing, when I give it the name "truth," what I'm doing compared with what *you're* doing when you call this same connection, or equivalence, "science."

The third question is more complex. It has to do with psychoanalysis, with the statement "There is psychoanalysis." The question can be formulated like so: There is thought in Lacan's work, but does that mean there is thought in psychoanalysis? This is where we find the *"there is"* again, the "there is" of thought. And "There is psycho-analysis" isn't a statement that includes, as such, the fact that "there is thought" in psychoanalysis. So we could hypothesize that there is thought in Lacan's work and that this includes the fact that there is psychoanalysis but doesn't allow us to conclude that there is thought in psychoanalysis.

At one point, you note, in a way that's consistent with your proof, that the individual affected by an unconscious, that is, by his coex-tension with the universe of what is contingent to him, is one thing, while the subject, in that it is the object of a number of Lacan's propositions, is another. Basically, you suggest that the thesis of psychoanalysis is that an absolutely contingent encounter between the two occurs. This encounter is the contingent encounter between individual, in the sense of contingency, and subject, in the sense of Lacan's propositions. The name Lacan gives the contingency of this encounter is "the psychoanalytic act."

So my question becomes: Is there or isn't there a relationship be-tween Lacan's work and this act? Because it could be assumed that Lacan's work exists only as a trace, itself contingent, of the contin-gency of the act. In that case, the work form itself needs to be re-thought, in such a way that it is uncertain whether it constitutes a corpus. If it doesn't, it's uncertain whether the impersonal proof that "there is thought"—a proof that, as you pointed out, requires this corpus to be circumscribed—can be undertaken regarding it. But if the corpus is only the contingent trace of the psychoanalytic act as a contingent encounter between the individual and the sub-ject, then there is no corpus, there is no work, strictly speaking, and therefore there can be no impersonal proof. Which would mean that the only proof there can be is a personal one!

What does it mean to say that the only proof there can be is a personal one? It means that the custodianship of the work of Lacan—which is not, in fact, a work—belongs by necessity to the psychoanalytic organizations. Why? Because only they can testify, personally, in accordance with the principles of the act, to the incompleteness of the work, or even to the irremediable weakness of the work of Lacan. And therefore your project, and mine as well, would be irrelevant.

I'll give my question its final form: Can the impersonal proof of "there is thought" in Lacan's work do without the act, without the reference to the act, by purely and simply excluding it, or is the impersonal proof relegated to being just a personal interpretation? Because, ultimately, only the organization could be the custodian of the act's impersonality. So that's it.

⸙

Jean-Claude Milner: As to the first question, I would answer: if there are only two possible options, the Mallarméan option and the Heideggerian one, I'd go with the former. I link thought and impersonality closely together. That's how I interpret Lacan's dictum "it thinks" [*ça pense*]. Whence it follows that, in effect, I don't directly decide on the being that the "there is" would or wouldn't involve. But are there only two options? Rather than to being, the locution *il y a de l'X* ["there is (some) X"]—which Lacan sought to reduce to a single word, *yad'l'*—alludes to a real.[7] To say that there is thought is to grant thought, or rather bursts of thought, the contingent possibility that they are inscribed as reals. To say that there is thought in Lacan's work is to claim that, in Lacan's textuality, there are points where a real of thought crops up.

As to the second question, I could limit myself to a simple affirmation: yes, I hold that, for Lacan, so-called modern science sets up a collision between contingency and infinity. So this is not a thesis *about* Lacan; I am presuming to reconstruct one of Lacan's theses. Since that's the case, I think I have a duty to distinguish between several subquestions.

The first has to do with infinity. In my opinion, Lacan doesn't speak about mathematical infinity, even if he's interested in it. It's much more a question of an infinity that I'd call philosophical. It's even more convoluted than that. I stressed the relationship Lacan entertained with Galilean physics. That physics has two distinctive features: for one thing, it is mathematized, and, for another, it groups earthly and celestial objects together into a self-homogenous universe. This universe is infinite, if only because it doesn't treat as a special case the reign of the finite that the sublunary world once was. I'll leave aside Descartes's caveats regarding the use of the term "infinite," even though they are crucial and show how far Descartes outstripped his contemporaries in depth of understanding. The paradox remains: in the age of Galileo or Descartes or Newton, no mathematician had a clear concept of infinity. On the contrary, after infinity obtained a clear status in mathematics, thanks to Bolzano, Weierstrass, and Cantor, it stopped playing a role in philosophical argumentation, as I've already pointed out, but it also stopped being an issue for mathematized physics. As can be observed in twentieth-century cosmologies, mathematized physics can assume without contradiction a finite universe, except that the finite concerned is a post-Cantorian finite, with no relation to Koyré's pre-Cantorian infinity. For, as I can never stress enough, in Koyré's phrase "the infinite universe" the infinite in question is not the mathematical infinite.

Admittedly, Cantor himself never gave up trying to connect the mathematical infinity he had introduced and the philosophers' infinity. Or even the theologians' infinity, which was much more important to him. After Cantor, however, the question of the connection between mathematical and nonmathematical infinity seems to have been abandoned. Either it was asserted, with no proof, that only mathematical infinity had meaning, or it was accepted, without much discussion, that the cumulative progress of knowledge enabled mathematical infinity to absorb a posteriori all the pre-Cantorian discussions about infinity. In his writings about the All, Lacan focused new light on the question. But we still have to make the effort to decipher his writings from this point of view. In any case, it's striking that Lacan's writings about the All opted for logic over mathematics, for Russell over Cantor. Moreover, what was taken from Russell was very narrow in scope since Lacan confined himself to the quantificational writing. If we remember how extensive Russell's mathematical project was, it could be said that Lacan treated it without much regard.

When Badiou and I quarrel about the equivalence between contingency and infinity, it's important to beware that, on my side at least, the substantive "contingency" encompasses the predicative use "X is contingent." Likewise, the substantive "infinity" encompasses the predicative use "X is infinite." However, the predicate "to be infinite" can involve something quite different from the mathematical concept of infinity. If infinity is incorporated into the series of cardinal numbers, a logician might argue that, in the phrase "infinite universe" or the proposition "The universe is infinite," the idea of "infinite" is no more a predicate than is "twelve" in "The apostles are twelve." In the latter, you can't apply the *dictum de omni et nullo* ["the maxim of all and none"] and deduce that "each apostle is twelve." By the same token, you could interpret "The universe is infinite" in strictly numerical terms: the universe would then be made up of an infinite number of entities, without each entity being, as such, infinite. But to say that the universe is infinite, making "infinity" a predicate, is to go beyond an enumeration; it is to assume that each object of the universe, insofar as it belongs to the universe, is assigned the predicate "infinite," that it bears its mark.

I'm not saying that this is peculiar to infinity. I often refer to the game of the three prisoners,[8] which Lacan assigned to collective logic. Without going into detail, I would say that it is based on an operation that turns the number three into a *ternary*: each of the three prisoners, taken one by one, is, as a one, affected by the three that he forms with the other two. Likewise, it can be argued that each entity of the infinite universe is, as an individual, affected by the infinity in which it is inscribed with each of the other entities.

But infinity of course raises more wrenching questions. Some philosophers have contended that the mark of infinity borne by every entity was freedom. Others have contended it was death. In other words, they went beyond physical entities, something which, in proper Greek, is called "metaphysics." What's very striking in both Freud and Lacan is that, in order to situate the mark of infinity borne by every individual, they turned to the universe as modern science has defined it—in other words, the physical universe. The two propositions—that the mark of infinity is neither freedom nor death but the unconscious, and, in addition, that the infinity in question is the one defined by so-called modern science—intersect. That's why the issue of science plays just as important a role in Freud as it does in Lacan, even though their ideas about it were very different.

What I claim about the predicate "to be infinite" I also claim about the predicate "to be contingent." The radical contingency of the universe of science imprints its mark on every entity in the universe. If I confine myself to the speaking being, its contingent-being is seen at the level of the zoological species, which might not exist or might exist otherwise (see Darwin), as well as at the level of the individual, who might be missing from his place; at the level of the sexuated body, which might not be sexuated at all, or might be a different sex than it is, or might be subject to polysexuation (Deleuze's thesis); and, finally, at the level of the subject, who is constantly in eclipse. Except that what might be otherwise is in fact not otherwise. Since "contingency" and "infinity" are the substantivations of the verbal phrases "to be contingent" and "to be infinite," we can understand how Lacan could call Koyré his guide, inasmuch as Koyré introduced the apparently predicative locution "the infinite universe"—even though Lacan dispelled many residual ambiguities. We can understand how Lacan could say Kojève was his master, since Kojève emphasized the contingent nature of the universe of modern science, as opposed to the necessary nature of the cosmos of the ancient *episteme*. With the understanding, here, too, that Kojève didn't say the last word about it.

<hr />

So I now come to the third question, that of psychoanalysis. What I understand on Badiou's part is a question about how the work of Lacan (given all the caveats I attach to the word "work") and the psychoanalytic act are connected. However, in the way that I connect them, there's a third term: the proposition "There is psychoanalysis." I make it play the role of the "whole" in charades, the word that has to be guessed, which doesn't in fact appear in the game.

If that proposition were to appear in *L'Oeuvre claire*, it would have to be its starting point. But that starting point would be observation, whereas my aim was to construct a chain of propositions, not to observe a state of fact, not even so as to develop the conditions of possibilities from it. If I may be a bit pedantic, I would refer more to a Cartesian order of reasons than to a Kantian-type critique. It is very important for the first proposition in the order of reasons to have to do with the subject. So there's a big advantage to linking the propositions in such a way that the proposition "There is psychoanalysis" appears only later on in the discursive apparatus. In fact, instead of acting as a starting point, it acts as an end point.

This allows me to explain the difference between the propositions "There is thought in Lacan's work," "There is psychoanalysis," and "There is thought in psychoanalysis." Let's take seriously the trajectory that led Freud and Lacan to use the work form. The proposition "There is thought in Lacan's (or Freud's) work" makes it possible to reconstruct the chain of propositions that structure their work. In this chain, as I have reconstructed it, the proposition "There is psychoanalysis" emerges in the final instance.

But the analogy with charades allows me to go a little further. In the same way as "the whole" in charades is not just a matter of adding together "my first," "my second," "my third," and so on, I allow for a step between *L'Oeuvre claire* and the proposition "There is psychoanalysis." I set Lacan up as a work, and in the process I encounter the affirmation of the existence of psychoanalysis, but in disguised form: this is what Lacan himself calls his hypothesis, in which the name "psychoanalysis" does not appear directly; only its metonymic placeholder, the unconscious, does. The explicit affirmation doesn't appear. This is because there is no transition between the set of propositions and the affirmation of existence.

Similarly, I don't think it's possible to go from the proposition "There is thought in Lacan's work" to a proposition of the type "There is thought in psychoanalysis." I think such a proposition is as meaningless as asserting "There is thought in physics" or "There is thought in poetry." Let's not confuse such a proposition, which is empty, with propositions of the type "There is thought in Baudelaire's work" or "There is thought in Einstein's work." Ultimately, I would venture the following paradox: the intrinsic impersonality of thought cannot be given concrete expression except by its being related to a proper name, simply because the proper name may have nothing to do with a person. Kripke's greatness lay in having attempted to show this. To put it another way, far from the potential personalization of the proper name affecting the thought in the proposition "There is thought in Lacan's work," it is the impersonality of the thought that affects the proper name and makes its antipersonal aspect stand out. When Kant thought, *he* didn't think personally; *thinking* thought through the medium of Kant. When Kant thought personally, he didn't think; he became the medium of his person, and even a passive medium, where we once again encounter Descartes and the *Treatise on the Passions*. If I had time, I would develop some related remarks on the pronouns called, equivocally, "personal," which can be "antipersonal" precisely to the extent that they involve the subject.

There remains the question of the psychoanalytic act. I refuse to do any more than accept the possibility of it. For someone who is not involved in psychoanalysis, it is impossible to take the step from the proposition "There is psychoanalysis" to the psychoanalytic act. What is that step actually? It is the step from a multiplicity to a unicity. I can understand how the possibility of any analytic act can be rejected. But I can't understand how the possibility of a psychoanalytic act that is supposedly unique in human history can be accepted. Just as, according to Christians, there was only one resurrection, accomplished by Christ. It is hard for me even to admit that psychoanalytic acts are few and far between. Consequently, to accept the possibility of the psychoanalytic act is to accept the possibility of an indefinite multiplicity of such acts. How does one go from there to the singular statement "There is psychoanalysis"? I don't know.

The only ones who know are the psychoanalysts and the analysands. What I nevertheless think I do know is that the statement "There is psychoanalysis" is not intended to deny the possibility of the psychoanalytic act. Despite appearances, I am not spouting a tautology here. To make my position clearer, let me refer to a theme that Badiou has developed in his work. In many historical cases, the statement "There is politics" was intended to prove that there was no political act. Conversely, the statement that one or more political acts were possible was intended to make the negative claim that there was no politics. In the case of psychoanalysis, I think that these contradictory relations are irrelevant. Thus, the psychoanalytic institutes can be situated more precisely. Their basic justification, possibly their only one, is that they limit the potential disaster of psychoanalysis and the psychoanalytic act coming into conflict with each other to the point of mutually and reciprocally canceling each other out. Taking full advantage of the analogy that I attempted to use with politics, I will turn Badiou's question back on him: Isn't the purpose of political institutions—I'm deliberately using one of Saint-Just's titles—to ensure that politics and the political act confirm each other mutually and reciprocally? Or at the very least that they don't cancel each other out? As for the statement "There is psychoanalysis," let me come back to it one last time so as to leave nothing in the dark. I think I provided the material proof of the existence of one or more propositions in thought in Lacan's work. I argued that the linking of these propositions led to the proposition "There is psychoanalysis." But even assuming I'm right about all the essential points, it still leaves the question of whether there is really psychoanalysis unresolved. The affirmation of existence or nonexistence cannot be inferred.

Alain Badiou: I'm in complete agreement with you about that. There is thought in Lacan's work only if there is the proposition "There is psychoanalysis." But the proposition—in thought—that there is psychoanalysis is part of the fact that there is, in general, thought. I, too, leave completely open the question of whether there is psychoanalysis, and I do so in accordance with the principle that the proof, in thought, of the "there is" doesn't resolve the question of the "there is." In other words, the "there is" of the "there is" is not a matter of thought.

Well, in any case, for our last session of 1994–95 we've had a real proof of the fact that "there is thought." It's like in a symphony, when the conclusion of the last movement attempts to show that there is indeed a tonal system on the basis of which this music can be played, and, to that end, amplifies and orchestrates, in the most subtle and emphatic way possible, the final occurrence of the themes.

I thought I'd be done with anti-philosophy this year. That *is* the case with the trio of major contemporary anti-philosophers, Nietzsche, Wittgenstein, and Lacan. But then the idea occurred to me of going all the way back to the prince of anti-philosophers, the one who directly confronted the philosophers of the time, on the public square in Athens, and who really gave them a good laugh thanks to his subjective preaching and his scathing polemic against argumentative thinking. I'm talking about the apostle Paul. We'll be dealing with *him* next year.

Have a good summer, everyone.

Acknowledgments

We [the French editors] would like to thank the people who provided the documents that allowed us to establish this text: François Duvert, first of all, whose transcription of Olga Rodel's original audio cassettes we used, and Annick Lavaud, who helped us fill in the blanks.

Notes

Editors' Introduction to the English Edition of the Seminars of Alain Badiou

1. On October 19, 2015, in a session from his final seminar on "The Immanence of Truths," Badiou describes two distinct but equivalent paths of entry into his work: the first "systematic approach" involves reading, preferably in order, his three or four great works (depending on whether one counts *Theory of the Subject* as part of that sequence or as the prelude to a trilogy). The second "methodical" but not systematic path [*le voyage ordonné*] involves beginning with his *Manifesto for Philosophy* and *Second Manifesto for Philosophy*, to establish the fundamental structure, ligatures, and knots of his thought, followed by, in no particular order, the seminars—now expected to extend to twenty volumes.

Introduction to the Seminar on Lacan

1. Alain Badiou, *Conditions*, trans. Steven Corcoran (New York: Continuum, 2008), 129. Originally published in French in *Conditions* in 1992 (Paris: Seuil) and based on a lecture from 1991 in Montpellier. Also cf. Badiou's *Manifesto for Philosophy*: "[T]he anti-philosopher Lacan is a condition of the renaissance of philosophy. A philosophy is possible today, only if it is compossible with Lacan." Trans. Norman Madarasz (Buffalo: SUNY Press, 1999), 84.

2. For more biographical accounts of Badiou's early exposure to Lacan's work, see Alain Badiou and Élisabeth Roudinesco, *Jacques Lacan, Past and Present: A Dialogue*, trans. Jason E. Smith (New York: Columbia University Press, 2014); and Peter Hallward and Knox Peden, eds., " 'Theory from Structure to

Subject': An Interview with Alain Badiou," in *Concept and Form: Volume Two* (New York: Verso, 2012).

3. Other philosophers in this category include, of course, Slavoj Žižek, Mladen Dolar, and Alenka Zupančič. On Badiou's concept of the "contemporary" or the "present time," see his seminar of 2001–2004, *Images du temps présent* (Paris: Fayard, 2014), English translation forthcoming from Columbia University Press.

4. See Didier Masseau, *Les ennemis des philosophes: L'antiphilosophie au temps des Lumières* (Paris: Albin Michel, 2000), cited by Bruno Bosteels in his very fine essay, "Radical Antiphilosophy," *Filozofski vestnik*, 39, no. 2 (2008): 155–87. The expression "anti-philosophy" apparently first appears in English when used by Samuel Taylor Coleridge in his *Philosophical Lectures* of 1818. Lacan uses the expression to define a position against university discourse in "Peut-être à Vincennes . . .," *Autres écrits*, ed. Jacques-Alain Miller (Paris: Seuil, 2001), 314–35. And in "Monsieur A." Lacan points to Tristan Tzara's use of the term in his manifesto "Monsieur Aa l'antiphilosophe" and declares "*I rebel*, so to speak, against philosophy" *Ornicar?* 21–22 (Summer 1980): 17.

5. Bruno Bosteels points out that sophistry and antiphilosophy constitute "partially overlapping" categories, rather than fully opposing ones, and the same can be said about anti-philosophy and religion (for Badiou, the originary figure of anti-philosophy, and the topic of the following year's seminar, is Saint Paul). But anti-philosophy, sophistry, and religion are all distinct from each other as well as from philosophy, despite these partial convergences. And whereas the affinities between Lacan and sophistry are quite clear—see, e.g., Barbara Cassin's book *Jacques le sophiste* (Paris: EPEL, 2012)—, Lacan is much more ambivalent about religion, which he predicts will "triumph" over psychoanalysis. See *The Triumph of Religion*, trans. Bruce Fink (Cambridge: Polity, 2013).

6. Steven Corcoran's translation of *traverser* as to "work through" aligns it with Freud's notion of *Durcharbeiten*, the analytic process that is usually translated as "working through." Lacan's key account of the "traversal of the fantasy" appears near the conclusion of *The Seminar of Jacques Lacan, Book XI: The Four Fundamental Concepts of Psychoanalysis*: "How can a subject who has traversed the radical phantasy experience the drive? This is the beyond of analysis, and has never been approached. Up to now, it has been approachable only at the level of the analyst, in as much as it would be required of him to have specifically traversed the cycle of the analytic experience in its totality." Trans. Alan Sheridan (New York: Norton, 1981), 273–74.

7. Lacan's notion of "the act" is complicated, involving the act of deciding to enter into analysis and the experience of transference in analysis;

moreover, the authentic act is always linguistic, never simply a mute gesture of "acting out." The notion of the act is developed in his Seminar 15, "The Psychoanalytic Act" (unpublished). For Lacan's notion of "subjective destitution" see his "Proposition du 9 octobre 1967 sur le psychanalyste de l'École," "Discours à l'École freudienne de Paris," and "L'acte psychanalytique," all in *Autres écrits* (Paris: Seuil, 2001). These Lacanian notions of "subjective destitution" and "traversing the fantasy" ultimately should be put into relation with Lacan's other key concept of the aim or conclusion of analysis (and the shift of an analysand into the position of an analyst), the "pass."

8. In *Theory of the Subject*, Badiou distinguishes between two temporal aspects of the subject, both derived from Lacan: the interruptive moment of "subjectivation" (or subjectivization) and the more extended work of the "subjective process." Trans. Bruno Bosteels (New York: Continuum, 2009), 241–74.

9. On Lacan's expression s'... *oupire*, see note 9 in session 2.

10. Badiou describes anti-philosophy as the "destitution" of philosophy, and in particular the philosophical category of truth, in his essay "Silence, solipsisme, sainteté," *BARCA! Poésie, Politique, Psychanalyse* 3 (1994): 23. Cited by Bosteels, 165.

11. The anti-philosopher, according to Badiou, addresses a primary "counterfigure" who is not necessarily a philosopher, but someone who must be *rescued* from the temptations of philosophy (see session 3). In Lacan's case, these are the psychoanalysts themselves, who can only be saved from philosophy by reading philosophy.

12. Lacan writes in his essay "L'Étourdit" that philosophy is "more than usable" to psychoanalysis.

13. From a letter to Georg Brandes from December 1888. Quoted by Badiou in "Who is Nietzsche?" *Pli* 11 (2001): 4.4 For Badiou this is an "archi-political" account of an act rather than a "political" one insofar as Nietzsche is not proposing a political act, but a radical "break" in the historical conditions of politics as such. See Bruno Bosteels's essay, "Nietzsche, Badiou, and Grand Politics: An Antiphilosophical Reading," in *Nietzsche and Political Thought*, ed. Keith Ansell-Pearson (London: Bloomsbury, 2013), 219–39.

14. See Badiou's *Wittgenstein's Antiphilosophy*, trans. and intro. Bruno Bosteels (New York: Verso, 2011), 80.

15. "What makes up for the sexual relationship is, quite precisely, love." *The Seminar of Jacques Lacan: Book XX, On Feminine Sexuality and the Limits of Love and Knowledge*, ed. Jacques-Alain Miller and trans. Bruce Fink (New York: Norton, 1998), 45. Lacan also suggests at points that there may be a real

mode of love, a "love . . . outside the limits of the law" (*The Four Fundamental Concepts of Psychoanalysis*, 276). For an account of Lacan on love, especially as presented in his transference seminar, see Bruce Fink, *Lacan on Love: An Exploration of Lacan's Seminar VIII, Transference* (Cambridge: Polity, 2016).

16. Badiou began to understand love as a fourth truth procedure soon after the publication of *Being and Event* in 1988, hence already a few years prior to the seminar on Lacan in 1994–95.

17. One way to understand the title of Lacan's *Seminar XIX . . . ou pire* [. . . or worse] is that the ellipses stand for the lack of the sexual relationship, the kernel of the real, which may not be very appealing as an account of the speaking be-ing, but the refusal to acknowledge such an impossibility is certainly "worse."

18. The pass is a non-cognitive procedure involving a passee, one or more pass-ers, and a committee or jury, which is meant to demonstrate whether or not there has been an analytic act in the process of a psychoanalysis. On the pass see Éric Laurent's essay, "The Pass and the Guarantee in the School," avail-able in English here: *http://www.lacan.com/essays/?page_id=470*.

19. See Lacan's essay, "On a Question Prior to Any Possible Treatment of Psychosis," in *Écrits*, trans. Bruce Fink (New York: Norton, 2006), 472.

20. On the relationship of sense, non-sense, and ab-sense in Lacan, see Alain Badiou and Barbara Cassin, *There's No Such Thing as a Sexual Relationship: Two Lessons on Lacan*, trans. Kenneth Reinhard and Susan Spitzer (New York: Columbia University Press, 2017).

21. In Seminar XVII Lacan says "If there is one thing that our entire approach delimits, and that has surely been renewed by analytic experience, it is that the only way in which to evoke the truth is by indicating that it is only accessible through a half-saying [*mi-dire*], that it cannot be said completely, for the reason that beyond this half there is nothing to say. That is all that can be said." *The Seminar of Jacques Lacan, Book XVII: The Other Side of Psycho-analysis*, trans. Russell Grigg (New York: Norton, 2007), 51.

22. In the famous opening lines of *Television*, Lacan declares, "I always speak the truth. Not the whole truth, because there's no way to say it all. Saying it all is literally impossible: words fail. Yet it's through this very impossibility that the truth holds onto the real." *Television*, trans. Denis Hollier, Rosalind Krauss, and Annette Michelson (New York: Norton, 1990), 3.

23. Although Lacan is a great admirer of many of Plato's texts, and devoted most of his Seminar VIII on transference to a reading of *The Symposium*, *The Republic* is not a text of which he speaks favorably.

24. Badiou discusses happiness as the affect of love in *Logics of Worlds*, trans. Alberto Toscano (New York: Continuum, 2009), 571 and *passim*. Also see Badiou's *Métaphysique du bonheur réel* (Paris: Presses universitaires de France, 2015).

25. The statement comes from the letter that Lacan wrote that appeared in *Le Monde* (January 26, 1980) along with the text of his seminar "The Other is Missing." *Television*, trans. Denis Hollier, Rosalind Kraus, and Annette Michelson (New York: Norton, 1990), 135.

26. First published in *Scilicet* 5 (1975), and republished in *Autres écrits*, 551.

27. *The Seminar of Jacques Lacan, Book VII: The Ethics of Psychoanalysis*, trans. Dennis Porter (New York: Norton, 1992), 112.

28. See "Truth: Forcing and the Unnameable," where Badiou writes, "I must admit, I am not nor have I ever been nor will I most likely ever be either an analyst, or an analysand, or analysed. I am 'unanalysed'. Can someone unanalysed say anything about psychoanalysis? You will be the judges of that" (122).

About the 1994–95 Seminar on Lacan

1. Unless otherwise indicated, all notes are by the translators. *Cahiers pour l'analyse* was a journal published by a group of young philosophy students at the École normale supérieure in Paris, many of whom (including Jacques-Alain Miller, Jean-Claude Milner, François Regnault, and Alain Badiou) would later become major figures in French intellectual life. A number of articles from the *Cahiers* have been translated into English and collected in *Concept and Form*, ed. and trans. Peter Hallward and Knox Peden (New York: Verso, 2012).

2. The phrase appears in a slightly different form in ". . . ou pire: Compte rendu du séminaire 1971–1972," in *Autres écrits*, 551. All further page references to *Autres écrits* will be in parentheses in the text. All translations from this work or other works that have not yet been translated and published in English are our own except where otherwise noted.

Session 1

1. Badiou discusses the term "archi-political" in greater depth in "Who is Nietzsche?," *Pli: The Warwick Journal of Philosophy* 11 (2001): 1–11. See also his seminar on Nietzsche, forthcoming from Columbia University Press.

2. Badiou referred to the archi-scientific status of the act for Lacan in his seminar on Wittgenstein's anti-philosophy the previous year (especially in session 4). Also see his comments in *Wittgenstein's Antiphilosophy*, trans. Bruno Bosteels (New York: Verso, 2011), and the Translator's Introduction, pp. 38–39.

3. See Jacques Lacan, "Logical Time and the Assertion of Anticipated Certainty," in *Écrits*, 161–75.

4. Friedrich Nietzsche, *Ecce Homo*, trans. Duncan Large (Oxford: Oxford University Press, 2007), 3.

5. Ludwig Wittgenstein, *Tractatus Logico-Philosophicus*, trans. Charles K. Ogden (New York: Dover, 1998), 5. Subsequent page references to this edition will be in parentheses in the text.

6. Friedrich Nietzsche, *Selected Letters of Friedrich Nietzsche*, ed. and trans. Christopher Middleton (Indianapolis: Hackett, 1969), 283–84; translation slightly modified to conform to the French.

7. Originally published in *Scilicet* 2/3 (1970) as "Discours de clôture du Congrès de l'École freudienne de Paris," this speech was later entitled "Allocution sur l'enseignement" (Address on Teaching) when published in *Autres écrits*.

8. Badiou will discuss Lacan's notion of "the pass" that marks the conclusion of a training analysis at length later in the seminar. See session 3.

9. Friedrich Nietzsche, *Twilight of the Idols* and *Anti-Christ*, trans. Reginald J. Hollingdale (New York: Penguin, 1990), 51; translation modified. Subsequent page references to this edition will be in parentheses in the text.

10. See Paul Celan, *The Meridian: Final Version—Drafts—Materials*, trans. Pierre Joris (Stanford: Stanford University Press, 2011).

11. Friedrich Hölderlin, "Bread and Wine," in *Selected Poems and Fragments*, trans. Michael Hamburger (London: Anvil, 2004), 319–21. The lines from "Yes, and rightly to her garlands we dedicate, hymns" on do not appear in the published version of the seminar, although they can be found in the seminar online (*http://www.entretemps.asso.fr/Badiou/94-95.htm*). We have included them here since they clarify some of Badiou's comments that would otherwise seem enigmatic.

12. The traversal of the night at the height of wakefulness that Badiou is referring to appears only in the French translation of the poem: "Et qu'ainsi, comme des amants, yeux jamais clos, coupes à pleins bords, audace à vivre et sainte souvenance, *nous traversions la nuit au comble de l'éveil*" (our emphasis).

13. Stéphane Mallarmé, "Igitur," in *Selected Poetry and Prose*, trans. and ed. Mary Ann Caws (New York: New Directions, 1982), 91–92.

14. "*Midi, roi des étés*" [Noon, king of summers] are the first words of the poem "Midi," by the nineteenth-century French poet Leconte de Lisle.

15. The French philosopher Jean Beaufret (1907–1982) introduced Heidegger to France after World War II and remained his staunchest defender throughout the so-called Heidegger wars in France.

16. See Jean Beaufret, "Heraclitus and Parmenides," in *Dialogue with Heidegger*, trans. Mark Sinclair (Indianapolis: Indiana University Press, 2006), 20–31.

17. Paul Valéry, *Charms and Other Pieces*, trans. and ed. Peter Dale (London: Anvil, 2007), 105–7.

18. Badiou discusses Valéry's "Le Cimetière marin" at length in *Logics of Worlds* (455–70) and in his seminar "Images du temps présent" (Paris: Fayard, 2014), forthcoming from Columbia University Press.

19. Paul Claudel first wrote *Partage de midi* in 1905, and greatly revised it in 1948–1949.

20. Paul Claudel, "*Break of Noon:* First Version", trans. Moses M. Nagy and Michael Gillespie, in *Claudel Studies* 3, no. 2 (1976): 6–7; translation slightly modified. Although this translation is of the first version of the play, most of the dialogue in this excerpt from the second version remains unchanged. We have incorporated one missing line ("The brontosaur is going to begin to bray") and certain stage directions from Wallace Fowlie's translation in *Paul Claudel Two Dramas* (Chicago: Henry Regnery, 1960).

21. *Break of Noon*, trans. Wallace Fowlie, 70.

22. Badiou actually cites an unpublished but widely distributed translation of the *Tractatus Logico-Philosophicus* by Étienne Balibar.

23. Ludwig Wittgenstein, *Tractatus Logico-Philosophicus*, trans. David F. Pears and Brian F. McGuinness (New York: Humanities Press International, 1992), 4.

24. Badiou here is alluding to Lacan's concept of "the subject supposed to know," a status usually attributed to the analyst in the initial phases of an analysis, but which may be active in other transferential situations as well, such as teaching.

25. "*Science sans conscience n'est que ruine de l'âme*" (Science without conscience is but the ruin of the soul) is a well-known line from François Rabelais's *Pantagruel*. The French word "*conscience*" can mean "moral conscience," as it no doubt does in Rabelais's phrase, but also "awareness" or "consciousness," which is probably closer to Lacan's use of the term here. See session 4, this volume.

26. The italicized words in brackets in this and other citations throughout this seminar are Badiou's interpolations.

27. Taking off from Lacan's remark about the philosopher being inscribed like a circumference in the discourse of the master, Badiou here devises a series of puns that defy easy translation into English. The root word involved is *rond*, "round," but the expressions in which the word is found have a variety of meanings, whose echoes can be heard better in French. Thus, one of the figurative senses of *rond*, "truthful," "honest," and so forth prevails in this passage, culminating in the image of the court fool, who, albeit unconsciously, speaks truth to power. The first pun occurs in Badiou's interpolated comment "He's an all-around truthful guy, isn't he?" [*il est rond, n'est-ce pas?*], which is subsequently expanded in the definition of the philosopher as "what is true (or truthful) in the discourse of the master" [*ce qu'il y a de rond dans le discours du maître*]. This is rounded out, so to speak, with two further

locutions, *tourner rond* and *tourner en rond*. The literal meaning of the first of these is "to turn round." In this sense, the philosopher can be imagined as someone turning round in the master's discourse, like a cog in a machine. Figuratively, however, *tourner rond* means "to go/work/function well" or "to run smoothly or true," as might be said of an engine, for example. The philosopher is therefore what runs true or functions properly in the master's discourse. Nevertheless, the more frequent negative use of the phrase, *ne pas tourner rond* ("to have something wrong," "not to work right," or even "to have a screw loose") must inevitably be heard at the same time. It is this latter sense that prefigures the Fool Lacan mentions in the latter part of his statement. So the affirmative *tourner rond* could also imply "to be sane." The philosopher might then be someone who keeps the master's discourse sane. The second locution, *tourner en rond*, similar in its literal sense to the first, means "to go or turn round," but its more negative connotation is "to go round in circles." There is moreover another figurative meaning of *tourner en rond*—"to be bored to death" or "to go crazy (out of boredom)"—an echo of which can be heard here. Last but not least, hovering in the background is the *empêcheur de tourner en rond*: the killjoy or spoilsport, the person who prevents something positive from occurring.

28. The French word *fou* used here [*Ne devient pas fou qui veut*] can mean both "fool," in the Shakespearian sense, and "insane, crazy" or "madman."

29. Lacan frequently comments in his earlier work that the unconscious is "structured like a language."

30. "Whereof one cannot speak, thereof one must be silent" is Proposition 7, the final one, of Wittgenstein's *Tractatus Logico-Philosophicus*.

31. The concept of "torsion" is central to Badiou's 1982 book, *Theory of the Subject*. In the glossary that concludes his translator's introduction to the text, Bruno Bosteels defines torsion as "the way in which a subject works back upon the structure that determines it in the first place" (xxxvi). Here it suggests more specifically the twist or doubling in the real between what can be said and formalized about it (mathematics) and what can only be written as an impasse in formalization (the matheme).

32. Cf. Rimbaud's prose poem "Vagabonds": "... *moi, pressé de trouver le lieu et la formule*" (" ... I, impatient to find the place and the formula"). Arthur Rimbaud, *Illuminations*, trans. Louise Varese (New York: New Directions, 1988), 64. Badiou discusses this line in *The Century*, trans. Alberto Toscano (Cambridge: Polity, 2007), 146, and alludes to it again in Alain Badiou and Barbara Cassin, *There's No Such Thing as a Sexual Relationship: Two Essays on Lacan*, trans. Kenneth Reinhard and Susan Spitzer (New York: Columbia University Press, 2017).

33. Élisabeth Roudinesco has written an influential, two-volume history of French psychoanalysis, *Histoire de la psychanalyse en France*, as well as a number of books specifically on Lacan. Those translated into English include: *Jacques Lacan & Co.: A History of Psychoanalysis in France, 1925–1985* (Chicago: University of Chicago Press, 1990); *Jacques Lacan* (New York: Polity, 1997), *Jacques Lacan: An Outline of a Life and History of a System of Thought* (New York: Polity, 1999); *Lacan: In Spite of Everything* (New York: Verso, 2014); and, most recently, with Alain Badiou, *Jacques Lacan: Past and Present* (New York: Columbia University Press, 2014). Roudinesco had in fact dealt with Heidegger's meeting with Lacan in 1955 in her 1993 book *Jacques Lacan: Esquisse d'une vie, histoire d'un système de pensée* (Paris: Fayard).

34. See session 2 for further remarks on this quote.

Session 2

1. "Lacan avec les philosophes" was a conference organized by the Collège international de philosophie in Paris on May 25, 1990. The papers delivered were collected in a volume of the same name, published the following year by Albin Michel.

2. Heraclitus, Fragment 50, in Thomas M. Robinson, trans. and ed., *Heraclitus* (Toronto: University of Toronto Press, 1987), 37.

3. Lacan uses the term *désêtre* at various points in his writings and seminar, beginning in the late 1960s, to indicate what we might call the "ontological disaster" of the analyst's fall from the position of the "subject supposed to know" to the *objet a*.

4. "Hontology" (*hontologie*) is a neologism combining *honte*, "shame," and *ontologie*, "ontology."

5. Badiou's rendering of the line (no doubt from memory)—*Je vais quand même dire un mot toute (h)onte bue*—is similar to Lacan's—*Toute onto bue maintenant, je répondrai . . ."* (*AE*, 426)—in that it plays on the same combination of "shame" and "ontology."

6. Martin Heidegger, "Sketches for a History of Being as Metaphysics," in *Martin Heidegger: The End of Philosophy*, ed. and trans. Joan Stambaugh (Chicago: University of Chicago Press, 1973), 55–71. Subsequent page references to this edition will appear in parentheses in the text.

7. Badiou discusses the ideas covered in the next few paragraphs at greater length in the first chapter of *Court traité d'ontologie transitoire*, which was translated as "The Question of Being Today" in Badiou's *Theoretical Writings*, ed. and trans. Ray Brassier and Alberto Toscano (London: Continuum, 2006).

8. "... ou pire. Compte rendu du Séminaire 1971–1972," in *Scilicet* 5 (1975) 5–10, reprinted in *Autres écrits*, 547–52. Page numbers in parentheses refer to the text in *Autres écrits*.

9. Lacan used the neologism *s'oupirer* in Seminar XX, *Encore*. In a note, Bruce Fink, the translator, commented: "*Soupirer* means 'to sigh,' but the apostrophe Lacan adds creates a neologism here, a reflexive: 'or-sighs itself,' 'or-is-sighed,' 'or-worsens itself.'" Lacan, *The Seminar of Jacques Lacan, Book XX, Encore: On Feminine Sexuality: The Limits of Love and Knowledge*, ed. Jacques-Alain Miller and trans. Bruce Fink (New York: Norton, 1975), 2, n. 4. However, when followed by *après*, as is the case here and elsewhere in this volume, *soupirer* may be translated as "to yearn for." We have accordingly invented the neologism "to yearsen," which combines "yearn" and "worsen," the two elements of Lacan's *s'... oupirer*.

Session 3

1. See Session 9, in which Jean-Claude Milner, Badiou's guest lecturer, discusses his thesis of an early and a late Lacan in his book *L'Oeuvre claire* (Paris: Seuil, 1995).

2. A detailed discussion of Lacan's concept of ab-sense can be found in Badiou's essay on "L'Étourdit" in the book he co-wrote with Barbara Cassin, *There's No Such Thing as a Sexual Relationship: Two Lessons on Lacan*, trans. Kenneth Reinhard and Susan Spitzer (New York: Columbia University Press, 2017).

3. The "pass" is the procedure for verification required for a candidate to be awarded the title of "Analyst of the School" in the École freudienne de Paris, which Lacan established in 1964, after his "excommunication" from the Société française de psychanalyse. Lacan presented the notion of the pass (which Badiou describes below) in his "Proposition du 9 octobre 1967 sur le psychanalyste de l'École" (*Scilicet* 1: 14–30/*Autres écrits*, 243–60), translated by Russell Grigg as "Proposition of 9 October 1967 on the Psychoanalyst of the School" in *Analysis* 6 (1995): 1–13. The pass procedure continues to be practiced within the World Association of Psychoanalysis, the school founded by Lacan's son-in-law, Jacques-Alain Miller.

Session 4

1. Immanuel Kant, "Second Preface," *The Critique of Pure Reason*, ed. and trans. Paul Guyer and Allen W. Wood (Cambridge: Cambridge University Press, 2000), 106.

2. See session 1, note 25 with regard to this phrase from Rabelais.
3. Lettrism was a French avant-garde movement of the 1940s founded by the Romanian immigrant poet Isidore Isou, a compatriot of Tristan Tzara's. With roots in Dada and Surrealism, its early works were characterized by strange arrangements of letters.
4. Lacan had dissolved his school, the École freudienne de Paris, three months earlier, in January 1980.
5. The sentence Badiou is referring to is: "Those long chains of utterly simple and easy reasonings that geometers commonly use to arrive at their most difficult demonstrations, had given me occasion to imagine that all the things that can fall within human knowledge follow from one another in the same way . . . ." René Descartes, *Discourse on Method* and *Meditations on First Philosophy*, 4th ed., trans. Donald Cress (Indianapolis: Hackett, 1999), 11.
6. In reference to this word *dit-mension* in another text, Alain Badiou and Barbara Cassin's *There's No Such Thing as a Sexual Relationship: Two Lessons on Lacan*, trans. Kenneth Reinhard and Susan Spitzer (New York: Columbia University Press, 2017), Ken Reinhard notes: "Lacan often writes the word 'dimension' as the homophonic *dit-mension*, which suggests two French words, *dit* ("what is said") and *mension*, which he associates with *mensonge* (a "lie"): '*Dit-mension* is *mension* of the said. This way of writing has an advantage, which is to allow *mension* to be extended into *mensionge*, which indicates that what is said is not at all necessarily true.' " Jacques Lacan, *Le Séminaire. Livre XXIII: Le sinthome* [The Sinthome], ed. Jacques-Alain Miller (Paris: Seuil, 2005), 144).

Session 5

1. See *The Seminar of Jacques Lacan, BookVIII: Transference*, ed. Jacques-Alain Miller and trans. Bruce Fink (Cambridge: Polity, 2015), 83.
2. The Cause freudienne was a psychoanalytic association established at Lacan's request in 1980 by some of his disciples after his dissolution of the École freudienne de Paris.
3. The lines Badiou quotes here can be found in *Ornicar?* 20–21 (1980), pages 15 and 18 respectively. The first line is from "D'Écolage" and the second from "Monsieur A." Both essays were collected in *Le Séminaire XXVII: Dissolution* (1979–80). Unpublished.
4. *The Seminar of Jacques Lacan, Book XVII: The Other Side of Psychoanalysis*, ed. Jacques-Alain Miller and trans. Russell Grigg (New York: Norton, 2007), 52; translation modified.

Session 6

1. From at least as early as 1958, Lacan frequently commented on and revised Descartes's famous declaration, "I think, therefore I am" (*Je pense donc je suis*). For Lacan, however, it is not the "ego" that thinks but the subject of the unconscious, the "it"—the French *ça*, from the German *Es*, the Freudian term translated in the *Standard Edition* as the "id." Hence for Lacan, "it thinks."

2. On the difference between *savoir* and *connaissance*, Adrian Johnston writes: "It is crucial to appreciate here the difference between knowing/knowledge involving conscious acquaintance or familiarity (*connaître/connaissance*) versus knowing/knowledge (*savoir*) as entailing conceptual, intellectual comprehension . . . The truths of the unconscious, situated in the register of the Real, defy *connaissance* but not (analytic) *savoir*." *Adventures in Transcendental Materialism: Dialogues with Contemporary Thinkers* (Edinburgh: Edinburgh University Press, 2014), 260.

3. Jean-Jacques Rousseau, *Émile, or On Education*, trans. Allan Bloom (New York: Basic, 1979), 274. Subsequent page references to this edition appear in parentheses in the text.

4. Søren Kierkegaard, *Either/Or*, Part 1 of 2, ed. and trans. Howard V. Hong and Edna H. Hong (Princeton: Princeton University Press, 1987), 32; translation slightly modified. Subsequent page references to both volumes of this edition appear in parentheses in the text.

5. Søren Kierkegaard, *Concluding Unscientific Postscript to Philosophical Fragments*, vol. 1 of 2, ed. and trans. Howard V. Hong and Edna H. Hong (Princeton: Princeton University Press, 1992), 316; translation slightly modified. Subsequent page references to this edition appear in parentheses in the text.

Session 7

1. In this citation from Lacan's " . . . ou pire. Compte-rendu du Séminaire 1971–1972," Badiou has omitted Lacan's parenthetical descriptions of impotence and logical impossibility and replaced them with his own descriptions in brackets, although when he cites the statement again he includes Lacan's parenthetical text.

2. "*Hic Rhodus, hic salta*" ("Here is Rhodes, jump here") is a phrase of ancient Greek origin, translated into Latin in one of Aesop's fables and meaning, more or less, "Prove what you can do here and now." It was famously used (if oddly translated) by Hegel in his *Philosophy of Right* and by Marx in *The Eighteenth Brumaire of Louis Bonaparte*.

3. Stéphane Mallarmé, "Variations on a Subject," in *Stéphane Mallarmé, Selected Poetry and Prose*, trans. Mary Ann Caws (New York: New Directions, 1982), 76.

4. Badiou is alluding here to Lacan's essay, "Logical Time and the Assertion of Anticipated Certainty" (*Écrits*, 161–75), an essay Badiou commented on in *Theory of the Subject* (248–58). In that commentary, Badiou supplements Lacan's version of the "prisoner's dilemma" (a thought experiment common in game theory) by arguing that the "haste" to act implies an anxiety that introduces an element of the real into the symbolic process of subjectivization.

Session 8

1. The titles Badiou cites here for Lacan are either real or reinvented titles of works by Lenin—*What Is To Be Done?; Imperialism: The Highest Stage of Capitalism; State and Revolution*—or titles that echo the gist of other works by him.

2. The comment here seems to refer to Lacan's description of the position of the analyst in *Television*: "[T]here is no better way of placing him objectively than in relation to what was in the past called: being a saint. During his life a saint doesn't command the respect that a halo sometimes gets for him . . . A saint's business, to put it clearly, is not *caritas*. Rather, he acts as trash [*déchet*]; his business being *trashitas* [*il décharite*]. So as to embody what the structure entails, namely allowing the subject, the subject of the unconscious, to take him as the cause of the subject's own desire." Lacan, *Television: A Challenge to the Psychoanalytic Establishment*, ed. Joan Copjec, trans. Denis Hollier, Rosalind Krauss, and Annette Michelson. (Norton: New York, 1990), 15.

3. On Badiou's comments on Lacan's essay on "logical time," see *Theory of the Subject*, 248–58.

4. The concept of the *hors-lieu*, often contracted as *horlieu*, is central in Badiou's *Theory of the Subject*. Bosteels translates *hors-lieu* as "out-of-place"; see also the commentary in his Translator's Introduction, xxxii–xxxiii. In *Theory of the Subject*, Badiou defines "contradiction" as a scission whereby "a term is included in the place as out-of-place [*hors-lieu*]" (15).

5. "Première lettre de convocation à un forum," in *Annuaire et textes statutaires 1982 de L'École de la Cause freudienne*: 93.

6. "Seconde lettre de convocation au forum," *Annuaire et textes statutaires 1982*: 94.

Session 9

1. The word *oeuvre* can refer to a single work of art or to the total output of an artist or writer. Here, Badiou uses it in the sense of an entire body of work.

2. *Ralentir travaux* (1930) is the title of a book of poetry by the three surrealists.

3. *Le cadavre exquis* ("the exquisite corpse") was a verbal collage game, invented by the surrealists, in which players would write in turn on a sheet of paper, fold it to conceal part of the writing, and then pass it to the next player for a further contribution.

4. Milner here is referring to Lacan's formulation that "a signifier represents a subject for another signifier," often presented as the relationship of three of the four terms of the "master's discourse":

$$\frac{S_1}{\cancel{S}} \to S_2$$

5. *Lalangue* is Lacan's coinage (made by collapsing the article *la* and the noun *langue*, "language" or, more literally, "tongue") and refers to speech as purely sonic chatter, the language the unconscious speaks and hears, speech as rife with jouissance. See Kenneth Reinhard, introduction to *There's No Such Thing as a Sexual Relationship: Two Lessons on Lacan*, by Alain Badiou and Barbara Cassin (New York: Columbia University Press, 2017), xiii.

6. Milner is alluding here to Mallarmé's poem "Un coup de dés jamais n'abolira le hasard" ("A Throw of the Dice Will Never Abolish Chance").

7. The nuance between the standard French *il y a de l'* and the more colloquial *y a d'l* in Lacan's dictum *Y a d'l'Un*, often translated as "There's some One" or "There's something like One," is not as perceptible in English.

8. On Lacan's version of the prisoners' dilemma, see session 7, note 4. Lacan presents it as a "logical problem," in which a prison warden summons three prisoners and asks them to undergo a test, which will result in one of them being set free. The warden has five disks, three white and two black; he attaches one disk to the back of each prisoner, so that each can see what color disk the others have but not his own. The first prisoner who correctly deduces the color of his disk on logical (not probabilistic) grounds will be released.

Bibliography

Badiou, Alain. *Being and Event.* Translated by Oliver Feltham. New York: Continuum, 2006.

——. *Conditions.* Translated by Steven Corcoran. New York: Continuum, 2008.

——. *Logics of Worlds.* Translated by Alberto Toscano. New York: Continuum, 2009.

——. *Manifesto for Philosophy.* Translated and edited by Norman Madarasz. Albany: State University of New York Press, 1999.

Beaufret, Jean. "Heraclitus and Parmenides." In *Dialogue with Heidegger*, translated by Mark Sinclair, 20–31. Indianapolis: Indiana University Press, 2006.

Celan, Paul. *The Meridian: Final Version—Drafts—Materials.* Translated by Pierre Joris. Stanford, CA: Stanford University Press, 2011.

Claudel, Paul. "*Break of Noon:* First Version." Translated by Moses M. Nagy and Michael Gillespie. In *Claudel Studies* 3, no. 2 (1976): 3–70.

——. *Paul Claudel Two Dramas.* Translated by Wallace Fowlie. Chicago: Regnery, 1960.

Deleuze, Gilles, and Félix Guattari. *What Is Philosophy?* Translated by Graham Burchell. New York: Columbia University Press, 1996.

Descartes, René. *Discourse on Method* and *Meditations on First Philosophy*, 4th ed. Translated by Donald Cress. Indianapolis: Hackett, 1999.

——. *Rules for the Direction of the Mind.* Translated by Laurence J. Lafleur. Indianapolis: Liberal Arts Press, 1961.

Hegel, Georg Wilhelm F. *Science of Logic.* Translated by Arnold V. Miller. New York: Prometheus, 1991.

Heidegger, Martin. "Sketches for a History of Being as Metaphysics." In *Martin Heidegger: The End of Philosophy*, edited and translated by Joan Stambaugh, 55-71. Chicago: University of Chicago Press, 1973.

Hölderlin, Friedrich. *Selected Poems and Fragments.* Translated by Michael Hamburger. London: Anvil, 2004.

Kant, Immanuel. *The Critique of Pure Reason.* Edited and translated by Paul Guyer and Allen W. Wood. Cambridge: Cambridge University Press, 2000.

Kierkegaard, Søren. *The Concept of Anxiety: A Simple Psychologically Oriented Deliberation in View of the Dogmatic Problem of Hereditary Sin.* Translated by Alastair Hannay. New York: Norton, 2014.

——. *Concluding Unscientific Postscript to Philosophical Fragments,* vol. 1. Edited and translated by Howard V. Hong and Edna H. Hong. Princeton: Princeton University Press, 1992.

——. *Either/Or.* 2 vols. Edited and translated by Howard V. Hong and Edna H. Hong. Princeton: Princeton University Press, 1987.

Lacan, Jacques. *Autres écrits.* Edited by Jacques-Alain Miller. Paris: Seuil, 2001

——. *Écrits: The First Complete Edition in English.* Translated by Bruce Fink. New York: Norton, 2006.

——. "Monsieur A." *Ornicar?* 21–22 (Summer 1980): 17–20.

——. "Première lettre de convocation à un forum." In *Annuaire et textes statutaires 1982 de L'École de la Cause freudienne,* 93.

——. "Seconde lettre de convocation au forum." In *Annuaire et textes statutaires 1982 de L'École de la Cause freudienne,* 94.

——. *Le Séminaire de Jacques Lacan. Livre XIX: . . . ou pire.* Edited by Jacques-Alain Miller. Paris: Seuil, 2008.

——. *The Seminar of Jacques Lacan, Book XI: The Four Fundamental Concepts of Psychoanalysis.* Edited by Jacques-Alain Miller. Translated by Alan Sheridan. New York: Norton, 1998.

——. *The Seminar of Jacques Lacan, Book XVII: The Other Side of Psychoanalysis.* Edited by Jacques-Alain Miller. Translated by Russell Grigg. New York: Norton, 2007.

——. *The Seminar of Jacques Lacan, Book XX: Encore: On Feminine Sexuality: The Limits of Love and Knowledge.* Edited by Jacques-Alain Miller. Translated by Bruce Fink. New York: Norton, 1998.

——. *Television: A Challenge to the Psychoanalytic Establishment.* Edited by Joan Copjec. Translated by Denis Hollier, Rosalind Krauss, Annette Michaelson, and Jeffery Mehlman. New York: Norton, 1980.

Lacoue-Labarthe, Philippe. "De l'éthique: à propos d'Antigone." In *Lacan avec les philosophes,* edited by Michel Deguy, 21–36. Paris: Albin Michel, 1991.

Mallarmé, Stéphane. *Stéphane Mallarmé, Selected Poetry and Prose.* Edited and translated by Mary Ann Caws. New York: New Directions, 1982.

Milner, Jean-Claude. *L'Oeuvre claire.* Paris: Seuil, 1995.

Nietzsche, Friedrich. *Ecce Homo.* Translated by Duncan Large. Oxford: Oxford University Press, 2007.

——. *Selected Letters of Friedrich Nietzsche*. Edited and translated by Christopher Middleton. Indianapolis: Hackett, 1969.

——. *Twilight of the Idols* and *Anti-Christ*. Translated by R. J. Hollingdale. New York: Penguin, 1990.

Plato. *Meno*. 2nd edition. Translated by George M. A. Grube. Indianapolis: Hackett, 1980.

——. *The Republic*. Translated by Desmond Lee. New York: Penguin, 2007.

——. *The Symposium*. Translated by Christopher Gill. New York: Penguin, 2003.

Rousseau, Jean-Jacques. *Émile, or On Education*. Translated by Allan Bloom. New York: Basic Books, 1979.

Valéry, Paul. *Charms and Other Pieces*. Edited and translated by Peter Dale. London: Anvil, 2007.

Wittgenstein, Ludwig. *Tractatus Logico-Philosophicus*. Translated by Charles K. Ogden. New York: Dover, 1998.

——. *Tractatus Logico-Philosophicus*. Translated by David F. Pears and Brian F. McGuinness. New York: Humanities Press International, 1992.

Index

Heraclitus, Parmenides on, 63–64;
personally, 225; pride of, 52–53;
unifying, 196
thought: Eliatic, 15; of Marx, 206–7;
midnight of, 12–13; process, 187–88;
proof, 216–17, 219, 227; proposition
in, 212; psychoanalysis in, 217–18
time: space and, 197–99; theory of,
197–99; of treatment, 187, 199–200
topology: of the Other, xxv; of
philosophy, xxv; of surfaces, 10;
time, space and, 197–99
torsion, 33, 204, 238n31
Tractatus (Wittgenstein), 5, 21–22
transcendental aesthetic, 197–99
Transcendental Dialectic, 43
transmissible knowledge, 77–78, 82–84,
86; ab-sense and, 89; mathemes in,
165
transvaluation of all values, 6
traversal, of anti-philosophy, xxviii,
30–31
traverser, xxv, xxvii–xxviii, 232n6
treatment: direction of, 172, 174,
188–89, 191, 193–96; process, 175,
196–97; space of, 178; time of, 187,
199–200
true world, 8–9
truth, xxv–xxvii, xxx; anti-philosophy
and, 20–21, 73–74, 81, 175; bone
of, 95, 104; category of, 22–23,
27; contingency, infinity and,
217; disclosure of being in, 58;
as extension, of generic, xxvii;
as half-said, xxxiv, 20–21, 26; as
harmful, 20, 22–23, 26; knowledge
and, 7–8, 23–25, 76, 91, 144, 147–49;
linguistic structure of, xxxi; love
of, xxxiv–xxxv, 90, 134–36, 234n16;

mathematics and, 105–6, 109, 120;
meaning and, 7, 45, 47, 73–76, 85,
91, 120–21; of propositions, 32; in
psychoanalysis, 144–46; the real
and, 145, 148, 163; realism and,
xxxv; sense and, 79–81; subjugation
of, 50; unconscious and, 145–47;
Wittgenstein on, 22
"Truth: Forcing and the Unnamable"
(Badiou), xxiii, 235n28
truthfulness, of philosopher, 28
truth/knowledge/real triad, 144–50,
165
truth procedures, xxix
Twilight of the Idols (Nietzsche), 8
tyrants, 129–30, 141
Tzara, Tristan, 96–97

unconscious, the, 24, 100, 145–48, 215
understanding, 70–71
unity, of action, 8
universe, as infinite, 220–22
unknowability, 150–53, 155, 158–59,
168
unknown, the, 24
utopia, 128

Valéry, Paul, 13–15
validation, 82–83
values, 6
veridicality, xxvii
victory, anticipated certainty of, 5–7
Voltaire, 71

wager, 191–92
wakefulness, 11, 236n12
weakness, 136, 182
"what-it-is," 50
will to power, 19

List of the seminars
(in chronological order)

Milton Keynes UK
Ingram Content Group UK Ltd.
UKHW040746121224
452420UK00004B/227